"Rightly relating the church .... ide-
ranging theological and herm............................. ...... volume provides
the most theologically rich entry point into the issue. It is clearly written, and the back-and-forth format allows the reader to weigh the
arguments for each view."

—Douglas J. Moo,
Kenneth T. Wessner Professor of New Testament,
Wheaton College

"The different angles on Romans 9–11 presented here will help
readers sharpen their own understanding of the biblical text. We
are reminded in reading a book like this that our own arguments
seem irrefutable until someone questions us. The authors don't
merely help us interpret Romans 9–11, but they also introduce us
to crucial discussions on typology, prophecy, and biblical theology.
This book is a valuable and important contribution to the debate
over Romans 9–11."

—Thomas R. Schreiner,
James Buchanan Harrison Professor of
New Testament Interpretation and Associate Dean,
The Southern Baptist Theological Seminary

"Everyone gains from respectful debate on a significant biblical issue.
Open discussion, disagreement, and debate help to encourage and
produce exegetical and theological accuracy. Compton and Naselli
have brought together four qualified defenders of three different views regarding Israel and the church in Romans 9–11. Their
irenic, though provocative, debate-style essays represent one side of
the potentially wide range of views—all take the side maintaining
a distinction between Israel and the church. This debate reminds
us of the need to read apparent agreement with extreme care since
points of strong disagreement may coexist alongside general agreement. Attention to detail must characterize both our exegesis and
our communication of the theological implications of our exegesis.
Evangelicals desiring greater food for thought regarding Romans
9–11 will find a feast in this volume."

—William D. Barrick,
Professor Emeritus of Old Testament,
The Master's Seminary

"Complex arguments require careful listeners. Intricate structures demand attentive readers. Big-picture patterns call for synthesizing insights. Equivocal words necessitate skilled interpreters. And when arguments, structures, patterns, and words are hotly contested, then only humble and patient practitioners can help us. This excellent and timely book offers us all these things. It charts the complex, intricate, big-picture and equivocal terrain of Romans 9–11 in three different ways, and it allows each of the exponents to interact with the plausibility of the other readings carefully, attentively, and with synthesizing skill. Their humility and patience allow the reader to stare at the map of Scripture and discern the way ahead. Any study of Romans 9–11 in biblical theology will benefit from the riches and wisdom in this book."

—David Gibson,
minister of Trinity Church in Aberdeen, Scotland

"Romans 9–11 is a superlative test of one's biblical-theological mettle. These three chapters compel readers to articulate their understanding of the relationship between the Old and New Testaments and between Israel and the church. Jared Compton and Andy Naselli have assembled a team of capable scholars who, by presenting their own views and by interacting with one another, help us to understand the important issues presented by Romans 9–11 with greater clarity. The editors' introductory and concluding chapters commendably set, in clear relief, areas where the contributors agree and disagree. Although these essays are not the last word in the debate, they merit wide reading and thoughtful reflection."

—Guy Waters,
James M. Baird Jr. Professor of New Testament,
Reformed Theological Seminary, Jackson, MS

"This book is not only an excellent contribution to the study of Romans 9–11, but it will serve those who are trying to wrestle through larger questions of biblical theology very well. Compton and Naselli have framed the discussion carefully (perhaps as well as any multiple-views book I've seen), and the writers engage the text and each other's view frankly and fairly. A very helpful work!"

—David M. Doran, Senior Pastor,
Inter-City Baptist Church, Allen Park, MI;
President and Chairman of the Practical Theology Department,
Detroit Baptist Theological Seminary

THREE
VIEWS
ON
ISRAEL
AND THE
CHURCH

Perspectives on Romans 9–11

JARED COMPTON • ANDREW DAVID NASELLI

EDITORS

MICHAEL J. VLACH • BENJAMIN L. MERKLE
FRED G. ZASPEL & JAMES M. HAMILTON JR.

CONTRIBUTORS

Three Views on Israel and the Church: Perspectives on Romans 9–11
© 2018 by Jared Compton and Andrew David Naselli

Published by Kregel Academic, an imprint of Kregel Publications, 2450 Oak Industrial Dr. NE, Grand Rapids, MI 49505-6020.

The Hebrew font, NewJerusalemU, and the Greek font, GraecaU, are available from www.linguistsoftware.com/lgku.htm, +1-425-775-1130.

ISBN 978-0-8254-4406-7

Printed in the United States of America

20 21 22 / 5 4 3 2

CONTENTS

CONTRIBUTORS

Jared Compton (PhD, Trinity Evangelical Divinity School) is pastor for discipleship at CrossWay Community Church in Bristol, WI. He is the author of *Psalm 110 and the Logic of Hebrews* and several articles.

James M. Hamilton Jr. (PhD, Southern Baptist Theological Seminary) is professor of biblical theology at Southern Baptist Theological Seminary and preaching pastor of Kenwood Baptist Church in Louisville, KY. He is the author of many books and articles, including *God's Glory in Salvation through Judgment*.

Benjamin L. Merkle (PhD, Southern Baptist Theological Seminary) is professor of New Testament and Greek at Southeastern Baptist Theological Seminary, editor of *The Southeastern Theological Review*, and an elder of North Wake Church in Wake Forest, NC. He is the author of many books and articles, including *Ephesians* in the Exegetical Guide to the Greek New Testament series.

Andrew David Naselli (PhD, Bob Jones University; PhD, Trinity Evangelical Divinity School) is associate professor of New Testament and theology at Bethlehem College & Seminary and an elder of Bethlehem Baptist Church in Minneapolis, MN. He is the author of many books and articles, including

How to Understand and Apply the New Testament: Twelve Steps from Exegesis to Theology.

Michael J. Vlach (PhD, Southeastern Baptist Theological Seminary) is professor of theology at The Master's Seminary in Los Angeles, CA, and editor of *The Master's Seminary Journal.* He is the author of several books and articles, including *He Will Reign Forever.*

Fred G. Zaspel (PhD, Free University of Amsterdam) is pastor of Reformed Baptist Church in Franconia, PA, adjunct professor of systematic theology at The Southern Baptist Theological Seminary in Louisville, KY, and executive editor of Books at a Glance. He is the author of several books and articles, including *The Theology of B. B. Warfield.*

ABBREVIATIONS

Bibles

CSB	Christian Standard Bible
ESV	English Standard Version
HCSB	Holman Christian Standard Bible
LXX	Septuagint
MT	Masoretic Text
NASB	New American Standard Bible
NEB	New English Bible
NET	New English Translation
NIV	New International Version
NJB	New Jerusalem Bible
NLT	New Living Translation
NRSV	New Revised Standard Version
RSV	Revised Standard Version

Extrabiblical Sources

Jub.	*Jubilees*
m. Sanh.	*Mishnah Sanhedrin*
Ps. Philo	Pseudo–Philo
T. Benj.	Testament of Benjamin
T. Jos.	Testament of Joseph
T. Levi	Testament of Levi

Periodical, Reference, and Serial

AB	Anchor Bible
BDAG	Bauer, W., F. W. Danker, W. F. Arndt, and F. W. Gingrich. *A Greek-English Lexicon of the New Testament and Other Early Christian Literature.* 3d ed. Chicago: University of Chicago Press, 2000.
BECNT	Baker Exegetical Commentary on the New Testament
BSac	*Bibliotheca Sacra*
CBQ	*Catholic Biblical Quarterly*
CTJ	*Calvin Theological Journal*
DPL	*Dictionary of Paul and His Letters.* Edited by Gerald F. Hawthorne and Ralph P. Martin. Downers Grove, IL: InterVarsity Press, 1993.
EvQ	*Evangelical Quarterly*
ExAud	*Ex Auditu*
HNTC	Harper's New Testament Commentaries
IBC	Interpretation
ICC	International Critical Commentary
JBL	*Journal of Biblical Literature*
JETS	*Journal of the Evangelical Theological Society*
JSNT	*Journal for the Study of the New Testament*
MSJ	*The Master's Seminary Journal*
NAC	New American Commentary
NICNT	New International Commentary on the New Testament
NIDNTT	*New International Dictionary of New Testament Theology.* Edited by C. Brown. 4 vols. Grand Rapids: Zondervan, 1975–85.
NIGTC	New International Greek Testament Commentary
NovT	*Novum Testamentum*
NovTSup	*Supplements to Novum Testamentum*
NT	New Testament
OT	Old Testament

PSB	*Princeton Seminary Bulletin*
RB	*Revue biblique*
RevExp	*Review and Expositor*
RTR	*Reformed Theological Review*
SNTSMS	Society for New Testament Studies Monograph Series
SwJT	*Southwestern Journal of Theology*
TDNT	*Theological Dictionary of the New Testament.* Edited by G. Kittel and G. Friedrich. Translated by G. W. Bromiley. 10 vols. Grand Rapids: Eerdmans, 1964–76.
TNTC	Tyndale New Testament Commentary
TynBul	*Tyndale Bulletin*
WBC	Word Biblical Commentary
WUNT	Wissenschaftliche Untersuchungen zum Neuen Testament

INTRODUCTION

Andrew David Naselli

This debate-book is a window into a larger debate about how the NT uses the OT, especially regarding how the church relates to Israel.[1] Is the nation Israel a *type*? Is the church the new Israel? Is Jesus the true Israel?[2] This book addresses that larger debate by focusing on Romans 9–11—a passage in a letter that we think is the single most important piece of literature in the history of the world. When you do biblical and systematic theology, just about all roads lead through Romans. "Paul's letter to the church at Rome is the greatest letter ever written because of its great impact in history, its grand theology about Christ,

---

1. For an introduction to how the New Testament uses the Old, see G. K. Beale and D. A. Carson, eds., *Commentary on the New Testament Use of the Old Testament* (Grand Rapids: Baker Academic, 2007); Kenneth Berding and Jonathan Lunde, eds., *Three Views on the New Testament Use of the Old Testament*, Counterpoints (Grand Rapids: Zondervan, 2008); G. K. Beale, *Handbook on the New Testament Use of the Old Testament: Exegesis and Interpretation* (Grand Rapids: Baker Academic, 2012); Douglas J. Moo and Andrew David Naselli, "The Problem of the New Testament's Use of the Old Testament," in *The Enduring Authority of the Christian Scriptures*, ed. D. A. Carson (Grand Rapids: Eerdmans, 2016), 702–46.

2. Cf. Michael J. Vlach, "What Does Christ as 'True Israel' Mean for the Nation Israel? A Critique of the Non-Dispensational Understanding," *MSJ* 23 (2012): 43–54; Brent E. Parker, "The Israel-Christ-Church Relationship," in *Progressive Covenantalism: Charting a Course between Dispensational and Covenant Theologies*, eds. Stephen J. Wellum and Brent E. Parker (Nashville: Broadman & Holman, 2016), 39–68.

and its practical instructions for Christian living."[3] Romans 9–11 is an ideal passage to consider in light of the larger debate because Paul frequently quotes the OT and addresses Israelites and Gentiles in light of what God promised Israel in the OT.

1. What This Debate-Book Is About

Paul's letter to the Romans takes about sixty minutes to read aloud. And what we refer to as chapters 9–11 takes about fifteen minutes to read aloud.[4] Romans 9–11 is about one-fourth of Paul's magnificent letter. That one-fourth is what this debate-book is about: three views on Romans 9–11.

"Everything about Romans 9–11 is controversial," notes N. T. Wright.[5] Unfortunately, we do not have space in this book to debate "everything about Romans 9–11." One controversial aspect of this passage, for example, is whether 9:6–29 refers to God's electing to save individuals (i.e., the "U" for unconditional election in the Calvinist acronym TULIP) or God's electing to save a group (i.e., corporate election).[6] But that issue is not what this book is preoccupied with. (Everyone who contributes to this book agrees that 9:6–29 supports that God unconditionally chooses to save individuals.) This book focuses more broadly on how Romans 9–11 helps us understand Israel's role in the Bible's storyline and the nature of the

---

3. Benjamin L. Merkle, "Is Romans Really the Greatest Letter Ever Written?," *The Southern Baptist Journal of Theology* 11, no. 3 (2007): 31.

4. "Chapters" in the Bible go back only to the 1200s, and "verses" didn't exist until about 1550.

5. N. T. Wright, "The Letter to the Romans: Introduction, Commentary, and Reflections," in *The New Interpreter's Bible*, 12 vols. (Nashville: Abingdon, 2002), 10:620.

6. E.g., John Piper, *The Justification of God: An Exegetical and Theological Study of Romans 9:1–23*, 2nd ed. (Grand Rapids: Baker Academic, 1993), esp. 56–73; William W. Klein, *The New Chosen People: A Corporate View of Election*, 2nd ed. (Eugene, OR: Wipf & Stock, 2015), esp. 138–40, 146–48, 161, 175–77, 181–82; Thomas R. Schreiner, "Does Romans 9 Teach Individual Election unto Salvation? Some Exegetical and Theological Reflections," *JETS* 36 (1993): 25–40; Brian J. Abasciano, "Corporate Election in Romans 9: A Reply to Thomas Schreiner," *JETS* 49 (2006): 351–71; Thomas R. Schreiner, "Corporate and Individual Election in Romans 9: A Response to Brian Abasciano," *JETS* 49 (2006): 373–86.

people of God in that story. This book's three main essays attempt to answer the following questions:

1. What is the big idea in Romans 9–11? What is Paul trying to do? How does the passage function in Paul's letter?
2. Who is Israel? What role does Israel play? Why?
3. What does Romans 9–11 imply for biblical theology?[7] What does it imply about Israel's role in biblical theology? How does it contribute to how we understand typology and the relationship between the covenants?[8]

2. Tracing the Argument of Romans 9–11

Romans 9–11 opens with Paul's grief (9:1–2) that the majority of Israelites have rejected the Messiah (9:3; cf. 9:30–10:4; 11:1, 11, 20, 23) even though they had unique privileges (9:4–5). That introduces the tension that Romans 9–11 addresses: (a) Israel's unbelief and (b) Israel's privileged status. God made promises to Israel, yet Israel is "cut off from Christ" (9:3a). So does that mean God's word is unreliable? Has God's word failed? No, "It is not as though the word of God has failed" (9:6a). That is the thesis of Romans 9–11. That thesis was so important to Paul's original audience because the predominantly Gentile church in Rome needed to think rightly about themselves in relation to ethnic Israelites and treat Israelites accordingly: "Do not be arrogant toward the branches" (11:18a).[9] In the history of salvation, God

---

7. Biblical theology is a way of analyzing and synthesizing the Bible that makes organic, salvation-historical connections with the whole canon on its own terms, especially regarding how the Old and New Testaments integrate and climax in Christ. For an introduction to biblical theology, see Chapter 9 in Andrew David Naselli, *How to Understand and Apply the New Testament: Twelve Steps from Exegesis to Theology* (Phillipsburg, NJ: Presbyterian & Reformed, 2017), 230–63.

8. Typology analyzes how New Testament persons, events, and institutions (i.e., antitypes) fulfill Old Testament persons, events, and institutions (i.e., types) by repeating the Old Testament situations at a deeper, climactic level in salvation history.

9. I intentionally refer to "ethnic Israelites" rather than "the nation Israel" because "ethnic Israelites" more closely corresponds with the language in Romans 9–11. *Nation* connotes that ethnic Israelites inhabit a particular country or territory.

set aside Israel in order to save more Gentiles and thus provoke
Israel to jealousy and thus save more Israelites (11:11–32).

3. Two Features in Romans 9–11 Significant for This Book's Debate

Two features of this passage are particularly significant for this
debate-book:

1. Paul's Use of the Old Testament in Romans 9–11

Romans 9–11 is probably the single most important passage
in the NT about how early Christians put their Bibles
together. The strongest evidence for this is how Paul uses the
OT throughout the passage to support his point. Not every
instance of Paul's quoting the OT directly relates to what this
debate-book addresses (e.g., quoting Ps. 14:4 in Rom. 10:18),
but many do. Figure 1 displays each time Paul quotes OT in
Romans 9–11.[10]

Fig. 1. Old Testament Quotations in Romans 9–11

Romans	Old Testament Quoted	Paul's Point
9:7	Gen. 21:12	Ethnic and spiritual Israel are distinct.
9:9	Gen. 18:10, 14	God caused Isaac's birth to fulfill his promise to Abraham.
9:12	Gen. 25:23	God chose Jacob over Esau after their conception but before their birth.
9:13	Mal. 1:2–3	God chose Jacob and rejected Esau.
9:15	Exod. 33:19	God can have mercy on whomever he wants.

---

10. The table's third column succinctly summarizes Paul's points at the risk of
oversimplifying them, and it is consistent with the exegesis in Douglas J. Moo, *The
Epistle to the Romans*, NICNT (Grand Rapids: Eerdmans, 1996), 574–744. Figure
1 is from Andrew David Naselli, *From Typology to Doxology: Paul's Use of Isaiah and
Job in Romans 11:34–35* (Eugene, OR: Pickwick, 2012), 142–43, with one change:
I tweaked the entry for Romans 11:26–27 to be impartial (used with permission).

Romans	Old Testament Quoted	Paul's Point
9:17	Exod. 9:16	God can harden whomever he wants to accomplish his purposes.
9:25	Hos. 2:23	God will include Gentiles as his beloved people.
9:26	Hos. 1:10	God will include Gentiles as his children.
9:27–28	Isa. 10:22–23	God will judge ethnic Israel and save only a remnant.
9:29	Isa. 1:9	God will preserve ethnic Israel's remnant by leaving "a seed."
9:33	Isa. 28:16; 8:14	Ethnic Israel will stumble over the Messiah, failing to believe in him.
10:5	Lev. 18:5	Righteousness by practicing the law is impossible.
10:6–8	Deut. 30:12–14	Righteousness by faith is accessible.
10:11	Isa. 28:16	Faith is necessary for deliverance from judgment (i.e., salvation). Righteousness by faith is universally accessible for "whoever believes in" Jesus—whether ethnic Israel or Gentiles.
10:13	Joel 2:32	Righteousness by faith is universally accessible for "whoever will call on the name of the Lord"—whether ethnic Israel or Gentiles.
10:15	Isa. 52:7	Ethnic Israel's rejection of Jesus is inexcusable because God fulfilled the first and second conditions for calling on Jesus: God sent preachers, and the preachers preached.
10:16	Isa. 53:1	Ethnic Israel's rejection of Jesus is inexcusable because they are responsible for not fulfilling the fourth condition for calling on Jesus: They must believe in Christ.
10:18	Ps. 19:4	Ethnic Israel's rejection of Jesus is inexcusable because God fulfilled the third condition for calling on Jesus: They have heard the preaching.

Romans	Old Testament Quoted	Paul's Point
10:19	Deut. 32:21	Ethnic Israel not only heard—they should have understood that God would (1) use the Gentiles to provoke them to jealousy and (2) include the Gentiles despite their disobedience after reaching out to Israel.
10:20–21	Isa. 65:1–2	
11:2	1 Sam. 12:22; Ps. 94:14	God has not rejected ethnic Israel (whom he foreknew).
11:3–4	1 Kings 19:10, 14, 18	Though ethnic Israel's condition may seem hopeless, the faithful God is preserving and will preserve a remnant.
11:8–10	Deut. 29:4; Isa. 29:10; Ps. 69:22–23	Ethnic Israel's rejection is partial—not total—because there is a remnant, the elect. God hardened the rest.
11:26–27	Isa. 59:20–21; 27:9	"In this way all Israel will be saved."
11:34	Isa. 40:13	God is incomprehensible and without counselors, so finite humans cannot understand his infinite ways or counsel him.
11:35	Job 41:11a	God is without creditors, so finite humans cannot place God in their debt.

2. Paul's Extended Metaphor of the Olive Tree in Romans 11:16b–24

Paul's metaphor teaches there is one people of God. God's people under both the old and new covenants—both Israelites and Gentiles—are part of the *same* tree rooted in the soil of God's redemptive work.

A metaphor is an implied comparison without "like" or "as." For example, "All flesh is grass" (Isa. 40:6). A metaphor has three parts: (1) the image; (2) the topic or item that the image illustrates; and (3) the point of similarity or comparison. Sometimes one or two of the three components may be implicit rather than explicit, as is the case with Romans 11:16b–24. Figure 2 shows how I understand that extended metaphor.[11]

---

11. Figure 2 is from Naselli, *From Typology to Doxology*, 20–21 (used with permission).

Fig 2. Extended Metaphor of the Olive Tree in Romans 11:16b–24

1. Image	2. Topic	3. Point of Similarity
a. One cultivated olive tree	The people of God	A living organism
b. Arboriculturist	God	Skillful cultivation
c. The root of the olive tree	Israel's patriarchs as recipients and conveyers of God's covenantal promises	Basic means of support and nourishment
d. Natural branches	Israelites	Natural extension of the living organism
e. Natural branches broken off	Non-Christian Israelites	Disconnected from the living organism
f. Wild olive shoot from an uncultivated olive tree	Gentiles	Not naturally related to the living organism
g. Wild olive shoot engrafted into the cultivated olive tree	Gentile Christians	Attached extension of the living organism

4. Three Views on Romans 9–11

The "Conclusion" to this book by my coeditor, Jared Compton, summarizes the book's three main views in more detail, so what follows merely introduces those views (see Fig. 3).

Figure 3. Three Views on Romans 9–11

Advocates	Will there be a future mass-conversion of ethnic Israelites?[13]	Does Israel play a typological role in biblical theology?[14]
Vlach	Yes	No
Zaspel and Hamilton	Yes	Yes
Merkle	No	Yes

---

12. That is, when Christ returns, God will save a significant number of the ethnic Israelites alive at that time.

13. That is, in Romans 9–11 does Christ (the antitype) fulfill Israel (the type) by repeating Israel's situation at a deeper, climactic level in salvation history?

1. A Non-Typological Future-Mass-Conversion View

Michael Vlach argues that Romans 9–11 promises a future salvation and role for national Israel. Israel, therefore, plays a non-typological role in biblical theology.

2. A Typological Future-Mass-Conversion View

Fred Zaspel and Jim Hamilton argue that Romans 9–11 promises a future salvation but not role for ethnic Israel. Israel, therefore, plays a typological role in biblical theology, even while maintaining a "special" status.

3. A Typological Non-Future-Mass-Conversion View

Ben Merkle argues that Romans 9–11 does not promise a future salvation or role for ethnic Israel. Israel, therefore, plays a typological role in biblical theology.

A fourth view is so similar to Merkle's view that we do not include it as a separate view in this book, since the overlap would be so great and because it is a minority view. Some argue essentially what Merkle does but with one significant exception: "Israel" refers not to ethnic Israel but to spiritual Israel, namely, the entire church—both Jewish and Gentile Christians.[14] Some of this book's contributors think Israel can refer to both Jewish and Gentile Christians in other literary contexts (e.g., Gal. 6:16), but they all agree that in Romans 9–11 Israel refers to ethnic Israelites.

Now as you read the rest of this book, may God's Spirit illumine your mind to understand what Paul meant in Romans 9–11 and to rightly connect that with the rest of the Bible. And after you climb the perilous mountain of Romans 9–11, be sure to exult in our glorious God when you take in the panoramic view from Romans 11:33–36.

---

14. Cf. John Calvin, *Commentaries on the Epistle of Paul the Apostle to the Romans*, ed. and trans. John Owen (Grand Rapids: Eerdmans, 1947), 437; Wright, "Romans," 10:687–93; Wright, *Paul and the Faithfulness of God*, 2 vols., Christian Origins and the Question of God 4 (London: SPCK, 2013), 2:1231–52.

A NON-TYPOLOGICAL FUTURE-MASS-CONVERSION VIEW

Michael J. Vlach

The issue of Israel, Gentiles, and the church in God's plans remains a hotly debated topic in Christian theology. Is Israel as a people and nation still significant in God's purposes, or has the mostly Gentile church inherited Israel's identity and role? How does Jesus relate to both Israel and the Gentiles? Romans 9–11 is important for addressing these questions.

My purpose is to present what I believe is Paul's argument in Romans 9–11. I will argue for a "non-typological future-mass-conversion view" concerning Israel. By "non-typological" I mean Paul's understanding of Israel is continuous with the expectation of the OT prophets that Israel is an ethnic and national entity with a role to the world.[1] National

---

1. A nation consists of people united by common descent, history, culture, language, laws, and leadership who inhabit or are related to a particular territory. This applies to Israel. Genesis 12:1–3; 18:18; 22:18 predicted Abraham's descendants would become a nation with its own land. At Sinai the Hebrew people became a "holy nation" set apart for service (Exod. 19:6; Deut. 7:6–7). Even though individual Jews believed in him, Jesus addressed Israel as a nation concerning its response to him (Matt. 23:37–39; Luke 19:41–44). The Jews of Jesus's day were conscious that Jesus affected both "our place and our nation" (John 11:48).

Israel remains strategic to God's purposes and does not lose its significance with the arrival of Jesus and the church. Paul reaffirms that Israel is a people and nation composed of ethnic descendants from Abraham, Isaac, and Jacob. And God made promises to Israel that will be literally fulfilled. This coincides with God keeping a remnant of believing Israelites, even while Israel as a whole is in unbelief. These promises are and will be fulfilled through Jesus the Messiah, the ultimate Israelite, who through his two comings, blesses Gentiles, saves and restores Israel, and fulfills all that the prophets predicted for the world (Isa. 49:3–6; Rom. 11:26–27; 15:8–9).

This argument contrasts with typological approaches to Romans 9–11 that see a shift from OT expectation to NT fulfillment. Typological approaches often view Israel and physical and national promises to Israel in the OT as types and shadows that are transcended by greater spiritual realities in the NT era. Jesus and the church are perceived as fulfilling or superseding national Israel's identity and role in God's purposes so that Israel does not have future significance as a nation.[2]

A non-typological approach, however, is different. It asserts that the temporary Mosaic covenant with its sacrifices and priesthood were inferior types and shadows that were superseded by the new covenant and Jesus's superior sacrifice and priesthood (Heb. 8:5; 9:23–24; 10:1). But the people and promises connected with the Abrahamic, Davidic, and new

---

Israel still possesses national privileges given to it in the Old Testament (Rom. 9:4–5). When Jesus returns, he will come to rule the nations, of which Israel will be one (Acts 1:6; Rev. 19:15). So both "ethnic Israel" and "national Israel" are appropriate designations for Israel in Romans 9–11.

2. Mark W. Karlberg, "The Significance of Israel in Biblical Typology," *JETS* 31 (1988): 259: "If one grants that national Israel in OT revelation was truly a type of the eternal kingdom of Christ, then it seems that, according to the canons of Biblical typology, national Israel can no longer retain any independent status whatever." Bruce K. Waltke, "Kingdom Promises as Spiritual," in *Continuity and Discontinuity: Perspectives on the Relationship between the Old and New Testaments*, ed. John S. Feinberg (Wheaton, IL: Crossway, 1988), 275: "The Jewish *nation* no longer has a place as the special people of God; that place has been taken by the Christian community which fulfills God's purpose for Israel."

covenants are not inferior types that pass away. Israel is not a type that is transcended in significance by the church. Nor does Jesus's rightful identity as the ultimate Israelite remove or transcend national Israel's significance. The opposite is true. Jesus's role as the true Israelite involves the restoring of Israel as a nation (Isa. 49:3–6; Rom. 11:26–27).

Paul's message in Romans 9–11 is supported by over thirty quotations and thirteen themes from the OT, which he relies upon in a contextual way. Paul does not transform, reinterpret, or redirect the original intentions of the OT prophets. He pulls together several OT themes and connects them to new covenant realities and Israel's current rejection of Jesus. In these three chapters Paul explains various OT expectations concerning the Messiah, national Israel, the remnant of Israel, and Gentiles and shows how these work together in God's purposes.

I also argue for a climactic "future mass-conversion" of national Israel in connection with the second coming of Jesus. This coming salvation of Israel (Rom. 11:26) will bring the nation into the new covenant and allow it to fulfill its role of bringing more blessings to the world (11:12, 15, 26–27), just as the prophets predicted (Isa. 27:6).

This perspective differs from the view that the "all Israel" to be saved in Romans 11:26 is the church or the remnant of believing Jews throughout history. It also differs with the position that Israel's coming salvation is limited to incorporation into the church with no implications for a continuing role for Israel as a nation. If predictions concerning Israel's salvation must come true, so too must prophecies concerning Israel's role as a nation since the two concepts are inseparably connected (see Deut. 30:1–10; Isa. 2:2–4). Jesus is coming to rule the nations (Rev. 19:15), and this includes Israel and its role.

These truths are consistent with the church, which is the new covenant community of believing Jews and Gentiles in Christ between the two comings of Jesus. Believing Jews and Gentiles are united in salvation through faith in Jesus and participation in the covenants of promise (11:17–24). Yet

ethnic distinctions are not erased. Paul still distinguishes Israelites and Gentiles both in this age and in the future. This reveals
wonderful unity and diversity within the people of God.

Paul's Big Idea in Romans 9–11

In Romans, Paul proclaims the gospel of Christ as the power
of God unto salvation to the Jew first and then to Gentiles
(Rom. 1:16). He then explains the sinfulness of man (1:18–
3:20), justification (3:21–5:21), sanctification (6:1–8:17), and
glorification (8:18–25). Yet a major issue remained. If God is
true to his word, what about his promises to Israel? The Scriptures contain many predictions concerning Israel's coming
salvation and restoration with increased blessings to the world
(Deut. 30; Isa. 2:2–4; Ezek. 36; Amos 9:11–15).[3] About twenty
years passed since Jesus ascended to heaven. The new covenant
ministry of the Holy Spirit was operating, and many Gentiles
were coming to faith. Yet the majority of Israel remained in
unbelief. Some in the increasingly Gentile church concluded
God had permanently rejected Israel. This concerned Paul.
But how does Israel's unbelief harmonize with God's promises?
And if God could break his promises with Israel, how could
Christian Gentiles be sure God would keep his promises to
them? As Wolfhart Pannenberg observes, "How could Christians be certain of their own comparatively new membership
in the circle of God's elect if God for his part did not remain
faithful to his election in spite of Israel's unbelief?"[4]

In Romans 9–11, therefore, Paul addresses the problem
of Israel's unbelief and the erroneous view that God rejected
Israel (cf. 11:1–2). He explains how Israel's current rejection
of Jesus is consistent with God's commitment to Israel and
Israel's great privileges (9:1–5). He also reveals how Israel's
present unbelief relates to Gentiles and the believing remnant

---

3. "Restoration" concerns fixing or restoring a marred entity. In this context
restoration concerns Israel's renewal as a nation with a role to other nations.
4. Wolfhart Pannenberg, *Systematic Theology*, trans. Geoffrey Bromiley (Grand
Rapids: Eerdmans, 1993), 3:471.

of Israel. When done, Paul will harmonize the following: (1) national Israel's unbelief; (2) Gentile inclusion in the Abrahamic covenant; (3) the current believing remnant of Israel; (4) national Israel's coming salvation; and (5) what Israel's salvation will mean for the world.

Paul argues from past, present, and future realities. Concerning the past, Paul contends that God has not rejected Israel since God sovereignly chose and granted Israel many irrevocable privileges and gifts. Also, God has not rejected Israel because of his commitment to Israel's patriarchs (9:4–13; 11:28–29).

Concerning the present, Paul asserts that Israel as a whole missed righteousness in Christ while many Gentiles found it (9:30–10:21). But a current believing remnant of ethnic Israelites shows that some within Israel believed and that God is still committed to Israel (11:1–6). This remnant guarantees God will not reject the nation (9:29) and points to a future salvation of Israel as a whole (11:16a). Also, God is using the present unbelief of Israel to bring spiritual blessings to believing Gentiles (11:17b; 15:27). This Gentile salvation is used by God to provoke Israel to jealousy. Paul's ministry to Gentiles also provokes Israel (11:13–14).

Concerning the future, Paul claims God will save the mass of Israel in connection with Jesus's return and the fullness of God's purposes for Gentiles in this age. Israel's salvation involves the nation's entrance into the new covenant and the bringing in of greater world blessings (11:12, 15, 26–27).

In sum, Paul reveals a divinely orchestrated progression of events that shows God's word has not failed. Israel is partially and temporarily cut off from experiencing covenant blessings, although a believing remnant remains. God uses Israel's unbelief to include Gentiles in the covenants of promise. This present era when Gentiles are coming to saving faith will lead to a time when the nation Israel as a whole will be saved. Paul's angst for the nation (10:1) will give way to joy and an outburst of praise to God (11:33–36). Therefore, Gentiles should understand their place in history and not be "arrogant" against Israel (11:18).

Israel's Identity in Romans 9–11

Paul mentions "Israel" eleven times and "Israelite(s)" twice in Romans 9–11. Of his eleven uses of "Jew" or "Jews" in Romans, only two occur in chapters 9–11 (9:24; 10:12). Two ideas are significant here.

First, the titles "Israelite" and "Jew" refer to ethnic descendants of Abraham, Isaac, and Jacob. In 9:6, Paul says there is a subset of believing ethnic Israelites within the broader pool of all ethnic Israelites. At times Paul refers to a current believing remnant of Israel, and on other occasions he discusses the nation Israel as a whole.

Second, it is not coincidental that all of Paul's uses of "Israel" or "Israelite" occur in Romans 9–11, when outside of these chapters in Romans he uses "Jew(s)." While the designation "Jew" comes from the single tribe of Judah, without excluding the other tribes, the title "Israel" often carries national implications and emphasizes the broader twelve tribes of Israel stemming from Jacob (i.e., "Israel"). Pablo Gadenz notes that Paul's switch from "Jews" to "Israel" in these chapters shows Paul "is considering the situation not just of individual Jews but of Israel as a collective whole."[5]

The Structure of Romans 9–11

Romans 9–11 contains five main sections:

- The problem of Israel's unbelief (9:1–5)
- Selectivity as a reason God's word has not failed (9:6–29)
- Why Israel missed righteousness (9:30–10:21)
- The remnant and national Israel in God's plans (11:1–32)
- Praise for God's great plans (11:33–36)

---

5. Pablo T. Gadenz, *Called from the Jews and from the Gentiles: Pauline Ecclesiology in Romans 9–11*, WUNT 267 (Tübingen: Mohr Siebeck, 2009), 48. Jason A. Staples argues that "Israel" more so than "Jews" "more specifically refers to all twelve tribes as a whole." See "What Do the Gentiles Have to Do with 'All Israel'? A Fresh Look at Romans 11:25–27," *JBL* 130 (2011): 376.

Romans 9:1–5 launches Paul's argument by introducing the problem of Israel's unbelief in Jesus even though Israel possesses great privileges.

Romans 9:6–29 reveals God's selective purposes as evidence God's word has not failed. God has selected (1) a remnant of believing Israelites, (2) the seed line of promise from Abraham, and (3) saved people from both Israel and the Gentiles.

Romans 9:30–10:21 explains Israel's problem. Israel missed righteousness in Jesus, who is the end of the law. Gentiles, though, found righteousness in the Messiah and are currently provoking Israel to jealousy while Israel as a whole is characterized by unbelief.

Romans 11:1–32 shows God has not rejected Israel. The believing remnant of Israel is a "firstfruits" of the salvation of the nation that will occur when Jesus returns (11:16, 26). Gentiles are currently becoming God's people through faith. When this era of Gentile salvation is over, the people of Israel will be saved, resulting in greater world blessings.

Romans 11:33–36 is a doxology concerning God's wonderful ways as explained in Romans 9–11.

Summary of Paul's Argument in Romans 9–11

The Problem of Israel's Unbelief (9:1–5)

Romans 9:1–5 introduces the problem of Israel's unbelief. With deep sincerity, Paul addresses his fellow "Israelites," his "kinsmen according to the flesh" who are unbelieving (9:3). Paul wishes he could be cursed on Israel's behalf (9:3). Then he mentions Israel's great privileges:

> to whom belongs the adoption as sons, and the glory and the covenants and the giving of the Law and the temple service and the promises, whose are the fathers, and from whom is the Christ according to the flesh, who is over all, God blessed forever. Amen. (9:4–5)

This list of eight privileges currently "belongs" to "Israelites." It is not that they once belonged to Israel or have been
transferred to another. Israel still possesses them, even while in
unbelief. These privileges are (1) adoption as sons, (2) the glory,
(3) the covenants, (4) the giving of the law, (5) temple service,
(6) the promises, (7) a relationship with the "fathers," and (8)
being the vessel for the Messiah.

To further explain, Israel has a familial relationship to God as
adopted sons. Earlier Paul linked adoption with Christians (8:15,
23), showing adoption can apply to individuals and Israel as a
nation. "Glory" refers to God's *shekinah* glory that dwelt in the
presence of Israel. The "covenants" probably include the Abrahamic, Davidic, and new covenants. Closely related are the "promises." The Hebrew Scriptures contain many promises concerning the Messiah and blessings for Israel and the nations. Cranfield
observes that Paul probably "had in mind many other OT promises, particularly the eschatological and messianic promises."[6]

Paul's mention of "covenants" and "promises" raises the
issue of their content. Since he offers no qualifications, all
dimensions of the covenants and promises as explained in the
prophets are probably in view. No indication exists that only
salvation blessings are intended or that physical and national
aspects have been spiritualized or made into something else.
In Galatians 3:15 Paul says that once a covenant is ratified, "no
one sets it aside or adds conditions to it." So the spiritual, physical, and national components of God's promises as originally
revealed are significant because of God's character.

Paul does not explicitly repeat all the details of Israel's
restoration that exist in the OT such as agricultural prosperity,
the land, the city of Jerusalem, and other areas (although he
does mention temple service). But this is not significant since
these matters would be covered under the broader categories
of "covenants" and "promises" and since Paul need not repeat

---

6.   C. E. B. Cranfield, *A Critical and Exegetical Commentary on the Epistle to the Romans*,
     2 vols., ICC (Edinburgh: T&T Clark, 1975–1979), 2:464.

previous revelation on these matters. If the broad categories of the "covenants" and "promises" still belong to Israel, so too would the details of these.[7] Concerning 9:3–4, Zaspel rightly asks, "What exegetical warrant is there for allowing only a part of the covenants' promises (i.e. the forgiveness of sins) and not the whole of them?"[8]

Also, there are themes associated with the "covenants" and "promises," such as Israel's vocational role to the nations (Deut. 4:5–8; Isa. 2:2–4), Israel's disobedience and dispersion followed by salvation and restoration (Lev. 26:40–45; Deut. 30:1–10), and blessings to the nations under the Messiah and a restored Israel (Isa. 27:6; Amos 9:11–15). If these themes are included in the "covenants" and "promises," these need to be fulfilled as well. If not, then some NT author probably would tell us. As Saucy notes, "We would expect the apostle to give some explanation if the nature of these promises have been altered from their OT meaning, but nowhere does he give such indication."[9]

Paul also mentions the detail of "temple service" (*latreia*) that still belongs to Israel. Israel was the custodian for "service" of the Jerusalem temple. Paul, with approval from the church in Jerusalem, continued devotion to Jerusalem and the temple (Acts 21:17–26).[10] While Jerusalem and temple service intersected with the Mosaic covenant era, their relevance seems to go beyond to the new covenant era as well.[11] Some passages link Jerusalem and temple service with new covenant condi-

---

7. See Genesis 12; 15; 17; 22; Leviticus 26:40–50; Deuteronomy 30:1–10; 2 Samuel 7; Isaiah 2; 11; 59–66; Jeremiah 30–33; Ezekiel 36–37; Luke 1:32–33, 54–55, 67–74.

8. Fred G. Zaspel, *Jews, Gentiles and the Goal of Redemptive History: An Exegetical and Theological Analysis of Romans 9–11* (Hatfield, PA: Interdisciplinary Biblical Research Institute, 1995), 26.

9. Robert L. Saucy, "Does the Apostle Paul Reverse the Prophetic Tradition of the Salvation of Israel and the Nations?," in *Building on the Foundations of Evangelical Theology: Essays in Honor of John S. Feinberg*, ed. Gregg R. Allison and Stephen J. Wellum (Wheaton, IL: Crossway, 2015), 78.

10. After Jesus's ascension the apostles "were continually in the temple" (Luke 24:53).

11. The new covenant has been inaugurated in this age, yet some details await future fulfillment.

tions when Israel is restored (Isa. 2:2–4; Jer. 33:14–18; Ezek. 40–48; Zech. 14:16).[12] In reference to the coming day of the Lord, Paul mentions a "temple of God" that a future man of lawlessness will desecrate (2 Thess. 2:1–4). The concept of "temple" also applies to Jesus (John 2:19–21), the Christian's body (1 Cor. 6:19), and the church (Eph. 2:21), yet the importance of the Jerusalem temple and Israel's relationship to it remains. Paul's use of "temple service" reveals implications for national Israel since the temple is linked to Jerusalem and the land of Israel. Vanlaningham points out that Paul's mention of "temple service," along with "covenants," "promises," and the "fathers," shows that four privileges in 9:4–5 "have special implications for the land."[13]

Israel's patriarchs, "the fathers," also belong to Israel. Paul will again connect "the fathers" to Israel in 11:28. The patriarchs are probably also tied to the "rich root" Paul mentions in 11:16b. Lastly, Paul mentions "Christ," the most important of all the privileges. Israel was the vessel for the Messiah. Israel's belief in Jesus the Messiah is predicted in 11:26.

To summarize, Romans 9:1–5 reveals the problem (from the human standpoint) of Israel's unbelief while Israel still possesses all the great privileges given to them by God. But instead of concluding that God had rejected Israel, Paul will show how Israel's unbelief can be explained from Scripture. This section also reveals Israel's continued importance in God's plans.

Selectivity as a Reason God's Word Has Not Failed (9:6–29)

God's Word Has Not Failed (9:6a)

Does Israel's rejection of its Messiah mean God's word failed? Paul refutes this idea in 9:6a: "But it is not as though the word

---

12. If future temple service occurs, this would be done in light of Christ and his sacrifice and not in contrast to him and his work.

13. Michael G. Vanlaningham, "The Jewish People according to the Book of Romans," in *The People, the Land, and the Future of Israel*, ed. Darrell L. Bock and Mitch Glaser (Grand Rapids: Kregel, 2014), 121.

of God has failed." This statement is the springboard for the rest of Paul's discussion through chapter 11.

Selection as Means for Accomplishing God's Purposes (9:6b–13)

With Romans 9:6b–13 Paul introduces *selection* as part of God's means to accomplish his purposes. If God's plans from the beginning involve selection and distinction, then the present unbelief of Israel is not evidence God has failed; it is proof God's plans are proceeding.[14] Two examples show this. First, God is selective within Israel (9:6b). And second, God is selective in choosing the promised seed line from Abraham (9:7–13).

Paul begins, "For they are not all Israel who are descended from Israel" (9:6b). The two references to "Israel" here involve ethnic Israelites, yet a distinction exists. Contrary to what many Jews believed, being a biological Israelite alone was not enough to be right with God. Israelites needed to be people of faith (see John 1:47). So there is a broader pool of all ethnic Israelites, but then there is a narrower group of ethnic Israelites who believe. These are Israelites in the full sense.[15] Paul's point, as Leon Morris bluntly stated this: "It was stupid to think that, since the whole nation had not entered the blessing, the promise of God had failed."[16]

Some believe Paul redefines the first "Israel" in 9:6b to include believing Gentiles.[17] Yet Paul maintains a distinction between Jews and Gentiles throughout chapters 9–11, and the context indicates ethnic Israelites are in view. John Murray is

---

14. See Cranfield, *Romans*, 2:474.
15. Romans 2:28–29 and Galatians 6:16 also teach true Israelites are ethnic Israelites who believe.
16. Leon Morris, *The Epistle to the Romans*, Pillar New Testament Commentary (Grand Rapids: Eerdmans, 1988), 353.
17. See Herman Ridderbos, *Paul: An Outline of His Theology* (Grand Rapids: Eerdmans, 1997), 336n30; Wayne Grudem, *Systematic Theology* (Grand Rapids: Zondervan, 1994), 861.

correct that Romans 9:6 teaches, "There is an 'Israel' within ethnic Israel."[18]

Next, the conjunction "nor" in 9:7a introduces another example of selection: "nor are they all children because they are Abraham's descendants." Here Paul stresses God's sovereignty in choosing the promised physical seed line from Abraham. This example is not the same as 9:6b since Paul does not distinguish between believing and unbelieving Israelites. Instead, he compares physical descendants of Abraham who fathered various non-Israelite people groups with descendants of Abraham who became the patriarchs of Israel. Ishmael is the father of various Arab groups, and Esau is the father of the Edomites. Isaac and Jacob, however, are part of the promised seed line that culminates in God's chosen nation, Israel.

God's selectivity is highlighted. Being ethnically related to Abraham alone did not make one part of the promised seed line. Both Ishmael and Esau would be blessed and father great people groups, but they were not children of promise. They were not the promised seed line God would use to bless the world.[19] Abraham tried to control matters on his own when he fathered Ishmael through Sarah's maid, Hagar (Gen. 16). But God said it was through Sarah that the child of promise, Isaac, was to come. Paul quotes Genesis 21:12 to emphasize this point— "For this is the word of promise: 'AT THIS TIME I WILL COME, AND SARAH SHALL HAVE A SON'" (Rom. 9:9; cf. Gen. 17:15–21). God would bless Ishmael (Gen. 17:20), but Ishmael was a child of the flesh, not promise. Thus, God's selecting purposes are seen in his choosing of Isaac not Ishmael (9:7b–9).

Next, God's selectivity is seen in his choice of Jacob over Esau even though they were twins, and Esau was born first (9:10–13). Paul quotes Genesis 25:23 in Romans 9:12: "it was

---

18. John Murray, *The Epistle to the Romans*, 2 vols., NICNT (Grand Rapids: Eerdmans, 1959–1965), 2:9.
19. Abraham also sired sons with Keturah, who were not part of the special seed line (Gen. 25:1–4).

said to her [Rebekah], 'THE OLDER WILL SERVE THE YOUNGER.'" Paul also references Malachi 1:2–3 in Romans 9:13—"Just as it is written, 'JACOB I LOVED, BUT ESAU I HATED.'" Both Genesis 25:23 and Malachi 1:1–5 emphasize God's corporate election of Israel, and that is Paul's point here.[20] Paul will soon discusses individual election within Israel and the Gentiles (9:24–26), but here his point is that God sovereignly selected Israel's patriarchs and the people of Israel.

Romans 9:6b–13 shows in two ways that selectivity is part of God's means to accomplish his purposes. First, only ethnic Israelites with faith constitute the true Israel. And second, God chose the promised seed line from Abraham.

God's Selectivity over Israel and Gentiles (9:14–29)

With 9:14–18, Paul addresses the issue of God's fairness concerning his choosing purposes. God shows compassion to and hardens whomever he desires. He is not subject to man's concerns about fairness (9:19–23). Using the potter and clay analogy, which in Jeremiah 18:1–11 addresses God's sovereignty over nations, Paul asserts God can do as he wills with his creation. God endures with much patience "vessels of wrath prepared for destruction" and makes known "the riches of His glory upon vessels of mercy" prepared for glory (9:22–23).

God's electing purposes relate to both Jews and Gentiles according to 9:24–26, where Paul quotes Hosea 2:23 and 1:10 to show God can make outsiders his people. The Hosea passages were written to the disobedient northern tribes of Israel facing judgment and the loss of their kingdom. Since Paul applies these passages from Hosea to believing Jews and Gentiles, some believe Paul is redefining the concept of Israel

---

20. The first part of Genesis 25:23 states, "Two nations are in your [Rebekah's] womb." Malachi 1:1–5 discusses the descendants of Jacob (Israel) and descendants of Esau (Edom).

and identifying the church as Israel.[21] But Paul's point in 9:24–
26 is not to redefine Israel to include Gentiles. In this section
emphasizing God's sovereignty, *Paul uses Hosea to emphasize
God's calling purposes to make a non-people his people*: "'I will call
those who were not My people, 'My people'" (Rom. 9:25).
Vessels of mercy exist because God chooses and calls some to
be his people. This principle, found in Hosea 2:23 and 1:10,
applies to both believing Jews and Gentiles. Concerning Paul's
use of Hosea, S. Lewis Johnson explains,

> It is the sovereign purpose of grace in the salvation of both Israel
> and the Gentiles that is the point. In other words, the analogy is
> not a national or ethnic one; it is a soteriological one. . . . Paul
> thus lays stress from Hosea on the electing grace of the calling
> of both the Gentiles in the present time and the mass of ethnic
> Israel in the future. This is the point that he finds in Hosea, and
> it is most appropriate.[22]

While I would also apply 9:24–26 to believing Jews in the
present, Johnson is correct that Paul's main point concerns
God's "electing grace" of saved Jews and Gentiles. Paul is not
transforming the concept of *Israel*. He distinguishes believing
Gentiles from Israel before and after 9:24–26. The next verse
explicitly refers to ethnic Israel—"Isaiah cries out concerning
Israel" (9:27a). If Paul redefines Israel in 9:24–26, it would be
odd that he immediately uses "Israel" in the traditional sense of
ethnic Jews in the next verse and throughout Romans 10–11.

The idea of Gentiles becoming God's people alongside
believing Israel is rooted in the OT. Isaiah 19:24–25 predicted,

---

21. George Eldon Ladd, "Historic Premillennialism," in *The Meaning of the
    Millennium: Four Views*, ed. Robert G. Clouse (Downers Grove, IL: InterVarsity
    Press, 1977), 24.
22. S. Lewis Johnson, "Evidence from Romans 9–11," in *A Case for Premillennialism:
    A New Consensus*, ed. Donald K. Campbell and Jeffrey L. Townsend (Chicago:
    Moody, 1992), 209.

> In that day Israel will be the third party with Egypt and Assyria, a blessing in the midst of the earth, whom the LORD of hosts has blessed, saying, "Blessed is *Egypt My people*, and *Assyria the work of My hands*, and *Israel My inheritance*." (emphasis added)

Isaiah predicted that Gentiles someday would become the people of God ("Egypt my people") alongside Israel, who is also God's people ("Israel My inheritance"). *God's plans involve the expansion of the people of God concept, but not the expansion of Israel to include Gentiles*. God's plan is to bless Gentiles as Gentiles alongside believing Israel. And believing Gentiles in this age are becoming God's people in Christ. Romans 9:24–26 affirms this truth.

Why Israel Missed Righteousness (9:30–10:21)

Paul explains why Israel did not believe in its Messiah while some Gentiles did. According to Romans 9:30–10:4, *Gentiles who were not looking for righteousness found righteousness through faith in Jesus. But Israel did not find God's righteousness since it pursued righteousness by works of the Mosaic law and not by faith in Jesus, who is the end of the law* (10:4). Christ is the "stone" who brings righteousness, yet Israel stumbled over him (9:33). Some Gentiles were on the right side of history. But Israel was not. The law pointed to Jesus, but Israel passed him over, opting to establish their own righteousness through the Mosaic law. But because Jesus is "the end of the law for righteousness" (10:4), righteousness must be pursued through faith in him who is now near. That is Paul's main point in 10:5–13. The word of faith in Christ is near, so everyone who believes in him will be saved (10:9). This is true for both Jews and Greeks (10:12). Both now have the gospel preached to them. Using a principle from Psalm 19:4, Paul says the word of Christ is going forth and is accessible (10:18).

In addition to finding righteousness, Gentiles currently have a strategic role—provoking Israel to jealousy. With 10:19–21 Paul quotes Deuteronomy 32:21 and Isaiah 65:1–2

to show Gentiles would be blessed and provoke Israel to jealousy. Referencing Deuteronomy 32:21, Paul declares, "I WILL
MAKE YOU JEALOUS BY THAT WHICH IS NOT A NATION, BY A
NATION WITHOUT UNDERSTANDING WILL I ANGER YOU" (10:19).
This quotation reveals what Saucy calls a "minor theme of
the salvation of the Gentiles when Israel is in disobedience."[23]
This is an important part of Paul's argument in Romans 9–11
and is strategic to the "mystery" concept Paul mentions in
11:25—Gentiles will be blessed before the salvation of Israel
to provoke Israel to jealousy.

On one hand, the Scriptures often affirmed the major
theme that Israel's future repentance will usher in greater
world blessings (Isa. 2:2–4; 27:6; Amos 9:11–15). But the idea
of Gentiles experiencing blessings while Israel is disobedient
as a means to provoke Israel to jealousy is also taught in the
OT, although not as prominently. Saucy notes, "The OT not
only contained revelation of Israel's rebellious unbelief issu-
ing in the rejection of their Messiah. It also hinted that the
salvation that would come through the life and death of Christ
would go out to the Gentiles when Israel as a nation was in
disobedience and under the judgment of partial hardening."[24]
Also noting Paul's use of Deuteronomy 32:21 concerning
Gentile salvation before Israel's salvation, Beale and Gladd
state, "Paul identifies present Israel's judgment of hardening
and the Gentiles' salvation followed by Israel's redemption
with the same prophesied storyline in Deuteronomy."[25] The
expectation of Gentile salvation during Israel's disobedience
also appears in Isaiah 65:1–2, which Paul quotes in Romans
10:20–21:

---

23. Saucy, "Does the Apostle Paul Reverse the Prophetic Tradition of the Salvation
     of Israel and the Nations?," 71.
24. Ibid.
25. G. K. Beale and Benjamin L. Gladd, *Hidden but Now Revealed: A Biblical Theology
     of Mystery* (Downers Grove, IL: InterVarsity Press, 2014), 90–91. Beale and Gladd
     do not affirm the overall scenario I am presenting.

And Isaiah is very bold and says,

"I WAS FOUND BY THOSE WHO DID NOT SEEK ME,
I BECAME MANIFEST TO THOSE WHO DID NOT ASK FOR ME."

But as for Israel He says, "ALL THE DAY LONG I HAVE STRETCHED
OUT MY HANDS TO A DISOBEDIENT AND OBSTINATE PEOPLE."

Debate exists whether Isaiah 65:1 refers to Gentiles or Israel. That Isaiah often refers to Gentile salvation (19:24–25) and the situation in 65:1 contrasts with that of unbelieving Israel in 65:2 reveals Gentiles could be in view. So Isaiah 65:1–2 and Paul's use of this text support the idea of Gentiles seeking the Lord while national Israel was obstinate.

Also, Isaiah 52–53 could support the idea of Gentile salvation before the salvation of Israel. Paul quotes Isaiah 53:1 in Romans 10:16: "However, they did not all heed the good news; for Isaiah says, 'LORD, WHO HAS BELIEVED OUR REPORT?'" This shows that Israel would reject the good news for a time. Isaiah 52–53 predicted the suffering servant and Israel's rejection of this Servant. Yet Isaiah 52:15 says the servant will "sprinkle many nations," which means new covenant atonement will extend to Gentiles. The verse also says, "Kings will shut their mouths on account of Him; For what had not been told them they will see, And what they had not heard they will understand." Thus, Isaiah 52–53 foretells Israel's rejection of the suffering servant (Jesus) and his death extending to and benefiting Gentiles.

Put together, Deuteronomy 32:21 and possibly Isaiah 65:1–2 and 52–53 predicted Gentile blessings before the salvation of Israel. Paul draws on this theme and claims this development would provoke Israel to jealousy.

The Remnant and National Israel in God's Plans (11:1–32)

In Romans 11 Paul explicitly refutes the idea that God rejected Israel:

I say then, God has not rejected His people, has He? May it
never be! (11:1a)

God has not rejected His people whom He foreknew. (11:2a)

Paul's argument focuses on "His people," which is Israel as a
whole, the nation currently in unbelief as the verse before indicated (10:21). Paul will soon introduce the remnant as evidence
God has not rejected Israel in 11:1–6, but the nation is in mind
here. Paul's Gentile readers probably knew Jewish believers and
that Paul was a Jew, so they were aware of a Jewish remnant. Yet
they still concluded that God rejected Israel (11:18).

Paul offers two reasons why God has not rejected Israel:
(1) the present remnant of believing Israelites guarantees God
has not rejected Israel (11:1–6); and (2) God will save the mass
of national Israel in connection with Jesus's return (11:11–32).

Before looking at these two reasons, though, it is significant that Paul says God has not rejected Israel because Israel
is foreknown (11:2a). In Romans 8:29 Paul used "foreknew"
(*proegnō*) in regard to saved individuals. Peter also used the
term in relation to Jesus in 1 Peter 1:20. Paul now applies the
same term to Israel as a corporate entity. This highlights God's
unbreakable covenantal love for the nation Israel. In Amos 3:2
God told Israel, "You only have I *known* of all the families of the
earth" (ESV, emphasis added).

The Remnant as Evidence (11:1–6)

With 11:1–6 Paul says a remnant of believing Jews is proof God
has not rejected Israel. This includes Paul himself (11:1b). He
then refers to a previous time of apostasy when the prophet
Elijah believed he alone was faithful. But a remnant existed
then as seven thousand faithful Israelites did not worship Baal
(11:4). This principle of a remnant of Israel applies to the present: "In the same way then, there has also come to be at the
present time a remnant according to God's gracious choice"
(11:5). This choosing of a remnant is by God's grace (11:6). So

not only is there national election of Israel (11:2; Deut. 7:6); there is individual election within the nation.

Yet the remnant is not all there is to God's plans for Israel. The remnant guarantees Israel will not be destroyed. Isaiah 65:8 states, "So I will act on behalf of My servants [i.e., remnant] in order not to destroy all of them." Paul quotes Isaiah 1:9 in Romans 9:29 to show the remnant exists to preserve Israel from permanent destruction, "And just as Isaiah foretold, 'UNLESS THE LORD OF SABAOTH HAD LEFT TO US A POSTERITY, WE WOULD HAVE BECOME LIKE SODOM, AND WOULD HAVE RESEMBLED GOMORRAH.'" The remnant is a means to God purposes for the nation as a whole. As Rydelnik states, the remnant "is designed to be the earnest that God has given that one day God will fulfill the promise that 'all Israel will be saved.'"[26]

The Present State of the Remnant and National Israel (11:7–10)

Romans 11:7–10 addresses the present situation of both the remnant of Israel and Israel as a whole. Verse 7 states, "What then? What Israel is seeking, it has not obtained, but those who were chosen obtained it, and the rest were hardened." Paul then quotes Deuteronomy 29:4 and Psalm 69:22–23 to explain God's sovereignty over Israel's unbelief (Rom. 11:8–10).

Israel's Salvation and More Blessings for the World (11:11–15)

Verse 11 is a transitional verse. The pronouns "they," "their," and "them" here push the discussion from the remnant to the hardened mass of Israel mentioned in 11:7–10. Paul begins, "I say then, they did not stumble so as to fall, did they? May it never be!" (11:11a). He does not speak of the remnant as having stumbled, but Israel as a whole has stumbled. So, starting with v. 11 Paul shows that God's plans for Israel involve more than the remnant.

---

26. Michael Rydelnik, "The Jewish People: Evidence for the Truth of Scripture," in *The People, the Land, and the Future of Israel: Israel and the Jewish People in the Plan of God*, ed. Darrell L. Bock and Mitch Glaser (Grand Rapids: Kregel, 2014), 264.

Paul's "May it never be!" (11:11b) emphatically reveals that Israel's stumbling is not a permanent fall. A reversal is coming which is a major theme of 11:11–32. Verses 12, 15, 23, and 26 will explain what this reversal will mean.

With 11:11c, Paul states what Israel's current stumbling means for Gentiles: "But by their transgression salvation has come to the Gentiles, to make them jealous" (11:11c). This is the first of four times when Paul states that Israel's stumbling is used by God to bless Gentiles in this age (see also 11:12, 15, 30). This emphasizes that Israel's stumbling is a strategic part of God's plans. This development has a divine purpose—to make Israel jealous (10:19–21).

With v. 12 Paul offers a lesser to greater argument regarding national Israel's influence on the world, both now and later:

> Now if their [Israel's] transgression is riches for the world and their failure is riches for the Gentiles, how much more will their fulfillment be!

Israel's current "transgression" and "failure" bring "riches" for "the world" and "the Gentiles." The "riches" probably includes Gentile salvation and inclusion in Abrahamic covenant blessings in the present. But Israel's coming "fulfillment" will bring "much more" to the world.

The term for "fulfillment" is *plērōma*, best translated "fullness" or "completeness" in Paul's writings (see Rom. 15:20; Gal. 4:4). This is a rich, multidimensional term; it "is not easy to attribute a single, unambiguous meaning to it."[27] Also, no clear example exists where *plērōma* is understood quantitatively as "full number," and to interpret it this way in 11:12 (or 11:25) is not preferable.[28] Manfred Brauch notes, "the idea of a divinely predetermined number . . . is not within Paul's purview

---

27. Reinier Schippers, "πληρόω" *NIDNTT* 1:739.
28. Douglas J. Moo, *The Epistle to the Romans*, NICNT (Grand Rapids: Eerdmans, 1996), 689–90: "occurrences of *plērōma* with a straightforward numerical sense are rare, and entirely absent in biblical Greek elsewhere."

here. . . . When non-canonical Jewish apocalyptic literature speaks of a 'full number' of Israelites in relation to end events, the word used is not *plērōma*, but *arithmos*" (see Rev. 7:4).[29]

The qualitative sense of "fullness" or "completeness" is likely and in this context refers to Israel's salvation and everything God intends for Israel to be. This involves a full relationship and the great privileges of 9:4–5, including "the covenants," "the promises," and most importantly a saving relationship with the Messiah. This "fullness" includes national Israel's restoration and role in blessing other nations (Deut. 4:6–8; Isa. 2:2–4). Moo observes that if the qualitative connotation of *plērōma* is accurate, the word could mean "completion" in the sense of "the full restoration to Israel of the blessings of the kingdom that she is now, as a corporate entity, missing."[30] These matters associated with "fullness" are opposite to Israel's "transgression" and "failure," which led to Israel being "broken off" from fully experiencing God's privileges (Rom. 11:17).

The words "much more" show that Israel's completeness is linked with greater world blessings to come and points to an era better than the present one. Something like Isaiah 27:6 is probably in mind here: "In the days to come Jacob will take root, Israel will blossom and sprout, and they will fill the whole world with fruit."

Paul's point in 11:12 is that Israel's coming "fullness" (i.e., everything God intended for the nation) will bring better conditions for the world. This present age is not the complete fulfillment of God's purposes for Israel and the Gentiles. Jesus referred to a coming "regeneration" or "renewal" of the world (*palingenesia*) in connection with his second coming and a restored Israel:

---

29. Walter C. Kaiser Jr., Peter H. Davids, F. F. Bruce, and Manfred Brauch, *Hard Sayings of the Bible* (Downers Grove, IL: InterVarsity, 1996), 569.

30. Moo, *Romans*, 689. Moo believes this "fullness" "is attained through a numerical process" (ibid.).

> Truly I say to you, that you who have followed Me, in the regen-
> eration when the Son of Man will sit on His glorious throne,
> you also shall sit upon twelve thrones, judging the twelve tribes
> of Israel. (Matt. 19:28)

In a similar way, Acts 3:19–21 also speaks of a coming "restoration of all things" linked with Israel's repentance and the
second coming of Jesus. Speaking to "Men of Israel" (3:12),
Peter declared,

> Therefore repent and return, so that your sins may be wiped
> away, in order that times of refreshing may come from the
> presence of the Lord; and that He may send Jesus, the Christ
> appointed for you, whom heaven must receive until the period
> of restoration of all things about which God spoke by the mouth
> of His holy prophets from ancient time. (Acts 3:19–21)

The word for "restoration" in Acts 3:21 is *apokatastasis*, a term
used in verb form in Acts 1:6 concerning the kingdom being
restored to Israel. To restore something is to renew a marred
entity. The close connection of "restore" in Acts 1:6 and 3:21
indicates the coming "restoration" of Acts 3:21 includes the
restoration of Israel.

Murray notes that Israel's "fulfillment" in 11:12 must refer
to Israel as a whole and "cannot be the total of the elect of
Israel" since it "is contrasted with Israel's trespass and loss and
must refer to the restoration of faith and repentance of Israel as a
whole."[31] This also includes "restoration to the blessing of God's
kingdom."[32] The same Israel that committed the "transgression" must be the people who will experience the "fullness."
Also, if national Israel brought current riches to the world, the
greater blessings to follow must come from the nation as well.

---

31. Murray, *Romans*, 2:94.
32. Ibid., 2:79.

This greater result associated with Israel's salvation is further explained in v. 15:

> For if their [Israel's] rejection is the reconciliation of the world, what will their acceptance be but life from the dead?

Israel's rejection brought "reconciliation" to the world. But when Israel accepts the Messiah, the result will be "life from the dead." This "life from the dead" could be greater blessings to Gentiles or Israel or both. Or it could refer to physical resurrection from the dead. The Bible teaches both concepts, and they are not mutually exclusive. The world will be a better place, and physical resurrection will occur. The former is taught in passages like Isaiah 2:2–4 and 27:6. Also, Revelation 20:4 states that physical resurrection will occur for some at the first resurrection following Jesus's return. Narrowing "life from the dead" to just one thing is not necessary. The coming better era or kingdom brings a variety of blessings. "Life from the dead" probably includes more blessings for Gentiles and Israel, physical resurrection, and the restoration of creation, which Paul discussed in Romans 8:19–22. Since Paul speaks of national Israel here, some like Gadenz think he may have Ezekiel 37:1–14 in mind,[33] which speaks of resurrection, restoration, land, and new covenant inclusion for Israel.

Only one group can bring blessings to the world while in unbelief and then greater blessings for the world when this group believes. This cannot be true of the church since the church is not in unbelief and does not bring a global restoration of all things. Nor can it be said of the remnant of Israel, since the remnant alone does not usher in global blessings, and historically the remnant often suffered when Israel as a whole suffered. But it can be said of the nation Israel that is currently characterized by unbelief but will one day be saved.

---

33. Gadenz, *Called from the Jews and from the Gentiles*, 49n114.

A cause and effect relationship with chronological progression exists in Romans 11:11–15. Paul's argument can be stated thus ("→" means "leads to"):

> Israel's unbelief → Gentile salvation → Israel's belief → greater world blessings

How Israel and Gentiles Relate to the Abrahamic Covenant (11:16–24)

With 11:1–15 Paul explains the importance of a remnant of Israel and what the restoration of Israel will mean for the world. Then with 11:16 he offers two illustrations concerning why God has not rejected Israel: (1) a lump of dough and (2) an olive tree. The first is found in 11:16a: "Now if the firstfruits offered up are holy, so is the whole batch" (HCSB). This lump of dough analogy with its firstfruits alludes to Numbers 15:17–21. Paul uses this analogy to connect either Israel's patriarchs or the believing remnant of Israel with Israel as a whole. Both understandings are possible although the remnant view is more likely. The remnant was the focus of 11:1–6, and Paul uses the "firstfruits" concept concerning initial converts in 1 Corinthians 16:15. This understanding fits well here.

The remnant of Israel functions as a "firstfruits" of what God will do for the "whole batch," that is, the nation. Because the remnant of Israel is holy, the nation is holy too. The remnant influences the whole of Israel and preserves it for a better destiny. This shows the remnant is not an end in itself but guarantees and anticipates the salvation of the nation (11:26).

Next, Paul offers an olive tree analogy in Romans 11:16b–24. The root of this tree is connected to its branches. Some natural branches were broken off from the tree. Then a wild olive branch that was separate from the olive tree is grafted into the tree to partake of its rich root. Yet the wild olive branch is warned not to become arrogant toward the natural branches since God is able to graft the natural branches back into their own tree. Unbelief of the wild branch could lead to its removal from the tree. Also, if the natural branches cease their unbelief, then God is able to graft them back into the tree. The point is that the wild branch should not be arrogant and think the natural branches are forever cut off from the tree since God can graft the natural branches into their own tree again.

A progression of events is evident: (1) branches are naturally connected to the olive tree; (2) some natural branches were broken off from the tree because of unbelief (11:17a, 20a); (3) a wild branch is grafted into the tree (11:17b, 19); and (4) natural branches will be grafted into the olive tree if/when they believe (11:23).[34]

This analogy concerns how Israel and Gentiles historically relate to Abrahamic covenant blessings. The reason for this analogy was Gentile arrogance (11:18). Some adopted a replacement position against Israel. As Moo observes, "these Gentile believers were apparently convinced that they belonged to a new people of God that had simply replaced Israel."[35]

What do the components of the olive tree illustration represent? The natural branches refer to Israelites, and the wild branches represent believing Gentiles. The "rich root" is the Abrahamic covenant with the patriarchs. Paul's mention of Israel's "fathers" in 9:5 and 11:28 and their links with the "covenants" and "promises" show the importance of the patriarchs and Abrahamic covenant in Paul's thinking. Plus the concept of "root" referring to Abraham and the patriarchs is well-established in Jewish literature.[36]

Finally, the olive tree refers to the place of blessing stemming from the patriarchs and the Abrahamic covenant. There are around twenty references to "olive tree(s)" in the Bible.

---

34. The condition of belief is necessary for this fourth step to occur, but the context of 11:12, 15, 26 indicates that belief of the branches (Israel) will occur. Context indicates a predictive element.

35. Moo, *Romans*, 704.

36. See Christian Mauer, "ῥίζα," *TDNT* 6:987–89; Moo, *Romans*, 699n13. Some believe Jesus is the "root." But while covenant promises are fulfilled in Jesus, the Messiah comes from the patriarchs and Israel to fulfill God's covenant purposes (9:4–5).

The olive tree is often linked with fruitfulness, prosperity, and blessing. Israel is called a green olive tree in Jeremiah 11:16. The "olive trees" in Revelation 11:4 refer to two witnesses who prophecy for 1,260 days. Context will determine which meaning of olive tree is meant. In Romans 11, the "olive tree" is the place of blessing from the Abrahamic covenant. The Abrahamic covenant contains dozens of promises—some personal (Abraham), some national (Israel), and some international (Gentiles). It also involves spiritual and physical blessings. The Abrahamic covenant is also the foundational covenant for the Davidic and new covenants.[37] The Abrahamic covenant reveals that the nation from Abraham (Israel) will be a vehicle for blessing the families and nations of the earth (Gen. 12:2–3; 18:18). This covenant was designed to eventually include both Israel and the Gentiles (Gal. 3:7–9). Paul reaffirms this truth in Romans 4 when he states that Abraham's justification before circumcision qualified him to be both the father of believing Gentiles and the father of believing Jews (Rom. 4:9–12). Both groups are related to Abraham even though they maintain their unique identities.

Some claim the olive tree represents Israel so that when Gentiles are grafted into the tree, they become part of Israel.[38] But, again, the olive tree is often used of blessings (Hag. 2:19), and the main point of Paul's illustration is to show the relationship of Israel and Gentiles to the blessings of the Abrahamic covenant, not to identify all grafted into the tree as "Israel." Plus, "Israel" is represented by the natural branches, organically connected to the tree, that are broken off and later grafted in again. Israel is connected to the olive tree but is not the tree itself. The "olive tree" must be broader than Israel since it encompasses both Israel and Gentiles. And after this illustration Paul consistently distinguishes believing Gentiles from Israel.

---

37. The new covenant, which replaces the Mosaic covenant, emphasizes Holy Spirit-enablement so that God's people can obey him from the heart. This covenant results from the Messiah, who inaugurates the new covenant.

38. See O. Palmer Robertson, *The Israel of God: Yesterday, Today, and Tomorrow* (Phillipsburg, NJ: Presbyterian & Reformed, 2000), 188.

The broken off branches (11:17a) represent unbelieving Israel temporarily removed from experiencing covenant blessings. Yet Gentiles, as represented by "wild olive" branches, have been "grafted in" and are now partakers of the rich root of the olive tree (i.e., Abrahamic covenant) (11:17b, 19). They are now grafted into covenant blessings. Gentiles have become the people of God as predicted in Genesis 12:3 and 22:18 (Gal. 3:7–9). Gentiles experience the spiritual benefits of the covenants. As Romans 15:27 reveals, "the Gentiles have shared in their [Jews'] spiritual things." But the story does not end here. Israel will be grafted back into covenant blessings. Romans 11:23 states, "and they [Israel] also, if they do not continue in their unbelief, will be grafted in, for God is able to graft them in again." A coming grafting in of Israel will occur in the future.

In summary, the olive tree analogy presents a progression of events:

Israel naturally related to the olive tree (Abrahamic covenant) (v. 16b)

then

Unbelieving Israel cut off from the olive tree (v. 17a)

then

Believing Gentiles grafted into the olive tree (v. 17b)

then

Believing Israel grafted back into the olive tree (v. 23)

Paul's olive tree analogy warns Gentiles against concluding they had replaced Israel. *Gentile inclusion does not mean national Israel's exclusion.* The patriarchs/Abrahamic covenant supports the Gentiles. And if God grafted Gentiles into the place of blessing, he certainly can graft Israel back into covenant blessings connected with Israel's patriarchs (11:21–24). This will occur when "all Israel" is "saved" (11:26). This analogy parallels Leviticus 26:40–45, where God stated that Israel's repentance will lead to Israel's reinstatement to Abrahamic covenant blessings, including the land:

> *If they confess their iniquity and the iniquity of their forefathers, in their unfaithfulness which they committed against Me*, and also in their acting with hostility against Me . . . or if their uncircumcised heart becomes humbled so that they then make amends for their iniquity, *then I will remember My covenant with Jacob, and I will remember also My covenant with Isaac, and My covenant with Abraham as well, and I will remember the land.* (Lev. 26:40–42, emphasis added)

The Abrahamic covenant was meant to include both Israel and Gentiles (Gen. 12:2–3). Some claim that when Gentiles become related to Abraham, they become spiritual Jews or Israel.[39] But when Gentiles participate in the Abrahamic covenant, they do not become Israel—they *partake* in the covenant *with* believing Israelites. This is consistent with Ephesians 3:6: "that the Gentiles are *fellow heirs* and *fellow members* of the body, and *fellow partakers* of the promise in Christ Jesus through the gospel" (emphasis added). Believing Gentiles share with believing Jews in the great privileges of God, yet they do so as Gentiles, not as Israel.

Unity and diversity exist within the people of God. Believing Jews and Gentiles are united in salvation through faith in Jesus. Both are sons of Abraham (Rom. 4:9–12; Gal. 3:29), and both benefit from the blessings of the Abrahamic covenant. Yet Israel remains Israel, and Gentiles remain Gentiles. While both the "natural" and "wild" branches have a relationship to the same olive tree through faith in Christ, the branches are still distinguished.[40]

The Coming Salvation of National Israel (11:25–26a)

With 11:25a Paul mentions a "mystery." The concept of "mystery" in the NT is multi-faceted and can refer to

---

39. Ladd says, "If Abraham is the father of a spiritual people, and if all believers are sons of Abraham, his offspring, then it follows that they are Israel, spiritually speaking" (Ladd, "Historic Premillennialism," 24).

40. See A. Andrew Das, *Solving the Romans Debate* (Minneapolis: Augsburg Fortress, 2007), 245.

(1) hidden meanings found in symbols (Rev. 1:20; 17:5, 7), (2) a completely new truth not found in previous Scripture (1 Cor. 15:51), or (3) an earlier truth in the OT that is now coming to fruition with Jesus (Eph. 6:19). Beale and Gladd define "mystery" generally as "the revelation of God's partially hidden wisdom, particularly as it concerns events occurring in the 'latter days.'"[41] This third sense of "mystery" fits in 11:25–26 since the components of Paul's "mystery" have tentacles in the OT.

What is this "mystery"? It relates to the order of salvation concerning Gentiles and Israel, with particular focus on Gentile salvation before the salvation of national Israel. Paul says, "a partial hardening has happened to Israel until the fullness of the Gentiles has come in; and so all Israel will be saved" (11:25b–26a). There are three components to this "mystery":

- A partial hardening has happened to Israel.
- This partial hardening of Israel exists until the fullness of the Gentiles comes in.
- It is "in this manner" or "then" that all Israel will be saved.

First, a "partial hardening has happened to Israel." Some within Israel have not believed. Second, this partial hardening exists only for a time—"until the fullness of the Gentiles has come in." Like 11:12, the qualitative sense of *plērōma* ("fullness") is the best understanding here. While some prefer the quantitative sense of "full number," this interpretation is too narrow and does not grasp the richness of this term in this context. The "fullness of the Gentiles" refers to the completion of God's purposes for Gentiles in this present age. This includes Gentile salvation and the role of Gentiles in provoking Israel to jealousy. Thus, when God's plan for saving the Gentiles as provokers of Israel's jealousy in this age is over, Israel as a whole will be saved. Concerning *plērōma* in v. 25, James Denney states,

---

41. Beale and Gladd, *Hidden but Now Revealed*, 20.

"When the Gentiles in their full strength have come in, the power which is to provoke Israel to jealousy will be fully felt, with the result described in verse 26."[42]

The term "until" (*achris hou*) in 11:25 is important. In the NT, "until" usually indicates a coming change or reversal of circumstances after a period of time. If the usual meaning of "until" exists in 11:25, Israel's partial hardening will be reversed. Israel as a whole will go from unbelief to belief. As Schreiner observes, "The word 'until' implies that the hardening of the majority of Israel will be lifted *after* the full number of Gentiles are saved."[43]

Some, however, believe *achris hou* ("until") in 11:25 should be understood in a terminative sense.[44] Allegedly, the partial hardening of Israel continues up to the fullness of the Gentiles without a change of circumstances thereafter. So "until" would mean "up to a certain point" or "until a certain goal is reached."[45] But most cases of *achris* ("until") in the NT indicate a reversal or change in previous conditions after a period of time. *Achris* occurs 48 times outside of Romans 11:25 in the NT. Eleven times a spatial understanding occurs, so 37 uses relate to time. In his study of *achris*, Waymeyer observes that 27 of the 37 uses likely refer to a period of time that will come to an end followed by a change in circumstances.[46] Thus, reversal is predominately connected with this term. Sam Storms, who himself adopts the terminative understanding of *achris hou* in Romans 11:25, admits "it should be openly acknowledged that this is not its most frequent sense," and that those who adopt

---

42. James Denney, "St. Paul's Epistle to the Romans," in *The Expositor's Greek Testament*, ed. W. Robertson Nicoll (Grand Rapids: Eerdmans, 1990), 2:683.

43. Thomas R. Schreiner, *Romans*, BECNT (Grand Rapids: Baker Academic, 1998), 618 (emphasis in original).

44. Robertson, *Israel of God*, 179.

45. Robert L. Reymond, *A New Systematic Theology of the Christian Faith*, 2nd ed. (Nashville: Nelson, 1998), 1028.

46. Matt Waymeyer, "The Identity of 'All Israel' in Romans 11:26" (ThM thesis, The Master's Seminary, 2003), 137. See Moo, *Romans*, 717n30.

the terminative understanding of *achris hou* are going with "an admittedly rare sense of 'until' in verse 25."[47]

But could *achris hou* in Romans 11:25 be an exception to the normal sense of reversal? Probably not. The temporal use of *achris* can function either as a preposition or a conjunction in the NT. Significantly, as Deere points out, when *achris* functions as a conjunction, it has the meaning "until," with a coming change of circumstances.[48] Thus, when *achris* is used as a conjunction, it "more than implies a change which 'occurs after the point to which it refers is reached.'"[49] This is important since *achris hou* functions as a conjunction in Romans 11:25. Israel is experiencing a partial hardening "until" the fullness of the Gentiles comes in. So even before 11:26a is considered, the normal sense of *achris hou* points to a reversal of circumstances for Israel. Then when 11:26a declares the salvation of "all Israel," there is little doubt Paul intends a reversal of circumstances for Israel. The

---

47. Sam Storms, *Kingdom Come: The Amillennial Alternative* (Fearn, Scotland: Mentor, 2013), 323.

48. Jack S. Deere, "Premillennialism in Revelation 20," *BSac* 135 (1978): 68.

49. When *achris* is used as a conjunction with the aorist subjunctive, it "more than implies a change which 'occurs after the point to which it refers is reached'" (ibid.). This applies to 1 Corinthians 11:26, where some, like Robertson, think a terminative sense of "until" exists (*Israel of God*, 179). This verse reads, "For as often as you eat this bread and drink the cup, you proclaim the Lord's death until He comes." But Paul's words are similar to Luke 22:15–20, where Jesus explicitly says the Lord's Supper will be replaced by a face-to-face banquet in the kingdom. Verses 15–16 state, "And He said to them, 'I have earnestly desired to eat this Passover with you before I suffer; for I say to you, I shall never again eat it *until* it is fulfilled in the kingdom of God'" (see also 22:17–18) (emphasis added). The Lord's Supper will be replaced by Passover celebration (22:16) and eating and drinking at Jesus's kingdom table when the disciples are ruling over the restored twelve tribes of Israel (Luke 22:29–30). Some also see a terminative understanding of "until" in 1 Corinthians 15:25 (Robertson, *Israel of God*, 180), where Paul says, "For He [Jesus] must reign until He has put all His enemies under His feet." But while Jesus certainly will reign in the coming eternal kingdom (Rev. 22:3), Paul is referring specifically to Jesus's successful mediatorial kingdom reign as the Last Adam (Ps. 8:6; 1 Cor. 15:45). After this phase of kingdom reign, Jesus will hand his kingdom over to the Father according to 1 Corinthians 15:24, 28. Jesus's mediatorial kingdom reign in 1 Corinthians 15:25 will transition to an eternal kingdom of the Father. It should not be assumed that 1 Corinthians 11:26 and 15:25 are clear examples of a terminal understanding of "until." A reversal of conditions occurs with both.

coming salvation of Israel will replace the current unbelief of the mass of Israel.

Also, Jesus used "until" in Luke 21:24 to indicate a reversal of circumstances for Israel after a time of calamity: "They [Jews] will fall by the edge of the sword, and will be led captive into all the nations; and Jerusalem will be trampled under foot by the Gentiles until [*achris hou*] the times of the Gentiles be fulfilled." Jesus's use of "until" means that the captivity of the Jewish people and the trampling of Jerusalem by the Gentiles will end and be replaced with positive conditions for the Jewish people and Jerusalem after the "times of the Gentiles" occurs (Luke 21:24).[50] The fate of Israel and Jerusalem is not trampling with no reversal, especially when the kingdom of God is near (Luke 21:31). As J. Bradley Chance notes, "Close examination of L. 21:24b,c provides a strong hint that Luke did foresee the restoration of Jerusalem."[51] George Ladd connects Luke 21:24 with a positive reversal of fortune for Israel in Romans 11:26:

> The divine judgment is to rest upon Jerusalem and upon the Jewish nation until the "times of the Gentiles," i.e., the divine visitation of the Gentiles is accomplished. When God's purpose for the Gentiles is fulfilled, so this verse implies, Jerusalem will no longer be trodden down. There will be a restoration of Israel; "all Israel will be saved."[52]

The third element of the "mystery" is the salvation of Israel— "and so all Israel will be saved" (11:26a). This statement involves

---

50. The "times of the Gentiles" (Luke 21:24) and "fullness of the Gentiles" (Rom. 11:25) both relate to Israel but are not exactly the same. The former refers to the period of Gentile domination over Jerusalem and Israel. The latter refers to the completion of Gentile salvation as a means of provoking Israel to jealousy.

51. J. Bradley Chance, *Jerusalem, the Temple, and the New Age in Luke-Acts* (Macon, GA: Mercer University Press, 1988), 134.

52. George Eldon Ladd, *The Gospel of the Kingdom: Popular Expositions on the Kingdom of God* (Grand Rapids: Eerdmans, 1959), 120. Ladd's concept of "restoration" is not the same as mine.

three strategic interpretive issues—the meaning of (1) "and so", (2) "all Israel", and (3) "will be saved."

"And So." Paul starts 11:26 with "and so" (*kai houtōs*). Two main interpretive options exist here. The first is temporal: *"then all Israel will be saved."* With this view a fullness of the Gentiles occurs, and then afterwards, all Israel will be saved.

The second is modal: *"in this manner all Israel will be saved."* With the modal option, some assert Paul is speaking only of the manner of the salvation of "all Israel." Those who hold this view argue that whether through God's saving Jews and Gentiles in this age or through saving the remnant of Israel throughout history until Jesus's return, it is in this *manner* that all Israel will be saved. Manner is the issue, not time.[53] Allegedly, the saving of Jews and Gentiles, or the remnant of Israel in history, is the way God saves all Israel. Adherents of this understanding often deny a temporal sense of *kai houtōs* and the implication that the salvation of Israel will occur *after* the fullness of the Gentiles.

Which understanding is correct, temporal or modal? The temporal view of *kai houtōs* has scholarly support. P. H. R. van Houwelingen notes, "the temporal interpretation [in Rom. 11:26a] is gaining favor and rightly so."[54] P. W. van der Horst argues, "Quite apart from the grammatical and lexical possibilities that the word *houtos* had, it is also the context of Romans 11 that makes it very probable that it was the temporal meaning of *houtos* that the author had in mind here."[55] Kenneth Gentry observes, "Many noted commentators accept the outright temporal significance of the term (M. Stuart, C. K. Barrett, E. Käsemann, B. Corley), while others allow its temporal nuance

---

53. See Alan S. Bandy and Benjamin L. Merkle, *Understanding Prophecy: A Biblical-Theological Approach* (Grand Rapids: Kregel, 2015), 255.

54. P. H. R. van Houwelingen, "The Redemptive-Historical Dynamics of the Salvation of 'All Israel' (Rom. 11:26a)," *CTJ* 46 (2011): 305.

55. P. W. van der Horst, "'Only Then Will All Israel Be Saved': A Short Note on the Meaning of καὶ οὕτως in Romans 11:26," *JBL* 119 (2000): 524.

here (O. Michel, J. D. G. Dunn, R. Schmitt, A. Feuillet)."[56]
Van der Horst believes it is a "false argument" to conclude *kai
houtōs* never has a temporal sense.[57] A temporal sense of *kai
houtōs* could exist in 1 Thessalonians 4:17: "Then we who are
alive and remain will be caught up together with them in the
clouds to meet the Lord in the air, and so [*kai houtōs*] we shall
always be with the Lord" (see also 1 Cor. 11:28).

So should *kai houtōs* in Romans 11:26 be translated in the
temporal sense of "then"? This is possible. Yet even if a modal
understanding of manner is in view, which is also possible, the
context of Romans 11:11–24 so heavily involves chronological progression that manner in this context involves a temporal
reference. As Schreiner says, "the temporal element of the text
is present regardless of the meaning of καὶ οὕτως [*kai houtōs*]."[58]
Also, since other chronological indicators are in the immediate
context, such as progression within the olive tree analogy and
the words "until" and "will be saved," it is likely a temporal
element exists with *kai houtōs* in 11:26a. If this is accurate, Paul
is speaking of a future salvation of ethnic Israel after the period
of Israel's partial hardening.

"All Israel." What does Paul mean by "all Israel?" That he refers
to ethnic Israel is certain since the designation comes in the
context of distinctions between ethnic Israelites and Gentiles
before and after 11:26. Attempts to make "all Israel" the church
regardless of ethnicity fail since the context before and after
does not allow this understanding. As Murray pointed out,
"It is exegetically impossible to give to 'Israel' in this verse any
other denotation than that which belongs to the term throughout this chapter. . . . It is of ethnic Israel Paul is speaking and

---

56. Kenneth L. Gentry Jr., "A Postmillennial Response," in *Three Views on the
    Millennium and Beyond*, ed. Darrell L. Bock, Counterpoints (Grand Rapids:
    Zondervan, 1999), 135.
57. Horst, "Only Then Will All Israel Be Saved," 524.
58. Schreiner, *Romans*, 618n16.

Israel could not possibly include Gentiles."[59] Plus, telling Gentiles they are really the true Israel would only fuel the fire of the original problem in Romans 9–11—namely, that Israel has been rejected and replaced. This would be like pouring gasoline on a fire one is trying to extinguish.

Ethnic Israelites are in view, but does Paul use "all Israel" in a diachronic sense of the entirety of Israel throughout history? Or does he use it in a synchronic sense of the whole of Israel at a particular time? The designation "all Israel" occurs almost 150 times in the Bible and is found most frequently in Deuteronomy, 1–2 Samuel, 1–2 Kings, and 1–2 Chronicles. Most if not all uses are synchronic—referring to the whole or majority of Israel at the time of the circumstances being described. For example,

> Moses chose able men out of *all Israel* and made them heads over the people. (Exod. 18:25a)

> Then Moses summoned *all Israel* and said to them: "Hear, O Israel. . . ." (Deut. 5:1a)

> Now the LORD said to Joshua, "This day I will begin to exalt you in the sight of *all Israel*." (Josh. 3:7a)

> And David assembled *all Israel* at Jerusalem to bring up the ark of the LORD. (1 Chron. 15:3)

Paul follows the synchronic sense of "all Israel" in 11:26 and predicts a mass-conversion of Israel at a future time. This does not mean every single Israelite, but the majority of Israel at the time. Just as the majority of Israel rejected Jesus at his first coming, but some believed (the remnant), so too the majority of Israel will believe in Jesus at his second coming, even if some

---

59. Murray, *The Epistle to the Romans*, 2:96.

do not. Also, this view does not mean all Israelites of all ages will be saved.[60]

"Will be saved." Since Paul links "all Israel" with a future tense verb ("will be saved"), he sees Israel's salvation occurring in the future connected with Jesus's return. When this will happen Paul does not know. The salvation of national Israel is a coming dramatic event that replaces the current unbelief. This future event is consistent with other references to national Israel's future in Romans 11:11–26:

> [H]ow much more *will* their fulfillment be! (11:12)

> [W]hat *will* their acceptance be but life from the dead? (11:15)[61]

> And they also, if they do not continue in their unbelief, *will be* grafted in. (11:23)

> [H]ow much more *will* these who are the natural branches be grafted into their own olive tree? (11:24)

> [A] partial hardening has happened to Israel *until* the fullness of the Gentiles has come in. (11:25)

> [A]nd so all Israel *will be* saved; just as it is written, "THE DELIVERER WILL COME FROM ZION, HE WILL REMOVE UNGODLINESS FROM JACOB." (11:26)

When Israel's coming salvation takes place, Paul's hope and prayer will be realized. Lament for Israel as a whole will give way to fulfillment for Israel:

---

60. Ezekiel 20:30–38 reveals that not every Israelite will enter the land and benefit from the new covenant.

61. There is no future verb in 11:12, 15 although the thrust is future-oriented.

> *Paul's hope*: "Brethren, my heart's desire and my prayer to God for them is for their salvation" (10:1).

> *Paul's hope realized*: "and so all Israel will be saved" (11:26a).

A coming corporate salvation of national Israel is also taught in Matthew 23:37–39. Even though a remnant of Jews had believed in him, Jesus told unbelieving Israel ("Jerusalem, Jerusalem") it would soon experience national judgment concerning its city and temple—"your house is being left to you desolate" (v. 38). But this unbelief and judgment for the people and their city would be reversed by belief. Quoting Psalm 118:26, a psalm of praise, Jesus declared, "For I say to you, from now on you will not see Me until you say, 'BLESSED IS HE WHO COMES IN THE NAME OF THE LORD!'" (Matt. 23:39). The word "until" indicates a transition for Israel. Jesus will remove his presence from Israel for a time because of Israel's unbelief. But one day Israel will experience his personal presence in a positive way. This occurs in connection with a heartfelt embrace of the Messiah. Ladd notes that Matthew 23:37–39 is evidence that "Israel is yet to be saved."[62]

Likewise, in Acts 3:19–20 Peter tells the "men of Israel" in Jerusalem that their repentance will lead to the return of Jesus: "Therefore repent and return, so that your sins may be wiped away, in order that times of refreshing may come from the presence of the Lord; and that He may send Jesus, the Christ appointed for you." Again, Israel's salvation is linked with the return of Jesus. Linking this text with Romans 11, Ben Witherington observes that "Christ's second coming is seen as in some sense dependent on Israel's repentance (cf. Rom. 11:12, 15, 26)."[63]

---

62. Ladd, *Gospel of the Kingdom*, 120.
63. Ben Witherington III, *The Acts of the Apostles: A Socio-Rhetorical Commentary* (Grand Rapids: Eerdmans, 1998), 187.

Israel's Salvation Predicted in Old Testament (11:26b–27)

Israel's coming salvation is consistent with the OT:

> "THE DELIVERER WILL COME FROM ZION,
> HE WILL REMOVE UNGODLINESS FROM JACOB."
> "THIS IS MY COVENANT WITH THEM,
> WHEN I TAKE AWAY THEIR SINS." (11:26b–27)

Paul links Israel's salvation with Isaiah 59:20–21, Isaiah 27:9, and probably Psalm 14:7 ("out of Zion"). Isaiah 59 describes Israel's sinfulness (59:1–8), national confession of sin (59:9–19), and the Lord saving and bringing his Spirit to Israel with the new covenant (59:20–21). Then the nations will be drawn to and blessed by Israel—"Nations will come to your light, and kings to the brightness of your rising" (Isa. 60:3). Isaiah 27 also speaks of Israel's salvation (27:9) and restoration that bring blessings for the world (27:6). Psalm 14:7 declares, "Oh, that the *salvation of Israel* would come *out of Zion!* When the LORD *restores* His captive people . . ." (emphasis added). Thus, the informing theology of Isaiah 59–60, Isaiah 27, and Psalm 14 points to a salvation and restoration of national Israel. The former two passages also include blessings to the nations.

The reference to the "Deliverer" coming "from Zion" concerns Jesus's second coming. The thrust of Romans 11:11–27 is on a future climactic event that reverses national Israel's unbelief and ushers in greater world blessings. Jesus's second coming, not his first, accomplishes this.[64] Paul's first reference to "Zion" in 9:33 concerned Israel's stumbling over Jesus at his first coming. However, Paul's second reference to "Zion" in 11:26 relates to Israel's salvation with Jesus's second coming.

---

64. For a defense of the first coming view, see Christopher R. Bruno, "The Deliverer from Zion: The Source(s) and Function of Paul's Citation in Romans 11:26–27," *TynBul* 59 (2008): 119–34.

Another issue concerns Paul's understanding of "from Zion." While Isaiah 59:20 says the Deliverer will come "to Zion," Paul says the Deliverer will come "from [*ek*] Zion." Is Paul changing Isaiah's message and adding a heavenly dimension to "Zion"? Not necessarily. Paul's use of "Zion" in Romans 9:33 concerned earthly Zion, and "Zion" probably has this same meaning in 11:26 too.

But why does Paul use "from" and not "to" concerning Zion? Paul may be conflating Psalm 14:7 ("out of Zion") with Isaiah 59:20. If so, he is not changing Isaiah's message. Yet even if there is no conflation, the different prepositions ("to" and "from"), while duly noted, should not be pushed to mean Isaiah and Paul have mutually exclusive ideas. Paul's use of "from" could emphasize Jesus's rule from earthly Zion (i.e., Jerusalem) stemming from Jesus's return to Jerusalem (Ps. 110:1–2). The statements that the Deliverer is coming "to Zion" (Isa. 59:20) and "from Zion" (Rom. 11:27) can be harmonized. Isaiah declared both concepts. In addition to saying the Deliverer comes "*to* Zion" (Isa. 59:20), Isaiah also says, "For the law will go forth *from* Zion" (Isa. 2:3, emphasis added). Psalm 110:2a states, "The LORD will stretch forth Your [Messiah's] strong scepter *from Zion*" (emphasis added). Thus, Romans 11:26 could refer to Jesus's rule "from Zion" (earthly Jerusalem) connected with his second coming to Jerusalem as stated in Isaiah 59:20.

The Dual Status of National Israel (11:28)

Romans 11:26–27 reveals that Israel as a whole will be saved in connection with the return of Jesus. Verse 28 confirms that Paul was speaking of the nation Israel: "From the standpoint of the gospel they are enemies for your sake, but from the standpoint of God's choice they are beloved for the sake of the fathers."

Here Paul reveals a *dual status* of Israel that exists simultaneously. The first status is that of enemy. The second is that of "beloved"—"from the standpoint of God's choice they are beloved for the sake of the fathers." This group who is both enemy and "beloved" in 11:28 is linked with the "all Israel" of

11:26, the "all Israel" who will be saved.[65] This verifies that the "all Israel" in 11:26 concerns Israel as a whole. Only the people of Israel in unbelief at the time of Paul's writing could simultaneously be both an enemy of the gospel and beloved by God.

Romans 11:28 shows "all Israel" cannot be the church since the church is not an enemy of the gospel. Also, "all Israel" cannot be the remnant of believing ethnic Israelites throughout history since the remnant is not both beloved of God and an enemy of the gospel at the same time. Perhaps the argument could be made that the remnant goes from being "enemy" to being "beloved," but this is not what Paul describes for "all Israel." As Waymeyer observes, "Paul's use of the correlative conjunctions indicates that these individuals are *simultaneously* 'enemies' and 'beloved,' not enemies for a time and then later beloved."[66]

Israel's Irrevocable Gifts and Calling (11:29)

Romans 11:29 further explains why God has not rejected Israel: "for the gifts and the calling of God are irrevocable." "Gifts" is plural and likely refers to the eight privileges mentioned in 9:4–5. Again this shows Paul has the nation as a whole in mind since these great gifts were given not just to a collection of individuals, but to the nation of Israel.

Also, Israel's "calling" is "irrevocable." This certainly includes God's election of national Israel. But Israel's calling also included vocational service to the nations (Gen. 18:18; Deut. 4:5–6; Acts 3:25). As Saucy observes, "There is no reason not to see in Israel's 'calling' also a function of service in salvation history for which they were originally called and made 'God's people.'"[67] Cranfield believes this "calling" refers to Israel being able to "fulfill a special function in history."[68]

---

65. It is not saved "all Israel" who is both enemy and beloved. It is the "all Israel" who will be saved who is both enemy and beloved.

66. Matt Waymeyer, "The Dual Status of Israel in Romans 11:28," *MSJ* 16 (2005): 65.

67. Saucy, "Does the Apostle Paul Reverse the Prophetic Tradition of the Salvation of Israel and the Nations?," 77.

68. Cranfield, *Romans*, 2:581.

If "calling" here includes a vocational element, this is further evidence that Israel's role as a nation continues.

Imminence and the Salvation of Israel (11:30–32)

With 11:30–32, Paul reminds his Gentile audience they were shown mercy because of Israel's disobedience. Yet because of God's working with Gentiles, Israel is now positioned to receive mercy. These cause and effect relationships in 11:30–31 affirm that Israel as a corporate entity is on Paul's mind. Verse 30 indicates Gentiles received mercy because of Israel's disobedience:

> For just as you [Gentiles] once were disobedient to God, but now have been shown mercy because of their [Israel's] disobedience.

Gentiles received mercy because of Israel's disobedience. Next, with v. 31 Paul reveals that the current mercy extending to Gentiles puts Israel in a position to receive God's mercy:

> so these [Israel] also now have been disobedient, that because of the mercy shown to you [Gentiles] they [Israel] also may now be shown mercy.

Just as Israel's disobedience led to God's mercy for Gentiles (v. 30), mercy for Gentiles now puts Israel in a position to be shown mercy. The "they" must be the people or nation as a whole currently in unbelief since the believing remnant of Israel did not need God's mercy to Gentiles to receive mercy themselves. As 11:1–6 indicated, God was extending mercy to the remnant long before his mercy extended to Gentiles. But the present blessing of Gentiles means the salvation of national Israel can now occur. Paul does not say Israel as a whole is currently experiencing God's saving mercy, but he says Israel "may now be shown mercy." Paul's shift to "may now" indicates imminence. Schreiner notes, "the salvation of the Jews can now occur at any time—in that sense it is imminent."[69] Moo says the meaning here is "now, at any time."[70] Just as Israel's temporary stumbling has brought blessings to Gentiles, so too, current blessings to Gentiles bring the reality that Israel's salvation can now occur. When exactly this will happen Paul did not know.

Praise for God's Great Plans (11:33–36)

Paul ends his discussion of Gentiles and Israel in God's purposes with an outburst of praise in 11:33–36. His doxology here rightly brings praise to God and highlights that no human could devise or implement such a wonderful plan.

Paul's Use of the Old Testament in Romans 9–11

A proper interpretation of Romans 9–11 must account for Paul's heavy reliance on OT quotations and themes. This is no secondary matter since much of the debate over Romans 9–11 concerns whether Paul is relying on the literal and contextual meaning of the earlier prophets or using a typological hermeneutic to transcend, transform, or reinterpret the storyline begun in the OT. The evidence lies with the former. Paul relies on the OT in a predominately contextual way consistent with the intent of the OT prophets. The facts and principles Paul draws upon are not disconnected from their intent, nor is there a reality shift from OT expectation to NT fulfillment. Not only does Paul teach a future salvation of Israel with a role for bringing blessings to the world in Romans 9–11; this message is consistent with the intention of previous Scripture writers.

Old Testament Quotations

Paul quotes the OT approximately thirty-three times and draws upon approximately thirteen OT themes in Romans

---

69. Schreiner, *Romans*, 628.
70. Moo, *Romans*, 735.

9–11. The most quoted books are Isaiah (15 times), Deuter-onomy (5 times), Genesis (4 times), and 1 Kings (3 times). There are also quotations from Exodus, Leviticus, Job, Psalms, Hosea, Joel, and Malachi.

Paul often employs the OT to document historical facts, apply principles, and connect prophecies to Gentiles and Israel. He also quotes the OT to show Jesus is the one who transitions God's purposes from the Mosaic covenant to the new covenant.

Paul's quotations in Romans 9:7–12 reveal a straightfor-ward reliance upon Genesis 21:12, 18:10, and 25:23 concern-ing Abraham, Isaac, and Jacob as the seed line of Israel. With Romans 9:13, Paul quotes Malachi 1:2–3 to show God chose the nation Israel as a corporate vessel for his purposes. Paul's quotations of Hosea 2:23 and 1:10 in Romans 9:25–26 draw upon the principle of God's sovereignty in making non-people his people. Paul uses Leviticus 18:5 and Deuteronomy 30:11–14 in Romans 10:4–8 to reveal a transition from the Mosaic covenant to the new covenant because of Christ. With Romans 10:13, Paul employs a principle from Joel 2:32 to show that all who call on the Lord will be saved. Paul quotes Deuteronomy 32:21 and Isaiah 65:1 in Romans 10:19–20 to explain that the prophets predicted God would save and use Gentiles to provoke Israel to jealousy. In Romans 11:3–4, Paul relies on three verses from 1 Kings 19 to highlight that God always keeps a believing remnant even when Israel as a whole is disobedient. With Romans 11:26b–27, Paul under-stands Isaiah 59:20–21 and 27:9 in a straightforward manner as support for the coming salvation of the nation Israel and its entrance into the new covenant. Paul also quotes Isaiah 40:13 in Romans 11:34 to draw upon the principle that God needs no counselor.

Paul's uses of the OT are largely contextual and consis-tent with the intent of the OT prophets. Paul does not use a typological hermeneutic that transforms the OT expectations. The storyline continues in a straightforward way, including the person and role of Jesus the Messiah. Israel is not redefined. Paul does not claim the church is the new or true Israel or that physical and national promises have been transformed. Nor does he indicate that Jesus's rightful identity as the ultimate Israelite means that promises to national Israel have been transcended.

Old Testament Themes

Also significant is Paul's straightforward reliance on OT themes in Romans 9–11:

- Israel is the ethnic people descended from Abraham, Isaac, and Jacob (Gen. 12–50; cf. Rom. 9:3–13).
- The Abrahamic covenant will produce the nation Israel that will bless Gentiles (Gen. 12:2–3; 18:18; cf. Rom. 11:17–24).
- God is sovereign in his electing purposes concerning Israel and the nations (Deut. 7:6–8; cf. Rom. 9:6–26).
- Great privileges belong to Israel (Lev. 26:40–45; cf. Rom. 9:4–5).
- Israel is an instrument for worldwide blessings (Gen. 12:2–3; Ps. 67:7; cf. Rom. 11:12, 15).
- Israel as a whole will be characterized by disobedience until Israel is saved and restored (Lev. 26:40–45; Deut. 30:1–10; cf. Rom. 11:17–26).
- God preserves a remnant of believing Israelites when Israel as a whole flounders in unbelief (1 Kings 19; cf. Rom. 11:2–10).
- The remnant exists to guarantee Israel will not be destroyed (Isa. 1:9; 65:8; cf. Rom. 9:29).
- Israel as a whole will be saved and restored because of the Messiah (Isa. 49:3–6; Amos 9:11–15; cf. Rom. 11:26–27).
- Israel's salvation will involve the coming of the Lord and inclusion of Israel into the new covenant (Isa. 59:20–21; cf. Rom. 11:26–27).
- Before Israel's salvation and restoration, God will bless Gentiles to provoke Israel to salvation (Deut. 32:21; Isa. 65:1–2; cf. Rom. 10:19–21; 11:11, 13).

- When Israel as a nation is saved and restored, great blessings will come to the world (Isa. 27:6; cf. Rom. 11:12, 15).
- God chooses and directs the nations to bring himself glory (Deut. 7:6–8; cf. Rom. 9:17; 11:33–36).

Paul brings these various themes together and relates them to the Messiah and new covenant realities. The "mystery" of Romans 11:25 emphasizes the minor theme of Gentile salvation before Israel's salvation.

Romans 9–11 and Other Restoration of Israel Passages

Romans 9–11 is the not the only passage addressing Israel. How do these chapters harmonize with others texts that speak of Israel's salvation and restoration? Space does not allow a full treatment of this issue, but a few words are necessary.

Paul's primary purpose in Romans 9–11 is to explain how Israel's unbelief in Jesus harmonizes with the great privileges that still belong to Israel (9:1–5). Paul does not repeat all the details concerning Israel's restoration as found in passages such as Isaiah 2, Isaiah 11, Isaiah 65, Jeremiah 30–33, Ezekiel 36–48, Amos 9:11–15, Zechariah 14, and others. These sections explain in more detail Israel's possession of the land, agricultural prosperity, and service to other nations. There are also NT passages, that contain implications for Israel as a nation such as Matthew 19:28, Matthew 23:39, Luke 1:32–33, Luke 21:24, Luke 22:29–30, Acts 1:6, Acts 3:19–21, and Revelation 7:4–8.

Some believe the lack of Jewish details in Romans 9–11 (i.e., Jerusalem, land, etc.) means national Israel's restoration should not be expected.[71] But this objection is problematic for

---

71. See Robertson, *Israel of God*, 191. Richard Lucas claims those who believe Romans 11 affirms a future restoration of national Israel are drawing unjustified implications from this chapter. See "The Dispensational Appeal to Romans 11 and the Nature of Israel's Future Salvation," in *Progressive Covenantalism: Charting a Course between Dispensational and Covenantal Theologies*, ed. Stephen J. Wellum and Brent E. Parker (Nashville: Broadman & Holman, 2016), 235–53.

two reasons. First, the details of previous revelation need not be repeated for their significance to remain. While addressing issues related to Israel, John Feinberg notes that "lack of repetition in the NT does not render an OT teaching inoperative during the NT era so long as nothing explicitly or implicitly cancels it."[72] Thus, "If an OT prophecy or promise is made unconditionally to a given people and is still unfulfilled to them even in the NT era, then the prophecy must still be fulfilled to them."[73] Walter C. Kaiser also observes that Christians "misjudge the revelation of God if we have a theory of interpretation which says the most recent revelation of God is to be preferred or substituted for that which came earlier."[74]

Second, Paul reaffirms that the "covenants" and "promises" still belong to national Israel (9:4–5). These broad categories appear to cover the details of promises to Israel in Scripture. Also, Paul mentions "temple service" (9:4), which has implications for Jerusalem and the land. Plus, Paul says the world will be a better place when Israel believes, which coincides with what the OT prophets predicted (Isa. 27:6). Paul's words about Israel harmonize well with what earlier prophets revealed. No transformation of the Bible's storyline occurs in Romans 9–11.

The view that Romans 9–11 affirms a future salvation and role for national Israel is not just found in this one section; it has much support from other Bible passages.

A Topical Summary of Romans 9–11
Jesus

Israel's unbelief in Jesus was the reason for Paul's concern in Romans 9–11 (9:1–5). Paul mentions "Jesus" once and "Christ" seven times in these chapters. Jesus is referred to as both the Messiah coming from Israel and God in 9:5. He is

---

72. John S. Feinberg, "Systems of Discontinuity," in *Continuity and Discontinuity*, 76.
73. Ibid.
74. Walter C. Kaiser Jr., "The Land of Israel and the Future Return (Zechariah 10:6–12)," in *Israel, the Land and the People: An Evangelical Affirmation of God's Promises*, ed. H. Wayne House (Grand Rapids: Kregel, 1998), 222.

also "Lord" (10:9). Jesus is the most important of Israel's eight privileges (9:4–5) and the one who confirms Israel's promises and blesses the Gentiles (see Rom. 15:8–9). He also is the end or goal (*telos*) of the Mosaic law and the one who brings the new covenant (10:4–7). Only through faith in Jesus can one find righteousness. This is true for Israelites and Gentiles (9:30–10:3). No one is saved apart from him.

That Paul discusses Jesus and Israel in Romans 9–11 shows the importance of both. It also shows that Israel's identity and role are not absorbed into the person of Christ in a way that makes national Israel irrelevant. Jesus is the ultimate Israelite, *and* Israel is significant as a people and nation. The relationship of Jesus to Israel is not that of an antitype who makes an inferior type irrelevant. Instead, it is that of corporate headship—the representative head of Israel (Jesus) restores the many (national Israel). As Isaiah 49:6a states, "He [God] says, 'It is too small a thing that You [Messiah] should be My Servant, *to raise up the tribes of Jacob and to restore the preserved ones of Israel*'" (emphasis added).

Because of Jesus, the true Israelite, promises to Israel will be fulfilled over the course of his two comings. Jesus's return will be connected with Israel's salvation and inclusion in the new covenant (11:26–27).

Israel

Like earlier prophets, Paul presents Israel as God's chosen people, composed of ethnic descendants from Abraham, Isaac, and Jacob. Israel is still related to all the great privileges given to them by God (9:4–5). Paul's discussion of Israel includes the nation as a whole and the believing remnant. Likewise, God's election applies to both the nation (9:7–13) and individuals within the nation (9:6; 11:1–6). Although national Israel is chosen for service, not every Israelite is elect for salvation. Belief is necessary to be a true Israelite (9:6). The believing remnant guarantees Israel as a national entity will not be destroyed. As a "firstfruits" of the whole

(Rom. 11:16), the remnant anticipates the salvation and restoration of the nation (Isa. 1:9).

Israel missed righteousness by striving for it through the Mosaic law and not in Jesus. But Israel will be saved and reinstated to covenant blessings (Rom. 11:23, 26). Yet even in the present God is using Israel's unbelief to bring spiritual blessings to Gentiles (Rom. 15:27). Israel will be saved in connection with the return of Jesus (11:26–27). Then Israel's salvation will result in magnified blessings to the nations (11:12, 15, 26). Israel is not a means in itself but a vehicle for universal blessings (Gen. 12:2–3; 18:18). As Psalm 67:7 declares, "God blesses us [Israel], that all the ends of the earth may fear Him."

Some believe national Israel possessed a typological role that found fulfillment in Jesus and the church. Allegedly, the nation Israel loses its significance as the concept of Israel is fulfilled through Jesus and the "new" or "true" Israel—the church. But this idea is not found in Romans 9–11. There are correspondences between Israel and the church, and similar language is used of both, but the church does not supersede or replace Israel in God's plans. The future of national Israel in Romans 9–11 shows Israel is not a transcended type.

Paul explicitly teaches Israel will be saved in Romans 11:26. But does Romans 9–11 also affirm a continuing role for the nation? What Paul says in Romans 9–11 is consistent with the restoration as a nation idea found in previous Scripture, especially that Israel's salvation will bring more blessings to the world. Nothing in Romans 9–11 indicates the restoration as a nation concept has been transcended. On the contrary, several evidences exist for Israel's restoration.

First, evidence for a continuing role for Israel is found Romans 9:4–5, where Paul affirms that the "promises," "covenants," and "temple service" still belong to Israel. These privileges carry restoration implications if their full content is allowed. Objections that Paul does not mention Israel's land, Jerusalem, or other Israelite matters here are not persuasive since the broader categories mentioned in 9:4–5 would cover these details. Plus the mention of "temple service" is a specific detail that carries implications for Israel's land and Jerusalem. That Paul mentions privileges for Israel along with discussion of a future for Israel in 11:11–32 indicates that national Israel's significance continues.

Second, Romans 11:12, 15. reveals that Israel's coming "fullness," which involves everything God intended for Israel to be, will bring even better conditions for the world. This is consistent with the expectation that Israel's salvation as a nation leads to holistic blessings for the world (see Isa. 27:6).

Third, Paul's quotations of Isaiah 59:20–21 and 27:9 in Romans 11:26–27 carry restoration implications. The contexts of both Isaiah passages predict national Israel's repentance and inclusion in the new covenant along with blessings to the Gentiles at a time when Israel is restored.

Fourth, that Israel's "gifts" and "calling" are irrevocable (11:29) shows God's purposes for national Israel remain. The "gifts" involve the eight privileges mentioned in 9:4–5, which include but involve more than salvation. Also, if "calling" includes Israel's vocational calling to the nations, this would involve the continuing role of the nation Israel to other nations when the Messiah reigns on the earth (Isa. 2:2–4).

A fifth argument concerns consistency. If ethnic Israel is saved in connection with God's promises, then why would Israel's restoration as a nation not be fulfilled as well, especially when the two ideas are so closely connected? According to Deuteronomy 30:1–10, when Israel repents and obeys God from the heart (30:2), "God will restore" Israel from captivity and "will bring you [Israel] into the land" to "possess it" (30:3–5). This restoration to the land is linked with circumcision of the heart in 30:6, which is a reference to salvation and new covenant inclusion for Israel. In Jeremiah 31:31–34, God promised a "new covenant" for Israel that involves a changed heart. Then Jeremiah 31:38–40 speaks of the restoration of Jerusalem. This shows both salvation and restoration. Also, Israel's salvation and inclusion in the new covenant are evident in Ezekiel 36:26–28: "Moreover, I [God] will give you a new heart and put a new spirit within you. . . . I will put My Spirit within you and cause you to walk in My statutes. . . . You will live in the land that I gave to your forefathers; so you will be My people, and I will be your God." Again salvation, new covenant inclusion, and restoration to the land occur together.

In sum, Romans 9–11 explicitly teaches a future mass salvation of national Israel, while also affirming the OT picture of a restoration of the nation with blessings for the world.

Gentiles

Paul views Gentiles as non-Jews, who, until Christ, were not connected to the covenants of promise (11:17a). But in God's timing, Gentiles, who were not seeking God's righteousness, found righteousness through faith in Jesus (9:30). They now experience salvific blessings of the Abrahamic covenant and a relationship with the Messiah (15:27). Believing Gentiles in this age possess the role of provoking Israel to jealousy (10:19–21; 11:11, 13). When the fullness of Gentiles in this age has occurred, ethnic Israel will be saved, and greater world blessings will transpire (11:12, 15). Yet Gentiles must not become arrogant toward Israel (11:18), or their present role in God's purposes will be removed (11:22). Paul views believing Gentiles not as incorporated into Israel but as participants with believing Israelites in the covenants of promise. Paul wants his readers to know that Gentile inclusion does not mean national Israel's exclusion.

Church

All five uses of "church" in Romans occur in Paul's greetings in Romans 16. Paul does not mention "church" in Romans 9–11, although participation of believing Jews and Gentiles in the spiritual blessings of the covenants of promise in Jesus relates to the church (11:17–24; 15:27). The church is the new covenant community of believing Jews and Gentiles in this age and is God's instrument for worldwide gospel proclamation. Yet this present age is not all there is to God's purposes. Jesus is coming again to earth to rule the nations with his saints (Rev. 5:10; 19:15).

When he does, Israel will be saved and restored and will bring further blessings to the world under the Messiah (Rom. 11:12, 15, 26–27). Both the church of believing Jews and Gentiles and national Israel are strategic in God's purposes. Romans 9–11 contains no doctrine of replacement or fulfillment theology in which the church supersedes national Israel as the new or true Israel. In fact, the replacement view is rebuked by Paul in 11:18.

Jesus's church encompasses both believing Israelites and Gentiles. Believing Israelites are still identified with Israel (11:1–6) as they participate in Jesus's church. Believing Gentiles also are part of Jesus's church with faithful Israelites. As Paul says in Ephesians 3:6, "the Gentiles are fellow heirs and fellow members of the body."

What Romans 9–11 Contributes to Biblical Theology

Romans 9–11 contributes to the Bible's storyline by explaining how national Israel's present unbelief in Jesus harmonizes with God's commitment to Israel and Israel's great privileges. Many OT passages predicted that the Messiah's arrival would involve both Israel's restoration and blessings for the nations. But the coming of the Messiah did not coincide with national Israel's belief and restoration. How can this development be explained? Paul reveals that selectivity is part of God's purposes and that God never promised that every Israelite of all ages would be saved (9:6). So Israel's unbelief cannot prove God's word has failed. Paul also shows that Gentiles are now being saved by faith in Israel's Messiah, even while Israel as a whole is not (9:30–10:4). The remnant of believing Israel also guarantees God has not rejected Israel (11:1–6).

Particularly significant is Deuteronomy 32:21, which predicted that God would use national Israel's unbelief to use Gentiles to provoke Israel to jealousy and salvation (Rom. 10:19–20). This was a minor, perhaps even partially hidden, OT theme. But it is key to understanding why Gentile salvation is preceding the salvation of Israel. This is the heart of

Paul's "mystery" concept in Romans 11:25. The "mystery" of 11:25–26 is this: When the present era of Gentile salvation as a means to provoke national Israel to jealousy is over, Israel will be saved and participate in the new covenant (11:26–27). This will bring even greater blessings to the world (11:12, 15). While many passages predicted that Israel's salvation would precede world blessing, the "mystery" of Romans 11:25 is that Gentile inclusion in God's blessings will precede national Israel's salvation.[75]

Another contribution to biblical theology concerns the reality of two stages of world blessing: (1) Gentile salvation and participation in Abrahamic covenant blessings in this age between the two comings of Jesus while Israel is in unbelief, and (2) greater blessings to the world with Israel's salvation (11:12, 15).

Romans 9–11 evidences strong continuity with the storyline of the OT. Because of Jesus the Messiah, Gentiles are becoming the people of God. Israel is composed of ethnic descendants of Abraham, Isaac, and Jacob. This includes both the remnant and Israel as a whole. There is no redefinition of Israel or expansion of Israel to include Gentiles. Nor is Israel viewed as a transcended type. Paul's views on the future of Israel also coincide with other NT references concerning the salvation and restoration of national Israel (see Matt. 19:28; 23:29; Luke 21:24; 22:29–30; Acts 1:6; 3:19–21).

Also, Romans 9–11 reveals that Jesus and prophecies concerning national Israel work in harmony. Jesus's identity as the ultimate representative of Israel does not erase or transcend national Israel's significance or alter the nature of the covenants and promises as they relate to Israel. The Bible's storyline has not changed. Jesus is the corporate representative of Israel who restores national Israel and blesses Gentiles (Isa. 49:3–6). The two comings of Jesus mean significant first coming fulfillment and significant second coming fulfillment of previous prophecies. Spiritual blessings extend to believing Israelites and

---

75. See Beale and Gladd, *Hidden but Now Revealed*, 91.

Gentiles with Jesus's first coming (Rom. 15:27). But the salvation of Israel, Israel's full inclusion in the new covenant, and greater global blessings await Jesus's return.

Conclusion

Romans 9–11 shows that God's word has not failed, and God has not rejected Israel. A proper application of these chapters involves accepting what God is doing presently with believing Gentiles and the remnant of Israel. It also involves understanding Israel's coming salvation and restoration and what this will mean for the world. This is especially true for Gentiles who historically have struggled with grasping God's future plans for Israel.

The commentator C. E. B. Cranfield once altered his views on Israel based on his study of Romans 9–11. With transparency and honesty he admitted, "I confess with shame to having also myself used in print on more than one occasion this language of the replacement of Israel by the church."[76] Yet Paul's words in Romans 9–11 changed his perspective. Cranfield's words on what these three chapters mean for the church are worth heeding:

> It is only where the Church persists in refusing to learn this message, where it secretly—perhaps quite unconsciously!—believes that its own existence is based on human achievement, and so fails to understand God's mercy to itself, that it is unable to believe in God's mercy for still unbelieving Israel, and so entertains the ugly and unscriptural notion that God has cast off His people Israel and simply replaced it by the Christian Church. These three chapters emphatically forbid us to speak of the Church as having once and for all taken the place of the Jewish people.[77]

---

76. Cranfield, *Romans*, 2:448.
77. Ibid., 2:448n2. Cranfield does not affirm all the assertions in this chapter.

RESPONSE TO VLACH

Fred G. Zaspel
and James M. Hamilton Jr.

It is a pleasure to interact with Mike Vlach's essay. His concern to interpret Romans 9–11 carefully on its own terms and within the larger context of Scripture's related teaching is obvious, a mark of faithful biblical interpretation for which we are always appreciative. And we gladly acknowledge essential areas of agreement with him. We agree that it is Israel as a people (not only the remnant) whom Paul holds in view, and we agree that the apostle presents the happy prospect of Israel's coming faith in our Lord Jesus Christ. We concur on many subsidiary points along the way. Questions related to Israel, the church, and eschatology have been a specialized interest for Vlach, and we commend him for his diligence and carefulness in that study.

It is of course expected that areas of disagreement arise in minor details, but for our response we will restrict our remarks to matters of larger significance. The biggest issue we have with Vlach is one of authorial intent. For him, reading non-typologically means reading in accordance with the intentions of the authors of the various OT materials. We are convinced *that the OT authors intended to communicate typologically*. This strikes at another one of Vlach's emphases, his concern to interpret things "literally." We think statements should be interpreted *as literally as their authors intended*. So, for instance, when Isaiah says that Yahweh "will utterly destroy the tongue of the Sea of Egypt" (Isa. 11:15), we think he means to refer back to the crossing of the Red Sea at the exodus in the process of treating that historical event as a type of the future exodus he expects Yahweh to accomplish for his people. The sea does not literally have a tongue, nor are we contravening Isaiah's intention to understand him typologically. Isaiah's point is that the Lord will bring his people back after the exile, just as he brought them out of Egypt: "there will be a highway from Assyria for the remnant that remains of his people, as there was for Israel when they came up from the land of Egypt" (11:16).

Interpretation of Hosea 1–2 in Romans 9:25–26

Paul's use of Hosea 2:23 and 1:10 in Romans 9:25–26 has puzzled many. On what ground does the apostle apply to the Gentiles this prophecy that was given regarding Israel? Vlach answers in terms of analogy: just as God sovereignly called "Not My People" Israel to be his own again, so he will call Gentiles also. The connection is one of analogy, linked by the common idea of sovereign election. It seems to us, however, that the connection goes deeper. As we explain in our essay, Paul seems to connect Hosea's prophecy, in context, to the Abrahamic promise of Genesis 22:17 and 17:4–5, which foresee the Abrahamic blessing extending to the nations. When he does this, Paul is simply taking his cues from Hosea. Hosea 1:10 says, "the children of Israel shall be like the sand of the sea," reaffirming Genesis 22:17 after the covenant-ending words of Hosea 1:9. Though the Mosaic covenant has failed, and the people will go into exile (Hos. 1:9), God will keep the covenant with Abraham (Hos. 1:10; Gen. 22:17), a covenant that promises blessings for all the families of the earth (Gen. 12:3). Viewed in this larger covenantal context, the Hosea prophecy may legitimately be understood as inclusive of Gentiles. The connection between Hosea's prophecy and Gentile inclusion is not merely parallel but of a piece.

The upshot of this is that conceptually, Israel and the church are brought into very close relation, even if they are not equated. We wonder whether Vlach's dispensational commitments would lead him to see the relationships between the Abrahamic, Mosaic, and new covenants the way we do, and whether dispensationalism disinclines interpreters from the interpretive perspective of the biblical authors, particularly with respect to typology. We would suggest that these two considerations, relating to the covenants and typology, better account for the details of these passages and lend support for our contention regarding a tighter relationship of Israel and the church than Vlach allows (see below).

Relation of Israel and the Church

The larger question concerns how these two entities—Israel and the church—are related. We agree with Vlach that the "olive tree" (Rom. 11:16b–24) is "the place of blessing" via God's covenant with Abraham, and we heartily agree that both Israel and the church have a part in this Abrahamic tree. But we would want to clarify this "place of blessing" and tweak the way he describes the resulting relationship between Israel and the church.

Vlach denies that a typological relationship exists between Israel and the church, but the NT's repeated characterizations of the church in Israel terminology lead us to understand that Israel was, in fact, a type of the church. As noted above, part of Vlach's objection to typology is that he seems to think that for Paul to interpret the OT typologically would be for him to depart from the intention of the OT authors. This fails to recognize that the OT authors themselves interpreted earlier Scripture typologically and intended to present installments in developing typological patterns. That both Israel and the church are referred to as God's people (Lev. 26:12; 1 Peter 2:10), the saints (Deut. 33:3; 1 Cor. 1:7), the chosen (Deut. 7:6; 1 Peter 2:9), and God's house (Heb. 3:5–6) seems at least to hint in this direction. More telling is the fact that the church is described as Abraham's seed (Exod. 33:1; Gal. 3:29) and as the (true) circumcision (Phil. 3:2–3). And Peter's description of the church as "a holy priesthood" (1 Peter 2:5) and as "a chosen race, a royal priesthood, a holy nation, a people for his own possession" (1 Peter 2:9) seems to shout of some kind of typological fulfillment. Israel was the church in picture.

Still the evidence runs deeper. Few would dispute that Jesus is presented as the new and true Israel (e.g., Matt. 2:15), and from this it is but a small step to see the church, his body, as the fulfillment of Israel also. Indeed, in 1 Corinthians 12:12, Paul drops the "body" imagery and refers to the church, simply, as "Christ" (cf. Gal. 3:16, 29). Moreover, that our Lord called out twelve apostles to found the church seems obviously to present the church as a fulfillment of Israel. We might dispute whether we should take the next step and refer to the church as a new "Israel,"[1] but that the NT presents the church as in some sense the realization of what ancient Israel only anticipated seems obvious. That is to say, Israel is a type of the church.

One consideration that may seem to threaten Vlach's contention—and ours—for a future mass-conversion of Israel is that, as Merkle asserts in his essay, when the antitype arrives, the older type falls away, having been fulfilled. We are not exactly sure what Merkle means here and want to deal with examples. It may be that covenantally constrained institutions, such as the levitical sacrificial system, fall away after the sacrifice of Christ, but we are not sure the same holds for people or events. Events and people retain their significance even if a later person or event fulfills the pattern they typified. For instance,

---

1. Many argue that Galatians 6:16 ("the Israel of God") in fact makes this equation, and while there may be considerations that favor this interpretation, we doubt that it can be demonstrated with finality. Indeed, if Romans 9–11 is the normative passage on the question of Israel and the church, and given that here Paul argues for both a continuity and discontinuity between Israel and the church, maintaining some distinction within unity (as illustrated in the distinct branches of the one olive tree), the presumptive evidence would seem to lead us to understand Galatians 6:16 in similar terms: a reference to believing Israelites (Rom. 9:6) in the church. We do not think, however, that the answer to this question has determinative weight with regard to our overall argument, so long as a distinguishable Israel within the unity of the Jew-Gentile church may be recognized.

the exodus from Egypt is typified in the life of Abraham[2]—and Moses intended his audience to note the correspondence and escalation—but after the exodus Abraham and his experience are no less significant than before. We noted Hosea's reference to Genesis 22:17 in Hosea 1:10 above. All across Hosea the prophet indicates that Israel is going into exile and that the exile to Babylon corresponds to the sojourn and enslavement in Egypt. Just as God brought Israel out of Egypt at the exodus, so he will bring the exiles back after a second exodus. Israel's return to the land of promise in Ezra is arguably presented as a new exodus.[3] But that takes nothing away from the original exodus, and when they return to the land, the people continue to relate to God in accordance with the Mosaic covenant.

Similar things can be said about the fulfillment of the exodus pattern in the death and resurrection of Jesus. He is the "Passover lamb" who "redeems" his people, buying them with a price, giving them a new law, the law of Christ, building them into a new temple of the Holy Spirit, setting them on a pilgrimage to the fulfillment of the land of promise, the lasting city, the new Jerusalem, in the new heaven and new earth. The NT authors are everywhere assuming this narrative undercurrent, and the inner logic of the narrative undercurrent is that Jesus and the church are the typological fulfillments of the new exodus and are engaged in the return from exile, strangers in

---

2. Both Abraham and Israel went down to Egypt in response to a famine. Sarah was taken into Pharaoh's house. The nation was enslaved. Both Abraham and Israel plundered Egypt, and both Sarah and Israel were liberated when God brought plagues on Pharaoh. Both Abraham and Israel left Egypt to return to the land of promise, and at Sinai Yahweh spoke the same words to Israel in Exodus 20:1 that he had spoken to Abraham in Genesis 15:7. In that same chapter, Genesis 15, Moses presents Yahweh prophesying of the sojourn in Egypt and exodus therefrom in vv. 12–20. Moses saw the correspondence between Abraham's experience and Israel's, saw how the significance was increased at the exodus from Egypt, and presented his narrative such that his audience would expect Yahweh to deliver them in the future the way he had in the past—in Abraham's day and at the exodus. In other words, Moses intended these narratives to be understood typologically.

3. See further James M. Hamilton, *Ezra and Nehemiah*, Christ-Centered Exposition (Nashville: Broadman & Holman, 2014).

this world on the way to the very presence of God in a new and better garden of Eden.

At several points Vlach mentions the temple service, so perhaps this is a good place to speak to the question of the temple in biblical theology. As Beale and others have shown,[4] the profound correspondence between the tabernacle and temple narratives and the creation account in Genesis 1–2 points to the conclusion that creation is a cosmic temple (cf. Pss. 78:69; 104:2–3; Isa. 66:1, etc.).[5] This indicates that when the man and woman were driven from the garden of Eden, there is a sense in which they were expelled from God's temple precincts. This way of looking at things suggests that the promise of land to Abraham is a promise that God will once again bring his people into his presence. When we understand the land promise typologically, we are not spiritualizing it or moving away from authorial intent. On the contrary, we are understanding that Moses intended to communicate that the land promised to Abraham was only the beginning of God making his people heirs of the world (Rom. 4:13). Along similar lines, the reason Ezekiel 40–48 is quoted so much in Revelation 21–22 is that Ezekiel did not intend to prophesy of a rebuilt temple during the millennium but of a new heavens and new earth.

After the exodus, on the way to Egypt, Israel is given instructions for the tabernacle, which is later replaced by the temple. It seems the temple in the land is to be understood by analogy with the garden of Eden and the earth that God commissioned the man and woman to fill with his image-bearers in Genesis 1:28.

---

4. See G. K. Beale, *The Temple and the Church's Mission: A Biblical Theology of the Dwelling Place of God*, New Studies in Biblical Theology (Downers Grove, IL: InterVarsity Press, 2004) and the literature he cites.

5. For a brief summary of the evidence, see Gordon J. Wenham, "Sanctuary Symbolism in the Garden of Eden Story," in *I Studied Inscriptions from before the Flood: Ancient Near Eastern, Literary, and Linguistic Approaches to Genesis 1–11*, ed. Richard Hess and David Toshio Tsumara (Winona Lake, IN: Eisenbrauns, 1994), 399–404.

At creation, God put man in his cosmic temple and charged him to fill the earth and subdue it. Man instead rebelled and was expelled from God's temple. God then made Israel his son (Exod. 4:22–23), identifying Israel as a kind of corporate new Adam. Then he gave them the temple in the land: here again the purpose was filling the dry lands with God's glory (Num. 14:21; Ps. 2:8). Like Adam, Israel rebelled and was exiled from God's presence, driven away from the temple precincts.

The prophecies of a new exodus are prophecies that God will again redeem his people and again pursue his purpose of filling the land—the whole earth—with his glory. David wanted to build the temple, and God promised him a son who would do so. Solomon built a temple, but the prophecy was fulfilled when Jesus came and built a spiritual house (1 Peter 2:4), a temple of the Holy Spirit (1 Cor. 3:16), the church (Matt. 16:18).

The purpose of the temple is not for God to have a place to dwell, nor does he need animal sacrifice once Christ has been crucified. The point of the temple, rather, was for God to establish his presence among a sinful people as a beachhead in the grand project of redeeming and reclaiming his defiled world. Viewed this way, the filling of the tabernacle and temple with God's glory when construction was complete was but a preview of what God is going to do in the whole world, which is exactly what Revelation presents when the New Jerusalem comes down from God out of heaven like a new holy of holies. All the earth will be God's temple.

The sacrificial system has served its purpose, and the time for the temple in the sense of a literal building came to an end when the new covenant was initiated. We should not look for a temple in the millennium or in the new heavens and new earth (Rev. 21:22). In the millennium, Jesus will be cleansing the defiled world and reclaiming this place as God's cosmic temple. After the final rebellion, the world will be renewed, and God's purpose in creation, of filling the world with his glorious presence, will have been achieved.

So we affirm a typological relationship between Israel and the church. Can we identify the precise relationship further? Some of course have argued in altogether continuous terms that Israel is the visible church of the OT and that the church today is Israel. In this view "the church" consists always in a mix of both believing and unbelieving members. But this view cannot account for Israel's "rejection" (Rom. 11:15) and the stripping away of the unbelievers that marks this age (Matt. 21:43), as Paul describes in Romans 11:16b–24. Jesus equipped the church to expel those who showed themselves to be unbelievers (Matt. 18:15–18), and Paul's letters show that he expected churches to follow those instructions (1 Cor. 5; 2 Thess. 3:14–15; Titus 3:10). That is, we agree with Vlach that the relationship of Israel and the church is not altogether continuous.

We agree that the presence of both natural and wild branches in the olive tree leaves us to recognize Israel's distinguishable presence in the Abrahamic "place of blessing." Yet it would seem that this analogy leaves us to recognize some organic relation also. The branches of this olive tree share a common trunk and are united in the same tree. The natural and the wild branches may be distinguishable, but they share in the patriarchal promise. This was Israel's tree naturally, but due to her prevailing unbelief she was cut off. And through their faith Gentiles are now being grafted in. Yet Israelites who believe rejoin this tree again also, as in the end Israel will do *en masse*.

So what is this olive tree in which Jews and Gentiles share the Abrahamic blessing? Certainly it is "the place of blessing," as Vlach repeatedly affirms. But just what is this place of blessing? Is it not the church? This conclusion seems to us to be unavoidable, for it is in the church that Jew and Gentile come together by faith and enjoy the Abrahamic blessing. This, illustrated in the tree analogy, is the explicit teaching of the same apostle in Ephesians 2:11–22: the church is a "new man" created "in place of the two," a body in which Jews and Gentiles alike share the promised blessing in Christ.

So there is a typological relationship and an organic relationship also. We do not object to the notion of diversity within unity: the relationship is not one of exact identity. But we would press the notion of unity further than Vlach allows.

Indeed, although Vlach acknowledges the unity of Israel and the church in the Abrahamic "tree," he sometimes describes their diversity in terms that seem to us too discontinuous. For example, in his definition of the church he restricts the church to "this age" (p. 70) "between the two comings of Jesus" (p. 23). This seems to reflect the older dispensational understanding of two peoples of God (Israel and the church) that continue into the eschaton. Vlach's statement on p. 70 is particularly restrictive:

> The church is the new covenant community of believing Jews and Gentiles in this age and is God's instrument for worldwide gospel proclamation. Yet this present age is not all there is to God's purposes. Jesus is coming again to earth to rule the nations with his saints (Rev. 5:10; 19:15). When he does, Israel will be saved and restored and will bring further blessings to the world under the Messiah (Rom. 11:12, 15, 26–27). Both the church of believing Jews and Gentiles and national Israel are strategic in God's purposes.

We don't know how to understand this except in terms of a supposed two peoples of God, a distinction that we think is just too sharp, one that fails to recognize the church as the new and remaining "place of blessing" for both Israel and the Gentiles.

Vlach continues similarly in his very next sentence: "Romans 9–11 contains no doctrine of replacement or fulfillment theology in which the church supersedes national Israel as the new or true Israel" (p. 71). We agree that the church has not replaced or superseded Israel, but we do see a kind of "fulfillment theology" in the way the ancient nation anticipated—typified—the church. That is, we think both the supersessionist and the dispensational understandings are overly simplified and fail to recognize the nuanced way the NT writers depict the relationship of Israel and the church. Vlach does affirm both continuity and discontinuity as per the distinguishable branches in the olive tree, and with that much we agree. But the discontinuity he describes is more discontinuous than we think is exegetically warranted. Israel cannot inherit the promises apart from "us" (Heb. 11:39–40). Both Jews (natural branches) and Gentiles (wild branches) are brought together in the one Abrahamic tree, which it seems must ultimately be the church.

Again, we do not object to the idea of diversity within the church. But we are convinced that Paul's handling of the Hosea prophecy and his extended olive tree analogy indicate a closer notion of unity than Vlach seems to allow.

RESPONSE TO VLACH

Benjamin L. Merkle

I want to thank Michael Vlach for presenting a well-organized and clearly written essay. He has offered a consistent and coherent view of Romans 9–11. He has thought deeply about this topic and is a stellar representative of his view. I also commend him for his high view of Scripture and his desire to give the OT a fair hearing instead of reinterpreting its meaning through the NT. But the purpose of my response is to note those places where we disagree and to highlight weaknesses in his view. In the following response, I first discuss Vlach's view of biblical theology and typology. In particular, I address his deficient understanding of OT restoration prophecies and of Jesus's first coming. Next, I discuss the problems with his exegesis of Romans 9–11, limiting my discussion to seven key texts.

Biblical Theology and Typology
Deficient View of Old Testament Restoration Prophecies

Vlach bases much of his understanding of Romans 9–11 on the unfulfilled status of OT restoration prophecies regarding the nation of Israel. In other words, the reason that Romans 11:26 *must* refer to a future mass-conversion of Israel is his prior commitment that many OT prophecies that predict a future restoration of Israel remain unfulfilled.[1] For example, in defense of his position that God will save and restore Israel as whole, Vlach cites Amos 9:11–15. This text describes a time in the future when God will restore the nation of Israel and grant them unprecedented peace and prosperity—a time when their cities are restored, their enemies are defeated, and their land yields abundant crops. But when James cites this passage in Acts 15, he cites it as proof that God has included the Gentiles as his own people, just as the prophets foretold (vv. 16–17).[2] Interestingly, James does not apply this text to some future salvation of the nation of Israel when they regain their independence and rebuild the city of Jerusalem. Instead, he uses it to justify accepting the Gentiles into the people of God without requiring them to be circumcised. Thus, James interprets the passage to mean that God fulfills his promise to rebuild Israel by expanding who can be included as his people. God restores Israel through the work of the Messiah, who has fulfilled the new covenant, which grants Gentiles access to the promises of Abraham.

Some might respond that James does not claim this text is fulfilled but merely highlights that Amos mentions the Gentiles (or nations) seeking the Lord. But James could have simply quoted v. 12 (which mentions Gentiles) and left out v. 11 (which mentions the fallen shelter of David). The reason James includes v. 11 is that he sees the salvation of Gentiles as part of the restoration processes of Israel. God is rebuilding the house of David—not just out of physical Jews but also out of spiritual Jews.[3] John Polhill rightly comments,

---

1. For example, Vlach states, "What Paul says in Romans 9–11 is consistent with the restoration as a nation idea found in previous Scripture, especially that Israel's salvation will bring blessings to the world" (p. 68).

2. See Benjamin L. Merkle, "Old Testament Restoration Promises regarding the Nation of Israel: Literal or Symbolic," *The Southern Baptist Journal of Theology* 14, no. 1 (2010): 14–25; Alan S. Bandy and Benjamin L. Merkle, *Understanding Prophecy: A Biblical-Theological Approach* (Grand Rapids: Kregel, 2015), 107–23.

3. See also texts such as Acts 2:29–3, 6, which indicate that Jesus is currently reigning on David's throne.

> In the Gentiles, God was choosing a people for himself, a new *restored* people of God, Jew and Gentile in Christ, the true Israel. In the total message of Acts it is clear that the rebuilt house of David occurred in the Messiah. Christ was the scion of David who fulfilled the covenant of David and established a kingdom that would last forever (2 Sam. 7:12f.; cf. Acts 13:32–34). From the beginning the Jewish Christians had realized that the promises to David were fulfilled in Christ. What they were now beginning to see, and what James saw foretold in Amos, was that these promises included the Gentiles.[4]

Therefore, because of his misunderstanding of the nature of fulfillment of OT prophecies (which is based on a priority of the OT over the NT and a commitment to an eternal distinction between Israel and the church), Vlach is forced to maintain that Romans 11:26 refers to a future mass-conversion of Israel. To be fair, Vlach does provide exegetical evidence from Romans 9–11 to support his view. But his approach to the text betrays an underlying need to justify his theological system.

Deficient View of Jesus's First Coming

When I say that Vlach has a deficient view of Jesus's first coming, I am not saying that he is intentionally minimizing the significance of Jesus's life, death, resurrection, and ascension. Instead, because of his pre-commitment to view Israel as the controlling hermeneutical paradigm, he inadvertently focuses his attention on the second coming of Jesus, often bypassing Jesus's first coming. At the beginning of his essay, Vlach comments, "National Israel remains strategic to God's purposes and does not lose its significance with the arrival of Jesus and the church" (p. 21). According to Vlach, whatever occurs in the NT cannot affect the fulfillment of OT promises given to Israel. If God gives Israel certain promises, not even the

---

4. John B. Polhill, *Acts*, NAC 26 (Nashville: Broadman & Holman, 1992), 330 (emphasis original).

coming of the Messiah or the institution of the church can alter our understanding of the nature and scope of those promises. Later Vlach adds, "Israel's identity and role are not absorbed into the person of Christ in a way that makes national Israel irrelevant" (p. 67). While there may be some truth to what Vlach says (no one is arguing that national Israel is irrelevant), he wants to acknowledge some fulfillment in Christ and yet still proceed with "business as normal" in regard to OT promises. According to the NT, however, because Jesus is the fulfillment of OT promises (Luke 24:25–27, 44–45; John 5:39–40; Acts 28:23; Rom. 1:1–4; 2 Cor. 1:20; Gal. 3:8; Heb. 4:2), there is a significant change. Since Jesus's first coming is the pinnacle of salvation history, and since the gospel authors portray Jesus as the fulfillment of Israel, it is natural to view Israel's identity and role as fulfilled in Christ. In the end, it seems that Vlach has embraced more of an Israel-centric hermeneutic rather than a Christo-centric hermeneutic.

An example of Vlach's Israel-centric hermeneutic is his understanding of Romans 9:4. In this text Paul catalogs eight privileges that Israel possessed including the "temple service" (CSB).[5] Vlach notes, "Some passages link Jerusalem and temple service with new covenant conditions when Israel is restored" (p. 29). Then in a footnote he adds, "If future temple service occurs, this would be done in light of Christ and his sacrifice and not in contrast to him and his work" (p. 30n12). The idea that in the future Israel will rebuild the temple and reinstate temple sacrifices in fulfillment of OT promises is a sure sign of hermeneutical misalignment. Does the final fulfill-

---

5. Vlach states that the list of privileges currently "belongs" to Israel. In the Greek text, however, the word "belongs" is not found but must be supplied. Paul seems to be reflecting on the past more than affirming what is currently theirs. This understanding of Romans 9:4 is reflected in the NJB ("it was they who were adopted as children, the glory was theirs and the covenants; to them were given the Law and the worship of God and the promises") and the NLT ("chosen to be God's adopted children. God revealed his glory to them. He made covenants with them and gave them his law. He gave them the privilege of worshiping him and receiving his wonderful promises").

ment of God's promises to Israel include reinstating a sacrificial system, a system that is similar to the one that was itself a type and shadow that pointed to the Messiah?[6] Strimple rightly notes, "With regard to any type—whether it be sacrifice, feast, temple, or land—when the reality is introduced, the shadow passes away. And it does not pass away in order to be at some future [time] restored; it passes away because in Jesus Christ it has been fulfilled!"[7] Vlach clarifies that the sacrificial system during the millennium is somehow distinct from what was done in the Mosaic covenant. But on what basis does he claim that the future temple and animal sacrifices are distinct from the Mosaic sacrificial system, while dogmatically affirming that future national Israel must be equal to Mosaic national Israel? On what basis does Vlach distinguish what has a typological connection to Jesus (and thus doesn't continue) and what does not have a typological connection (and thus continues)?

Part of the reason Vlach largely rejects typology is the role that types play: they point forward to a greater reality. But if Israel (or the land or the temple) is a mere type, then Vlach will be forced to acknowledge that such types give way when the reality arrives. He writes, "The relationship of Jesus to Israel is not that of an antitype who makes an inferior type irrelevant" (p. 67). Vlach fears that if Israel is a type, it will become insignificant in God's plan of redemption. In doing so, however, he fails to acknowledge that types are not irrelevant, but relevant as they point to greater realities. Although Vlach acknowledges that "there are correspondences between Israel and the church, and similar language is used of both" (p. 68), he seems to reject Israel as a type of either Jesus or the church. Interestingly, several times Vlach refers to Jesus as the "ultimate Israelite" (pp. 22, 23, 64, 67) and even as the "true Israelite" (p. 23). So, if Jesus is not a typological

---

6. The same question could be raised regarding Vlach's view of the fulfillment of land and temple promises.
7. Robert B. Strimple, "Amillennialism" in *The Millennium and Beyond*, ed. Darrell L. Bock, Counterpoints (Grand Rapids: Zondervan, 1999), 86.

fulfillment of Israel, what exactly does Vlach mean that Jesus is the "ultimate" or "true" Israel? It appears to mean nothing more than "the model Israelite." In the end, by insisting that Israel is not a type that points to Christ, the ultimate significance of Christ is diminished in Vlach's interpretation.

Exegesis of Romans 9–11

In this section I discuss seven areas of disagreement with Vlach's exegesis of Romans 9–11, focusing mostly on chapter 11. The deficiencies in Vlach's exegesis are closely related to his views of biblical theology and typology.

First, Vlach seems to misunderstand the main purpose of Romans 9–11. He writes, "Paul's primary purpose in Romans 9–11 is to explain how Israel's unbelief in Jesus harmonizes with the great privileges that still belong to Israel (9:1–5)" (p. 65). According to Vlach, the section is about Israel. As I note in my essay, however, the primary purpose of Romans 9–11 is to defend God's faithfulness (9:6). As Hafemann notes, "The central issue in Romans 9–11 is whether God's faithfulness to himself and to his promised redemptive, saving activity can be maintained in spite of Israel's rejection of Jesus."[8] Although this may seem like a small difference, there is an important underlying factor to consider. That is, instead of rightly emphasizing God's faithfulness, Vlach focuses on Israel's unbelief and privileges, which seems to indicate that from the outset Vlach is concerned about something that is a secondary rather than primary issue. This causes him to miss the central focus of the passage. The passage is first and foremost about God and his faithfulness and only secondarily about Israel.

Second, Vlach's reading of Romans 11:11 is flawed. Paul questions, "I say then, they did not stumble so as to fall, did they? May it never be!" (NASB). Paul asks whether Israel's rejection ("stumble") of the Messiah constitutes a complete rejec-

---

8. Scott Hafemann, "The Salvation of Israel in Romans 11:25–32: A Response to Krister Stendahl," *ExAud* 4 (1988): 43.

tion ("fall") from God's saving purposes. His answer is emphatically "No!" In other words, Israel did *not* stumble as to fall. They did stumble, but the stumbling did not result in them falling. Vlach's interpretation, however, misses the point Paul is making. Vlach states, "Paul's "May it never be!" (11:11b) emphatically reveals that Israel's stumbling is not a permanent fall. A reversal is coming which is a major theme of 11:11–32" (p. 40). But Paul's point is *not* that Israel's fall is not permanent but that Israel did not fall decisively to begin with. That is, they stumbled, but they did not fall. Although the majority of Israel have stumbled and have not embraced God's Messiah, they did not fall from God's saving purposes. Paul is asking whether Israel is completely out, and the answer he himself provides is "absolutely not." There is no hint of a reversal of Israel's fortunes since Paul's answer is that they did not fall. The fact that Paul mentions himself and the seven thousand of Elijah's day would be superfluous if Paul were trying to prove that Israel's rejection is not final. These examples make sense only if he is demonstrating that the rejection is not *total*. Thus, Paul is asking if Israel has completely forfeited its past privilege and is now an utterly rejected people. Paul is declaring that there is still a remnant of believing Jews, and there will always be until Christ returns. So Paul's question and answer in 11:11 do not introduce the theme of reversal, which Vlach suggests characterizes 11:11–32.

Third, Vlach's understanding of "fullness" (*plērōma*) in Romans 11:12 is unlikely. According to Vlach, the "fullness" of Israel refers to "everything God intended for the nation" (p. 41). That is, *plērōma* must be understood qualitatively ("fullness" or "completeness") and not quantitatively ("full number"). But the quantitative sense is found in Mark 6:43 and 8:20 ("baskets full of broken pieces") as well as Romans 11:25 ("fullness of the Gentiles"). In fact, there is a scholarly consensus that "the fullness of the Gentiles" refers to the full number of elect Gentiles throughout history. The full phrase in 11:25 is "until the fullness of the Gentiles has come in." The addition of the phrase "has come in" (*eiselthē*) virtually rules out a qualitative interpretation since the phrase intimates a certain number of people coming into God's kingdom ("full number"). In addition, the CSB, NIV, RSV, NRSV, NLT, and NET all render 11:25 as "the full number of the Gentiles." Even Doug Moo, who is cited by Vlach, disagrees with Vlach's interpretation of 11:11. Moo maintains that "the context and the parallel with v. 25 suggest that this 'fullness' is attained through a numerical process," even if there might be some "qualitative denotation."[9] If 11:25 is taken quantitatively, that would also seem to favor a quantitative view in 11:12. Kruse writes, "In light of the use of 'fullness' in respect to the Gentiles in 11:25 we are justified in concluding that Israel's 'full inclusion' means the full number of believing Jews, which will be made up when those yet to believe are added to the remnant that already believe."[10] Consequently, if the salvation of "all Israel" occurs *after* the full number of Gentiles have come to salvation, then how can there be a subsequent time of salvation and great blessing for the Gentiles (p. 40)? Schreiner rightly states, "If the fullness of the Gentiles enters in before Israel is saved, it is inconceivable that there will be a great ingathering among the Gentiles *after* this event."[11]

Fourth, Vlach asserts without sufficient exegetical support, "Some in the increasingly Gentile church concluded that God

---

9. Douglas J. Moo, *The Epistle to the Romans*, NICNT (Grand Rapids: Eerdmans, 1996), 690 (see also p. 719).

10. Colin G. Kruse, *Paul's Letter to the Romans*, Pillar New Testament Commentary (Grand Rapids: Eerdmans, 2012), 428–29. This is also the interpretation of C. E. B. Cranfield, *A Critical and Exegetical Commentary on the Epistle to the Romans*, 2 vols., ICC (Edinburgh: T&T Clark, 1975–1979), 2:575; James D. G. Dunn, *Romans 1–8*, WBC 38A (Dallas: Word, 1988), 655; Joseph A. Fitzmyer, *Romans*, AB (New York: Doubleday, 1993), 611; William Hendriksen, *Exposition of Paul's Letter to the Romans* (Grand Rapids: Baker Academic, 1981), 367; Robert Jewett, *Romans*, Hermeneia (Minneapolis: Augsburg Fortress, 2007), 678; Kruse, *Romans*, 428–29, 443; Thomas R. Schreiner, *Romans*, BECNT (Grand Rapids: Baker Academic, 1998), 598–99; N. T. Wright, "The Letter to the Romans: Introduction, Commentary, and Reflections," in *The New Interpreter's Bible*, (Nashville: Abingdon, 2002), 10:681.

11. Schreiner, *Romans*, 599.

had permanently rejected Israel" (p. 24).[12] This claim is based primarily on 11:18–20, where Paul warns the Gentiles not to be arrogant toward the natural branches. But Vlach is claiming more than is warranted by the text. Paul warns his Gentile readers not to be proud, but nowhere does Paul state that they thought God had permanently rejected Israel or that they embraced a type of replacement theology. Instead, it seems that Vlach has forced his hermeneutic onto the text. That is, because his position is the opposite of so-called "replacement theology," it is easy to assume that the arrogant Gentiles held a position similar to replacement theology.

Fifth, Vlach wrongly concludes that all ethnic Jews or at least the vast majority will be grafted back into the olive tree. In Romans 11:23 Paul states, "even they [i.e., the natural branches broken off], if they do not continue in their unbelief, will be grafted in, for God has the power to graft them in again." Again, Vlach claims more than the verses can bear. Paul is not making a prediction. Instead, Paul uses a third-class conditional statement (considered uncertain but still likely) in order to make his point that the Gentiles should not boast.[13] If God can graft in the wild branches, certainly he can do the same with the natural branches. Paul does not prophesy or predict that God will graft the unbelieving nation *as a whole* back into the tree of salvation. Rather, he is stating that whenever individual Jews have genuine faith in Jesus the Messiah, they will be grafted back in.

Sixth, Vlach assumes that *achris hou* ("until") should not be understood in a terminative sense because that is not the "normal" or "usual" sense of the word. In other words, he suggests that understanding "until" as indicating a reversal as opposed to eschatological completion is to be preferred because

---

12. See also p. 70 ("Yet they still concluded that God rejected Israel"), p. 45 ("Some adopted a replacement position against Israel"), p. 47 ("Paul's olive tree analogy warns Gentiles against concluding they had replaced Israel").

13. See Andreas J. Köstenberger, Benjamin L. Merkle, and Robert L. Plummer, *Going Deeper with New Testament Greek : An Intermediate Study of the Grammar and Syntax of the New Testament* (Nashville: Broadman & Holman, 2016), 443.

"most cases of *achris* in the NT indicate a reversal or change in previous conditions after a period of time" (p. 50). Or, to put it differently, Vlach claims, "reversal is predominately connected with this term" (p. 50). But when Vlach appeals to the "normal" or "usual" meaning of a word, he is guilty of committing an exegetical fallacy.[14] Specifically, this is the fallacy of "unwarranted restriction of the semantic field," which fails to take into account the wide range of meanings of a word. In this case, the range is limited by an unjustified appeal to the "normal," "usual," or "typical" use of a word.[15] The problem with such an appeal is that a word does not have a normal use. A word means what the context dictates. If we used this method of determining the meaning of a word, then the same word would always have the same meaning because the majority (normal use) would win out. As I demonstrate in my essay, *achris hou* is essentially terminative, and only the context can determine where the emphasis lies after the termination. In several texts the phrase occurs in an eschatological context where the termination envisioned involves not a reversal but an eschatological fulfillment (1 Cor. 11:26; 15:25).[16] In other words, what is important is not what will take place *after* the event is completed (reversal), but *that* the event is eschatologically fulfilled (terminative). The hardening of Israel will occur "until" the full number of Gentiles receive salvation, and then it will reach its eschatological termination. That is, a hardening will occur throughout the whole of the present age until the return of Christ. As such, Paul is not suggesting a time when the hardening will be reversed but a time when the hardening will be eschatologically fulfilled.

---

14. See D. A. Carson, *Exegetical Fallacies*, 2nd ed. (Grand Rapids: Baker Books, 1996), 57–60.
15. In his appeal for evidence for his view, Vlach cites Luke 22:15–16, which uses the term *heōs* and not *achris* (p. 51n49).
16. See also Matthew 24:38–39, where "until" (*achris hēs*) does not indicate a reversal but results in judgment and new creation.

Furthermore, Vlach is inconsistent in applying his principle of the "normal sense" of a word. Later, when he discusses the phrase *kai houtōs* ("and in this way"), he implicitly acknowledges that the normal meaning is modal and not temporal. Ironically, he still argues for the temporal view claiming that the view "has scholarly support" since some have demonstrated that a temporal view "could exist" in 1 Thessalonians 4:17 (p. 53). Since the modal use of *kai houtōs* is (by far) the more common use, why doesn't Vlach adopt such an interpretation?

Finally, Vlach's understanding of Romans 11:26 ("The Deliverer will come from Zion, he will banish ungodliness from Jacob") is difficult to accept for two reasons. First, he claims that the text refers to the second coming of Christ and not his first coming. Although it is true that Paul uses the future tense, the question is whether or not Paul understood it as future from his point in history. It was future from the perspective of Isaiah, but when Paul quotes the passage, he is quoting it because he sees it as past.[17] Second, Vlach maintains that at his second coming Jesus comes from the *earthly* Zion. Vlach departs from many who, while still holding his overall position, insist that Paul is referring to the heavenly Zion. It seems to me that Vlach is more consistent with his view. In the end, however, his view is still not persuasive. In what way does Jesus come from Zion at his second coming? Doesn't Jesus come from heaven? Vlach insists that the thrust of the passage suggests a future reversal of Israel's fortunes, and therefore the quote from Isaiah in Romans 11:26 must refer to Jesus's second coming. But this is perhaps another place where Vlach's arguments support his position only if one assumes his interpretation of other issues in the context. But such an argument begs

---

17. See, e.g., Reidar Hvalvik, "A 'Sonderweg' for Israel: A Critical Examination of a Current Interpretation of Romans 11.25–27," *JSNT* 38 (1990): 93; Fitzmyer, *Romans*, 627; Christopher R. Bruno, "The Deliverer from Zion: The Source(s) and Function of Paul's Citation in Romans 11:26–27," *TynBul* 59 (2008): 127; N. T. Wright, *Paul and the Faithfulness of God*, Christian Origins and the Question of God (Minneapolis: Augsburg Fortress, 2013), 4:1251.

the question. He even acknowledges that the earlier reference to Zion in 9:33 relates to Jesus's first coming.

Conclusion

Vlach is to be commended for his clear and consistent presentation of a dispensational view of typology and exegesis of Romans 9–11. Throughout his survey he presents an unwavering commitment to the distinction between Israel and the church and the underlying need for a future millennium after Jesus returns. Exegetically, I believe that Vlach (1) misses the primary focus of Romans 9–11 (God's faithfulness), (2) misunderstands the nature of Paul's question in 11:11, assuming that Israel has fallen but in the future will be restored (Paul clearly indicates that Israel has *not* fallen), (3) misinterprets the meaning of "fullness" in 11:12 and 11:25, (4) assumes that Gentiles held to a form of replacement theology, (5) concludes that all (or most) of ethnic Israel will be grafted back into the olive tree, (6) rejects that *achris hou* ("until") can be interpreted in a terminative sense (eschatological fulfillment) in 11:25, and (7) embraces the unlikely position that the Isaiah quote in 11:26 refers to the second coming. In the end, our disagreements relate not merely to the exegesis of a particular text (in our case Romans 9–11), but to our fundamental differences in the relationship between the covenants, the role and function of typology, and our understanding of God's eschatological kingdom.

A TYPOLOGICAL FUTURE-MASS-CONVERSION VIEW

Fred G. Zaspel
and James M. Hamilton Jr.

The apostle Paul wrote his epistle to the Romans in order to expound "the gospel of God" (1:1) in its various dimensions and applications. The heart of this gospel is that through Christ God promises to freely give a right standing with him—and every attending blessing—to all who believe in Jesus. God accepts sinners on the ground of the substitutionary work and righteousness of our Redeemer. And this, the apostle emphasizes, is for *all* who believe.

Paul explains the gospel in Romans with compelling precision. But his agenda is not simply to expound the gospel but, in doing so, to demonstrate that this gospel is grounded in the OT Scriptures. This good news of salvation in Jesus Christ is the salvation that God "promised beforehand through his prophets in the holy Scriptures" (1:2). It is a matter of greatest importance to the apostle to show that his gospel is not only in keeping with the older revelation; it is the very salvation that the older revelation promised.

God intended to offer this gospel grace to both the Jew and Greek (1:16), and through the ministry of this "apostle to the Gentiles" (11:13) it gained an ever-widening international reception. Even if Israel remained largely in unbelief, great numbers of Gentiles were coming to enjoy the divine favor in Jesus Christ.

Happy as all this seems, it raises a serious question. No one can read the OT carefully and fail to notice that God gave Israel a central role in his redemptive purpose (e.g., Gen. 12:2; Isa. 44:23; 60:1–3; cf. John 4:22). So it is now a surprising turn of events that while Gentiles are embracing Israel's Messiah and sharing in Israel's promised blessing, Israel itself is not! The OT Scriptures offer Israel a bright hope that would come to fruition in the time of the Messiah. But now that Messiah has come, Israel has rejected him, and the promised salvation— in the church—is largely a Gentile affair. It is the church that Paul now describes as "the seed of Abraham" (4:16). What has become of Israel?

More to the point, given this surprising turn of events, just how does all this square with the OT revelation? Paul has insisted from the outset that the gospel of Jesus is the Messianic salvation the OT Scriptures foresaw and foretold. But if it is the salvation of Israel's Messiah, why is Israel itself missing out? Has the church replaced Israel in God's program? What has come of God's promise? Has God changed his mind? Certainly Paul's claims cry for some kind of explanation.

Moreover, the apostle has just sounded a triumphant note regarding the eternal glory God promised to all who are in Christ. Are these promises sure? If God's promises to Israel have failed, what confidence can we have in the promises God gave *us*?

So while on the surface the outstanding theme of Romans 9–11 concerns Israel, its future, and God's redemptive purpose for this age, the larger theme and issue at hand is the integrity and faithfulness of God himself. Has he acted with Israel according to his word? Has he done what he has promised? Has he changed his mind? Is Paul's gospel, after all, in keeping with the OT revelation?

To answer this question, in Romans 9–11 the apostle leans heavily on OT Scriptures, citing passage after passage to demonstrate God's continued faithfulness to his word. The argument is driven by questions, declarative statements, Scripture citations and allusions, careful exegetical distinctions, and (sometimes surprising!) theological correlations—all with a close eye to the redemptive-historical advance that marks this age. Paul insists that the salvation in Christ he now proclaims is the salvation promised in Israel's Scriptures.

Why then—particularly at this point in history—is Israel lost? In addressing this question, Paul provides in Romans 9–11 his most extensive overview of God's purpose in redemptive history and Israel's role in it. All sides acknowledge, therefore, that Romans 9–11 is a "normative" kind of passage, a passage that provides the paradigm for understanding related passages that touch this subject more briefly. Indeed, it provides a paradigm of redemptive history with regard to this age and the unfolding of God's redemptive purpose for Israel and for the world.

Romans 9–11 vindicates the trustworthiness of God. God has kept and will keep his promises to Israel. Grounding his argument solidly in a string of OT passages, the apostle demonstrates not only that God has kept his promises to Israel but also that these promises embrace Gentiles too. In this sweeping overview of redemptive history, Paul not only vindicates the integrity of God but clarifies God's purpose for Israel and for the world. Israel and the church are organically yet typologically related, united though not equated, and within this union Israel's hope remains.

Exposition of Romans 9–11

This section traces Paul's argument in Romans 9–11 and examines the most critical exegetical turning points. Here is a brief outline of how we approach the passage:

I. The Problem of Israel's Failure (9:1–6a)

Because the gospel of salvation seems to have left Israel behind, it may have seemed that Paul himself had turned against his people. Is the apostle now anti-Jewish? Has he denied God's promises to Israel? Whether or not Paul is responding to critics, his opening affirmation is transparently heartfelt and born of deep conviction. He laments Israel's state of overwhelming-majority unbelief and thus its failure to attain the promised messianic salvation (vv. 1–3).

What makes Israel's failure so tragic is that they, above all other people, are divinely privileged (vv. 4–5). All these blessings from God "belong" to Israel. But that is the rub: Given all these promises, how can Israel now be losing out? It surely cannot be that "the word of God has failed" (v. 6a). That could never be! But does not Israel's failure seem to say so? Paul's opening response is passionate and reaffirming: Yes, tragically, Israel has failed and is presently cut off from its Messiah, but Israel is yet a blessed people to whom belong God's promises. The apostle now unpacks this response throughout the remainder of Romans 9–11.

II. The Nature of God's Promise (9:6b–29)

The first step in Paul's argument is to demonstrate from Israel's own Scriptures that the tension in this theological conundrum is overstated and misunderstands Israel's ancient promises.

A. A Narrowing Focus (9:6b–13)

The Abrahamic promise had not an all-inclusive but a narrowing focus. The promise was to Abraham's seed (Gen. 12:3, 7; 13:15–16; 15:5, 18; 17:4–8; etc.), but that does not mean that God would include every individual descended from the great patriarch. This is obvious just on the surface of the text of Genesis: only Isaac received the blessing, not Ishmael, and only Jacob received the blessing, not Esau. There is more to be said since God did make great sweeping promises to the nation, as Paul will recall in due course. But this simple observation of a narrowing focus within the divine promise immediately relieves tension and casts the question in a new light. The theological "problem" is not as acute as it might have seemed. "Birth to the right family was not enough; there must also be an election according to grace."[1]

If we may characterize this in terms that reflect the contemporary discussion, Paul affirms that a "true Israel" or "spiritual Israel" exists within the larger body of Israelites. He is not (here, at least) expanding the meaning of "Israel" to include Gentiles, but narrowing it:

vs. 6 "of Israel"	vs.	(true) "Israel"
vs. 7 "Abraham's seed"	vs.	"Abraham's (true) children"
		"Abraham's (true) seed"
vs. 8 "children of the flesh"	vs.	"children of the promise"
		(true) "seed"

---

1. Harold W. Hoehner, "Israel in Romans 9–11," in *Israel: The Land and the People: An Evangelical Affirmation of God's Promises*, ed. H. Wayne House (Grand Rapids: Kregel, 1998), 147.

Paul emphasizes that mere physical descent does not determine one's standing with God; God's appointment does. Yes, Israel is a blessed and chosen people. But not all within Israel receive the promised blessings. From the beginning God has sovereignly chosen among those "of Israel" who would be his. God has never been obligated to anyone but has always maintained the right to determine who would constitute his people. God never intended the promise to be all-inclusive in absolute terms; not all of Abraham's descendants would receive the blessing.

Paul's argument so far is that the present failure of Israel must not be overstated. There has been from the beginning a narrowing focus in God's promise that did not include all of Abraham's descendants. Physical descent does not determine one's standing with God, and God is never obligated to anyone. In choosing Isaac (not Ishmael) and Jacob (not Esau), God demonstrated from the beginning that his blessing is sovereignly distributed (v. 11).

B. Excursus: The Justice of God (9:14–24)

This observation, in turn, raises a potential question regarding divine justice: "What shall we say then? Is there injustice on God's part?" (v. 14). Is God merely arbitrary? Is it fair that God chooses whom he will bless, apart from any consideration of human involvement or merit? So now almost as an aside Paul digresses from his primary line of argument to address this new "problem."

His response, in brief, is to assert that God is never bound to anyone but is always free to show mercy at his own discretion. By the same token, however, as in the case of Pharaoh, God is also free to withhold grace and to harden (vv. 17–18). He is God over all, answerable to no one, and as a potter with clay (vv. 19–24) he is sovereign in all his dealings with his creatures and may bless or harden fallen humanity at his discretion.

The fundamental point in all this is that saving blessing depends ultimately not on anything human—not family heritage, not personal standing, not individual effort—but on God's sovereign call. Those who are saved, both Jew and Gentile, are "vessels of mercy" whom God "prepared beforehand for glory" and "called" to himself in grace (vv. 22–24).

C. An Expanding Vision (9:24–29)

If salvation depends ultimately on God's call and not physical descent, then it is entirely feasible that Gentiles also may be included in the promise. And this is what Paul affirms: "in order to make known the riches of his glory for vessels of mercy, which he has prepared beforehand for glory—even us whom he has called, not from the Jews only but also from the Gentiles" (v. 24). Here the apostle returns more closely to the question at hand, but his purpose is not merely to affirm Gentile inclusion, but to affirm that the OT itself tells us this. So in vv. 25–26 he cites Hosea 2:23 and 1:10, and in vv. 27–29 he cites Isaiah 10:22–23 and 28:16. In Hosea's context, Israel had violated God's covenant and thus had relegated itself to a status of rejection: its name now is "Not My People." By its unfaithfulness to the covenant stipulations, it had no claim on God and no right to presume that it was still "his people." Yet without obligation, God pledged to call "Not My People" "My People" once again. God is free to show mercy to whom he will show mercy.

Two observations are important here. First, Paul does not rescind God's eschatological promise to Israel. He assumes that God's promise to Israel still stands: "Not My People" Israel will in the day of God's mercy become "My People" yet again. God will not forget his people Israel. Second, Hosea's promise includes Gentiles: "not of the Jews only but also from the Gentiles."

The question of course arises how this move is warranted. How does Paul come to understand that Hosea's prophecy applies to Gentiles and not to Israel only?

At the very least, Paul sees a parallel between rebellious and therefore rejected Israel on the one hand and estranged Gentiles on the other.[2] Both may rightly be described as "Not

---

2. John Murray, *The Epistle to the Romans*, 2 vols., NICNT (Grand Rapids: Eerdmans, 1959–1965), 2:38.

My People." Now if "Not My People" Israel can become "My People," it is a very small step to affirm that "Not My People" Gentiles—if God so wills—can become "My People" also. God's favor comes not by mere bloodline but by sovereign election. God's "call" is what establishes his people as *his* people. And just as God can sovereignly call "Not My People" Israel to be his "sons," so also he can call "Not My People" Gentiles to share in his favor in Christ, as Paul presumably holds in view for the church at Rome throughout chapter 8. The same God who sovereignly called Israel to be his people has sovereignly called Gentiles also. What matters, ultimately, is God's call.

So Paul sees the Gentile inclusion as analogous to that of rebellious and rejected Israel. What both hold in common is (1) a former alienated status and (2) God's sovereign call. But it seems there is more to the answer. Gentile inclusion in the people of God is not a new concept to Paul. It is a hope rooted in the patriarchal promise itself: Abraham would be the "father of many nations" (Gen. 17:4–5). How did Paul get there from Hosea? The answer may be, simply, that Paul read Hosea 1:10 in the fuller light of its covenantal context. In its entirety, Hosea 1:10, which Paul cites only in part, reads, "Yet the number of the children of Israel shall be like the sand of the sea, which cannot be measured or numbered. And in the place where it was said to them, 'You are not my people,' it shall be said to them, 'Children of the living God.'" Hosea borrows the phrase "like the sand of the sea which, cannot be measured or numbered" from Genesis 22:17, which, it would seem, is itself building on the divine promise in Genesis 17:4–5, the promise regarding "many nations." It appears that for Paul the promise of Hosea 1:10b ("Not My People" becoming God's children) is informed by the language of Hosea 1:10a, which, in turn, harks back to the patriarchal promise of worldwide blessing. And here Paul brings it all together: God will also bring Gentiles to share in Israel's promised blessing. There is little question that in Hosea's prophecy Israel is in view, but it seems that the reference to Genesis 22:17 opens the door for extending the prophecy to Gentiles also.

Put another way, if inclusion in the Abrahamic promise ultimately depends on God's call, and if that promise entailed blessing to the world and assured that Abraham would be the father of many nations, and if "Not My People" Israel becomes God's children, then it is not difficult for the apostle Paul, putting all this together, to conclude that the prophecy entails Gentile blessing also.[3]

In vv. 27–28 Paul cites some prominent "remnant" passages from the prophet Isaiah. Isaiah also saw that Israel was largely a disobedient people, so, centuries before Paul and the particular problem he addresses, the prophet insisted, "only a remnant will be saved." This captures exactly what Paul is arguing here, so he quotes Isaiah to settle the matter. Apart from God's sovereign election of a remnant, Israel would have failed altogether. But God has shown mercy, and the remnant is saved.

More to the point, if Isaiah of old spoke of the salvation of only a remnant, then this "problem" of Israel's present large-scale failure is not so surprising after all. Once again, Paul's point in 9:6b–29 is that the "problem" of presently failed Israel is something the OT Scriptures themselves foresaw. The theological "rub" of presently lost Israel is not as acute as it might appear. God's word has not failed (v. 6b).

Still more important to Paul's overall argument is how his interpretive citations of Hosea 2:23 with 1:10 and Isaiah 10:22–23 with 28:16 and 1:9 reflect an appeal to these prophets' larger message of hope. "Not my people" becoming instead "My

---

3. Douglas J. Moo and Andrew David Naselli ("The Problem of the New Testament's Use of the Old Testament," in *The Enduring Authority of the Christian Scriptures*, ed. D. A. Carson [Grand Rapids: Eerdmans, 2016], 702–46) provide a careful, thorough discussion of this passage (743–45), and we agree with their conclusion: "One of Paul's hermeneutical axioms helps to explain how he applies these Hosea prophecies to God's including Gentiles in Paul's day: the Christian church embodies the ultimate fulfillment of God's promise to Abraham" (744). We would not understand this "ultimate fulfillment" to preclude a future mass-conversion of ethnic Israelites at the second coming.

People," "not beloved" becoming "beloved," "not my people" becoming "sons of the living God," the language of "sand of the sea" and even "remnant"—all these expressions resonate with hope for Israel following its exile. Wagner demonstrates that these prophecies, in context, tell the "story of a God who determines not only to judge, but also to redeem, his people."[4] The prophecy of Isaiah 10:22–23, for example, indeed sounds a note of judgment (Paul's immediate point at hand) but also in context functions to underscore the promise that Israel's judgment will come to an end. Indeed, in Isaiah and in the literature of the Second Temple period, the "remnant" embodies Israel's hope— it is a reminder of *both* divine judgment and promise. Paul retains both these ideas (judgment and hope) somewhat in tension here until reaching his climactic argument in Romans 11 (especially v. 26). But this "hopeful conclusion with which Paul's argument ends in Romans 11 is thus already foreshadowed in his appropriation of Isaiah's promise of a remnant in Romans 9."[5]

III. An Explanation of Israel's Failure (9:30–10:21)

In 9:30–10:21 Paul again steps just a bit aside of his main argument in order to address an important related question that his discussion has raised: *Why* has Israel failed? The promise may not include all Israelites, but as Paul himself has acknowledged (9:4–5), Israel as a people yet maintains a privileged status. These promises centered in Jesus and the messianic salvation he accomplished, but now that this salvation has come, Israel as a people has been largely left out. Why?

A. The Reason for Israel's Failure (9:30–10:13)

We might think that since Paul just emphasized God's sovereignty, he would say that Israel has failed because God has so

---

4. J. Ross Wagner, *Heralds of the Good News: Isaiah and Paul "in Concert" in the Letter to the Romans*, NovTSup 101 (Leiden: Brill, 2003), 94; cf. 78–117. See also Mark A. Seifrid, "Romans," in *Commentary on the New Testament Use of the Old Testament*, eds. G. K. Beale and D. A. Carson (Grand Rapids: Baker Academic, 2007), 649–50.

5. Wagner, *Heralds*, 109.

ordered it. But that is not the answer he gives. Rather, he insists that Israel's failure is entirely their own fault. The Gentiles, though so far off, have attained righteousness because they have submitted to that righteousness of God that comes through faith (9:30). Israel, on the other hand, has idolatrously preoccupied themselves with the law, as though they could attain righteousness themselves (9:31–10:4). Israel has proceeded as though righteousness were something that by their own law-keeping they could give to God; the Gentiles (speaking here again in broad strokes) have by faith received righteousness from God. God intended the law to point us to Christ (10:4), the one in whom we may freely obtain the righteousness the law requires; the Gentiles have received Christ, but Israel has stumbled over him as though they could accomplish a standing with God on their own.

Throughout this passage Paul emphasizes that God's saving blessing, announced universally in the gospel of Christ, is free to all—but enjoyed only by those who believe (10:12–13). Israel has failed to receive the promise simply because they have pursued an inadequate (self-)righteousness and refused to trust in Jesus.

B. Prophecies of Israel's Failure (10:14–21)

Before moving on to his climactic argument in chapter 11, Paul again appeals to the OT Scriptures to show that this present situation of Israelite failure and Gentile blessing is no surprise to God but in fact was prophesied centuries before. Moses himself (in Deut. 32:21) had warned that God would make Israel jealous by Gentile blessing (Rom. 10:19). Isaiah echoes this in 65:1–2, where he announces that God would show his favor to the Gentile nations who were not even seeking him while Israel stubbornly refused his kind offer (Rom. 10:20–21). Paul takes up this "jealousy" theme again in chapter 11, but here he highlights it to demonstrate once more that God's word has not failed but is being fulfilled.

So Paul has responded to the apparent problem that God's word has failed (9:1–6a). First, God never gave the ancient promises to all of Abraham's descendants (9:6b–29) but to those whom he calls. Second, Paul blames Israel (9:30–10:21). Israel pursued an inadequate (self-)righteousness, refusing to trust in the one to whom the law pointed. God has offered his mercy to Israel, but the nation stubbornly persists in unbelief (10:21).

IV. A Demonstration of Israel's Hope (11:1–32)

All this sets the stage (οὖν, 11:1) for the climactic response of chapter 11. Two questions frame Paul's discussion:

1. "Has God rejected his people?" (v. 1)
2. "Did they stumble in order that they might fall?" (v. 11)

The answer to both questions is an emphatic "No!" that Paul then explains. But in vv. 1 and 11 Paul asks two related but very different questions. The first question (v. 1) asks if God is finished with Israel as a people: whether God's rejection of Israel is complete. The second question (v. 11) asks if their rejection and present state of failure is permanent. In both cases the apostle proceeds to answer accordingly.

1. Question 1: Is Israel's failure total? (vv. 1–10)
2. Question 2: Is Israel's failure final? (vv. 11–32)

In vv. 1–10, Paul insists that God *has been and is* faithful to his promise. He has preserved a remnant, so Israel's failure is *not total*. Israel has failed (v. 7), but God has not altogether rejected them. In vv. 11–32, Paul affirms that God *will be* faithful to his promise and restore Israel to favor. "All Israel" will yet be saved (v. 26). Israel's present state of failure is *not final*. Israel has fallen, but not forever.[6]

---

6. Commentators commonly recognize this understanding of the two questions of vv. 1 and 11. See, e.g., Richard N. Longenecker, *The Epistle to the Romans: A Commentary on the Greek Text*, NIGTC (Grand Rapids: Eerdmans, 2016), 877–88; Michael F. Bird, *Romans*, Story of God Bible Commentary (Grand Rapids: Zondervan, 2016), 379–80, 384; Thomas R. Schreiner, *Romans*, BECNT

Some equate the two questions of vv. 1 and 11, understanding both to inquire whether Israel has failed altogether.[7] The issues that Paul raises in vv. 11–31, however, point to a shift in his thought, a new stage of his argument (see the two following sections).

There are also literary-structural indications that Paul's argument shifts to a new question in v. 11. In Romans 9–11, Paul advances each step of his argument by using interrogatives and quotations from the OT:

> Two complementary factors support this reading. First, Paul usually signals the beginning of a new section with the inferential conjunction *oun* and a question throughout Romans 9–11: *Ti oun eroumen* (9:30), *Lego oun* (11:1), *Lego oun* (11:11). The parallel way Paul begins 11:1–10 and 11:11–32 shows that these passages constitute two distinct stages in Paul's argument. Paul uses the formula *Lego oun* plus a question in order to raise and reject (*me genoito*) an apparent inference from the preceding discussion. Although Rom 9:14, 19; 10:14; and 11:7 also fit this formula, a second factor provides another objective basis for adopting the proposed structure. Paul alerts us to the presence of structural breaks with the use of scriptural catenas or mixed quotations. These quotations suggest that 9:25–29; 10:18–21; 11:8–10; and 11:26b–27 all serve as conclusions to their respective sections. S. Hafemann offers a similar structural analysis of Romans 9–11.[8]

(Grand Rapids: Baker Academic, 1998), 593; James D. G. Dunn, *Romans 9–16*, WBC 38B (Grand Rapids: Eerdmans 1998), 653; Douglas J. Moo, *The Epistle to the Romans*, NICNT (Grand Rapids: Eerdmans, 1996), 686–87; Murray, *Romans*, 2:75; C. E. B. Cranfield, *A Critical and Exegetical Commentary on the Epistle to the Romans*, 2 vols., ICC (Edinburgh: T&T Clark, 1975–1979), 2:554–55; William Sanday and Arthur C. Headlam, *The Epistle to the Romans*, 5th ed., ICC (Edinburgh: T&T Clark, 1907), 318; B. B. Warfield, *Syllabus on the Special Introduction to the Catholic Epistles* (Pittsburgh: Waters, 1883), 200–201.

7. E.g., O. Palmer Robertson, *The Israel of God: Yesterday, Today, and Tomorrow* (Phillipsburg, NJ: Presbyterian & Reformed, 2000), 172–73.

8. Jason C. Meyer, *The End of the Law: Mosaic Covenant in Pauline Theology*, NAC Studies in Bible and Theology (Nashville: Broadman & Holman, 2009), 178n2.

A. God Has Been Faithful to Preserve a Remnant (11:1–10)

In effect, the wording of v. 1 both asks and answers the same question. "Has God rejected *his people?*" The concept of the nation of Israel as "God's people" is a familiar one in the OT (e.g., Exod. 8:20; 19:5–6; 1 Kings 8:43) and is an expression for Israel both in its times of rebellion (e.g., Isa. 1:3; 5:13; 47:6; 58:1; Jer. 2:31–32) and in the anticipated time of blessing (Zech. 8:7–8; cf. Isa. 32:18; 65:19; Jer. 24:7; 30:22; 31:1, 33; 32:38; Ezek. 11:20; 14:11; 36:28; 37:23, 27).[9] Paul's question echoes this familiar sentiment, with its obvious eschatological overtones, and thereby answers itself. The very idea that God has rejected his own people—a people whom he had made his very own—is unthinkable. So Paul answers accordingly: "God has not rejected his people whom he foreknew" (v. 2; cf. 1 Sam. 12:22; Ps. 94:14).

To establish his answer, the apostle highlights that God has always preserved a remnant within Israel, as in the days of Elijah (vv. 1–6). Indeed, Paul himself, a descendent of Abraham, is evidence that God has not cast off his people altogether. Verse 5 summarizes Paul's point that God has remained faithful to Israel: "So too at the present time there is a remnant chosen by grace." Israel's failure is not total.

Once again Paul demonstrates that all this is in keeping with the OT Scriptures (vv. 7–10). In v. 8 Paul cites Deuteronomy 29:4 with Isaiah 29:10, prophecies of Israel's hardening, a theme with echoes elsewhere in Isaiah (see especially Isa. 6:9–10, quoted repeatedly in the NT with reference to Israel's rejection of Jesus; cf. Matt. 13:14–15; Mark 4:12; Luke 8:10; John 12:40; Acts 28:25–28).[10] The remnant theme reverber-

---

Meyer refers to Scott J. Hafemann, "The Salvation of Israel in Romans 11:25–32: A Response to Krister Stendahl," *ExAud* 4 (1988): 45–47.

9. Sam Storms asserts that "his people" (11:1) refers to the remnant and not to Israel as a nation (*Kingdom Come: The Amillennial Alternative* [Fearn, Scotland: Mentor, 2013], 307). This misses the point under discussion—the lostness of the nation—and the immediate connection (οὖν) to this theme from the previous verse.

10. Wagner (*Heralds*, 244–51) argues that Isaiah 6:9–10 is likely the bridge that in Paul's mind links Isaiah 29:10 and Deuteronomy 29:4.

ates with hope, and particularly in light of Paul's unfolding argument in Romans 11 we should note the recurrence of the same in the chapter's opening verses. In the language of Moses's prophecy, God will circumcise Israel's heart so that the nation at last will trust the Lord (Deut. 30:6). Paul's citation of Moses's "down to this very day" (v. 8; cf. Deut. 29:4) echoes this hope, marking "the current state of affairs as an anticipation of God's future work,"[11] a theme Paul expands on in v. 11.

B. God Will Be Faithful to Save Israel (11:11–32)

The continued existence of a remnant within Israel provides only a partial answer to the question of God's faithful promise to Israel. Thus, Paul asks further whether this present situation (in which only a remnant from Israel believes) is permanent: "Did they stumble in order that they might fall?" (v. 11).

Verse 11 differs from that of v. 1. Verse 1 asks whether God had rejected Israel outright; Paul responds that God has not and that the remnant proves it. Israel's failure is *not total*. Verse 11 is different. "Fall" denotes "irretrievable spiritual ruin."[12] Given Israel's present unbelief, is its failure *final*? Will this present status of failure continue? Does Israel's stumble signify its "complete downfall, never to rise again"?[13] As the NIV translates, "Did they stumble so as to fall beyond recovery?" And again the apostle answers with an emphatic "No!" Israel's unbelief will not persist—it is *not final*.

But Paul does more than deny that Israel's present unbelief will persist. He explains that its present failure serves a larger

---

11.   Seifrid, "Romans," 670; cf. 671–72.

12.   Moo, *Romans*, 687.

13.   George R. Beasley-Murray, "The Righteousness of God in the History of Israel and the Nations: Romans 9–11," *RevExp* 73 (1976): 446. Cf. Murray, *Romans*, 2:75; Schreiner, *Romans*, 593; James Denney, "St. Paul's Epistle to the Romans," in *The Expositor's Greek Testament*, ed. W. Robertson Nicoll, 5 vols. (New York: Doran, 1902), 2:678; Andreas J. Köstenberger and Peter T. O'Brien, *Salvation to the Ends of the Earth: A Biblical Theology of Mission*, New Studies in Biblical Theology 11 (Downers Grove, IL: InterVarsity Press, 2001), 187.

divine purpose: "through their trespass salvation has come to the Gentiles" (v. 11). Israel has been left to its unbelief so that the gospel would move out to the nations. This idea is reflected in the NT elsewhere (cf. Matt. 8:11–12; 21:41–43; Acts 13:46, 48; 18:6; 28:19–20). Israel had stubbornly refused its Messiah, but this was no surprise to God and was fulfilling his global redemptive purpose.

In turn, this gospel advance among the Gentiles serves a further purpose: "to make Israel jealous" (v. 11). Wagner summarizes Paul's point here nicely: "Although Gentiles do enter into the saga of God's relationship to Israel, they do so in a supporting role. The main plot line in Romans 9–11 remains the suspenseful story of how God is going about making good on his promises to redeem his people Israel."[14] Simply put, Israel has fallen, but God's ultimate purpose for it is not its fall but its recovery.

In v. 12 Paul expands, reasoning from the lesser to the greater: "Now if their trespass means riches for the world, and if their failure means riches for the Gentiles, how much more will their full inclusion mean!" That is, if Israel's *failure* brought worldwide blessing, what greater blessing must its final *salvation* bring! This echoes the familiar OT theme of the nations' sharing in God's blessing of Israel (Ps. 67:1–2). The goal of Paul's own ministry is to see "some" Jews of his own day provoked to jealousy and thus turn to Christ in faith (v. 14). But his fuller perspective here looks beyond this and anticipates a "fullness" (v. 12) and "acceptance" (v. 15) of "all Israel" (v. 26) that will yet come.[15] There is a larger, continuously heightening purpose—from Israel's failure to Gentile blessing to Israel's blessing to unprecedented blessing. As Michael Bird paraphrases, "If Israel's loss is the Gentiles' gain, Israel's gain will be the Gentiles' mega-super-duper-über gain!"[16]

---

14. Wagner, *Heralds*, 239.
15. Cranfield, *Romans*, 2:561; Murray, *Romans*, 2:80; Moo, *Romans*, 692.
16. Bird, *Romans*, 385.

1. v. 11: Israel's trespass → Gentile salvation → Israel made jealous
2. v. 12: Israel's trespass / failure → Gentile riches → Israel's inclusion → greater riches
3. v. 15: Israel's rejection → global reconciliation → Israel's acceptance → life from the dead[17]

The immediate point at hand pertains to Israel, so in vv. 16–24 the apostle employs two metaphors to expand on Israel's place in this grand redemptive purpose: "If the dough offered as firstfruits is holy, so is the whole lump, and if the root is holy, so are the branches" (v. 16). The holiness of the part (dough or root) renders the whole (lump or tree) holy also. The idea of hope lies on the surface. The first metaphor is drawn from the offering of the firstfruit "lump of dough" to the Lord in Numbers 15:17–21. The second is drawn from the practice in horticulture of grafting branches into an existing tree. The dough and the root represent the patriarchs (cf. v. 28; also 9:5), illustrating that the patriarchal promise stands: for the sake of the fathers the hope of Israel remains. The "holy" status of the patriarchs—that is, the promise made to Abraham, Isaac, and Jacob—pledges the salvation of "all Israel" (cf. Ezek. 16:60).

There were ethnic conflicts of some sort between Jew and Gentile in the church at Rome, which Paul now turns to address in this passage (vv. 17–22). Gentiles in Christ are indeed beneficiaries of the Abrahamic blessings, but this gift of divine grace must by no means be twisted so as to allow a sense of superiority over Jews. Gentiles are wild branches, grafted in as a result of Israel's unbelief. So the apostle reasons that if Israel, being a natural branch, was stripped away because of unbelief, then Gentiles likewise will stand only by faith—and if they do not believe, then surely they, being but wild branches, will be stripped away also. "Do not become proud, but fear" (v. 20)! Gentiles may boast only in God's gracious

---

17. Cf. Moo, *Romans*, 684.

kindness, but they must remember also his severity lest they also be cut off (vv. 21–22).

Paul's olive tree metaphor suits not only these relational questions in the church but also the larger point concerning God's ultimate saving purpose. So in vv. 23–25 the apostle reasons that the restoration of Israel to its promised blessing is more likely than the Gentile salvation already under way—if God grafted in wild branches, Gentiles, "contrary to nature," it is surely the more likely that he will graft the natural branches in again. God is indeed *able* to do (v. 23) and has *purposed* to do this (vv. 23–26). The present failure of Israel is only partial *and temporary* (v. 25) and will continue only until the full number of God's elect among the Gentiles has come in. As Paul has already indicated in vv. 11–12, so here in vv. 25–26: "The large scale conversion of the Gentile world is to be followed by the large scale conversion of Israel. . . . If their temporary stumbling was prophetically foretold, so was their ultimate and permanent restoration."[18]

So there will be a reversal. At present Israel remains largely in unbelief, failing to receive the Abrahamic blessing, and only a remnant believes. This succession of events (vv. 25b–26—Jewish failure, Gentile inclusion, Jewish regathering) is a surprising turn, but it is the "mystery" now revealed to the apostle (v. 25).[19] Having completed its course among the Gentiles, the gospel will succeed in Israel, and in this way (οὕτως) not just "some" (vv. 13–14) but "all Israel will be saved" (v. 26).[20]

---

18.   F. F. Bruce, *Romans: An Introduction and Commentary*, TNTC 6 (Downers Grove, IL: InterVarsity Press, 1985), 211, 216.

19.   Moo, *Romans*, 715–17; Robert Jewett, *Romans*, Hermeneia (Minneapolis: Augsburg Fortress, 2006), 899; Bruce, *Romans*, 217. Most commentators identify the content of the mystery with the three-fold proposition of vv. 25–26a: (1) the partial hardening of Israel, (2) the length of its duration ("until . . ."), and (3) the salvation of "all Israel." Longenecker includes two more items: (4) the coming deliverer from Zion to turn away godlessness from Jacob, and (5) God's covenantal promise to take away Israel's sin (*Romans*, 896).

20.   Read in conjunction with v. 23, this affirms specifically that Israel will be saved *in faith*.

It is worth pausing to point out the explanatory conjunction (γάρ, left untranslated in both the ESV and NIV) in v. 25. The sense is that there is warrant to anticipate Israel's restoration (v. 24) *because* of this mystery now revealed to Paul. Israel's hope is grounded in new as well as previous revelation.[21]

Ethnic Israel is consistently in view in Romans 9–11, so most acknowledge the ethnic sense in 11:26 also, although the question remains (which we discuss below) whether Paul in 11:26 has Israel itself or the remnant in view. Paul provides some indicators regarding the time of this re-grafting of Israel, but they are sufficiently vague that we cannot determine it ahead of time. These time indicators are (1) the fullness of the Gentiles (v. 25) and (2) the coming of the Deliverer from Zion to redeem Israel (v. 26). Paul grounds (οὕτως . . . καθώς) the latter affirmation in explicit OT promise (vv. 26b–27; cf. Isa. 59:20–21; 27:9; Jer. 31:33–34) that looks ultimately to the second coming of Christ for final realization. We take up this question more below.

In v. 28 the apostle provides a crisp summary of Israel's present situation, which he then supports with three brief statements of explanation (γάρ . . . γάρ . . . γάρ, vv. 29–32). Simply put, this is the status of Israel today: "As regards the gospel, they are enemies for your sake. But as regards election, they are beloved for the sake of their forefathers." Stumbling, hardened, disobedient, and rejected, yet Israel is God's beloved. In its rejection of Jesus, Israel remains God's enemy—"Not My People"—and as such it has no claim to the ancient promise. But its hope remains "on account of" (διά, v. 28) the patriarchal promise. We may be sure of it because (γάρ) "the gifts and the calling of God are irrevocable" (v. 29). Moreover, it was God's purpose that (1) Israel remain in unbelief in order that the gospel would move out to the Gentiles and, in turn, (2) that by this Gentile blessing Israel will again receive mercy also (vv. 30–31). Indeed, God has ordered all this so that his gracious saving purpose will reach its intended global dimensions (v. 32).

---

21. Moo, *Romans*, 713–14.

V. Concluding Doxology (11:33–36)

Paul has sketched out a grand drama of saving grace that runs from ancient times (Abraham) to the eschaton and that culminates in the redemption of all humanity. God chose a man from whom would come a uniquely blessed people. Yet by leaving this chosen but rebellious people in unbelief for a time, he determined to bring the promised blessing to Gentiles, a move that will provoke Israel to jealousy and also bring it to faith. Yes, indeed, as Paul has argued, righteousness may be attained freely, by faith alone, and this very faith God has determined to effect in the hearts of men and women the world over. In the end this once disobedient world will know and sing of divine mercy.

Rightly apprehended, all this must inevitably culminate in praise. So it is with the apostle Paul in vv. 33–36.[22]

In v. 33 he expresses his praise in three exclamations:

1. Oh, the depth of the riches and wisdom and knowledge of God!
2. How unsearchable are his judgments!
3. How inscrutable his ways!

In vv. 34–35 he expresses his praise in three questions, each drawn from the OT:

1. For who has known the mind of the Lord?
2. Who has been his counselor?
3. Who has given a gift to him that he might be repaid?

In v. 36 he explains (ὅτι), again in three prepositional phrases, that the sovereign and gracious God is the ground of all things:

---

22. For Paul's use of the OT in this passage, see Andrew David Naselli, *From Typology to Doxology: Paul's Use of Isaiah and Job in Romans 11:34–35* (Eugene, OR: Wipf & Stock, 2012).

1. For from him and through him and to him are all things.

Finally, in v. 36b he offers his own expression of ultimate praise:

2. To him be glory forever. Amen.

As S. Lewis Johnson aptly summarizes, Paul's marvel at the wonder and vastness of this redemptive purpose can be explained only in terms of God's "independent sovereignty. . . . He is the source, the means, and the goal of all the divine acts of creation, providence, and redemption."[23] It is the recognition of this divine greatness and mercy that brings the apostle, appropriately, to conclude in such exuberant doxology—a discussion that began with a note of tragedy (9:1–5) concludes with a note of joy.

Summary
Paul answers the "problem" of Israel's present failure, then, in two broad steps. (1) One cannot claim the Abrahamic blessing based on physical descent alone; it depends upon God's sovereign call, and one must receive it by faith in Christ. As the continued remnant testifies, God has not rejected his people Israel. (2) God will one day reverse this present situation—not just the remnant but "all Israel will be saved." God designed Israel's temporary unbelief and rejection to fulfill his global saving purpose, a purpose that reflects his marvelous grace, for which he is worthy of all praise.

Further Considerations
With this survey exposition of Paul's argument now in place, we can focus on some major exegetical points on which our

---

23. S. Lewis Johnson, "Evidence from Romans 9–11," in *A Case for Premillennialism: A New Consensus*, eds. Donald K. Campbell and Jeffrey Townsend (Chicago: Moody, 1992), 213.

reading turns and address some larger hermeneutical issues that this discussion affects.

The Time Frame

The succession of events that Paul outlines broadly (vv. 11–32) indicates that God's saving of "all Israel" (v. 25) is a climactic, end-time event. Paul highlights this succession of events several times over.

1. v. 11: Israel's trespass → Gentile salvation → Israel made jealous
2. v. 12: Israel's trespass / failure → Gentile riches → Israel's inclusion → greater riches
3. v. 15: Israel's rejection → global reconciliation → Israel's acceptance → life from the dead
4. v. 16a: The holiness of the dough → the eventual holiness of the whole batch
5. v. 16b: The holiness of the trunk → the eventual holiness of the whole tree
6. vv. 17–24: cutting off of Israel → grafting in of the Gentiles → re-grafting of Israel
7. vv. 25–27: Partial hardening of Israel → ("until") the fullness of the Gentiles → Israel's salvation in conjunction with the Deliverer coming from Zion
8. vv. 30–31: Israel's disobedience → mercy to the Gentiles → mercy to Israel

Just as Israel's historical disobedience and rejection resulted in this historical stage in which the gospel advances largely among the Gentiles, so this stage of Gentile blessing, in turn, will give way to Jewish ingathering. Paul paints with broad strokes, and in view throughout is corporate Israel and the historical succession of events it will experience—from Jewish rejection to Gentile blessing to Jewish acceptance. Israel's hardening will continue throughout this age "until" God's purpose for the Gentiles in this age is complete.

Understanding this flow of the argument helps us determine the meaning of καὶ οὕτως in v. 26. This expression is capable of a temporal force ("then").[24] That interpretation would make explicit the eschatological time frame expressed in the future tense verbs of vv. 24 and 26, implied in the "until" of v. 25, and outlined in the succession of events we highlight above. But οὕτως likely bears its usual modal force: "*in this manner* all Israel will be saved." Still, although not explicitly temporal in meaning, the expression retains the chronological sequence developed through this passage: it is "in this manner"—that is, the sequence of Israel's unbelief, Gentile ingathering, and then Jewish regathering—that Israel will be saved.[25] This succession of events will culminate in a glorious future for Israel, who, though now cut off because of unbelief, will in that day be re-grafted into its Abrahamic tree. In brief, God will again show mercy to Israel once his present program of Gentile salvation is complete.

This flow of argument also informs the significance of "until" in v. 25, which likewise retains its usual force, highlighting the temporary nature of Israel's partial hardness. Its partial hardness (i.e., the situation in which only a remnant is believing) will continue only "until" the full number of Gentiles have been gathered in. Moo summarizes,

> The hope of spiritual rejuvenation of the nation of Israel is endemic in the OT prophets and in Jewish apocalyptic. . . .

---

24. E.g., Ernst Käsemann, *Commentary on Romans*, ed. and trans. Geoffrey W. Bromiley (Grand Rapids: Eerdmans, 1980), 313; Bird, *Romans*, 392–93; C. K. Barrett, *A Commentary on the Epistle to the Romans*, HNTC (Peabody, MA: Hendrickson, 1987), 223. Bruce seems to argue that the expression indicates both time sequence and manner (Bruce, *Romans*, 218).

25. E.g., Denney, "Romans," 683; Moo, *Romans*, 720; Benjamin B. Warfield, "The Prophecies of St. Paul," in *Biblical Doctrines*, vol. 2 in *The Works of Benjamin B. Warfield*, 10 vols. (New York: Oxford University Press, 1932), 623–24; Walter C. Kaiser Jr., "Jewish Evangelism in Light of the New Millennium in Light of Israel's Future (Romans 9–11)," in *To the Jew First: The Case for Jewish Evangelism in Scripture and History*, eds. Darrell Bock and Mitch Glaser (Grand Rapids: Kregel, 2008), 49–50.

Paul's language in Rom. 11 seems deliberately calculated to restate this traditional hope for Israel's renewal. His point seems to be that the present situation in salvation history, in which so few Jews are being saved, cannot finally do full justice to the scriptural expectations about Israel's future. Something "more" is to be expected; and this "more," Paul implies, is a large-scale conversion of Jewish people at the end of the age.[26]

The apostle gives us another time indicator in vv. 25–27, where he connects the removal of Israel's hardness of heart to the coming of the Deliverer from Zion and the new covenant promise to banish Israel's sins—familiar themes that brim with eschatological overtones. "The Deliverer from Zion" (v. 26) alludes to Isaiah 59:20–21, and the covenant of forgiveness (v. 27) presumably refers to the new covenant (Isa. 27:9; Jer. 31:33–34), which Christ climatically fulfills when he returns.[27] Paul changes "for the sake of Zion" to "from Zion," perhaps influenced by Psalms 14:7, 53:6, and 110:2,[28] probably in order to signal that it is "heavenly" Zion (cf. Heb. 12:22) and thus Christ's second coming that is in view (1 Thess. 1:10).[29] This, combined with the future tense of v. 24 ($\dot{\epsilon}\gamma\kappa\epsilon\nu\tau\rho\iota\sigma\theta\dot{\eta}\sigma\sigma\nu\tau\alpha\iota$), as well as the "until" of v. 25 and the succession of events it entails, points us to the return of Christ and its attending events. All this accords well with what Jesus promised in Matthew

---

26. Moo, *Romans*, 724.

27. Christopher R. Bruno argues from Paul's use of Isaiah that in view is the first coming of Christ, the accomplishment of redemption, and its ensuing success "from Zion" ("The Deliverer from Zion: The Source[s] and Function of Paul's Citation in Romans 11:26–27," *TynBul* 59 [2008]: 119–34). But see Meyer, *End of the Law*, 186–87. On any view, of course, the accomplishments of Christ's first coming are necessarily in view in some measure: the purpose of his second coming is to bring the work of his first coming to its completion. But as the "until" of v. 25 signals, it is this final stage, the eventual reversal of Israel's fortune, that remains a key aspect of Paul's hope. Cf. A. Andrew Das, *Paul, the Law, and the Covenant* (Grand Rapids: Baker Academic, 2000), 107.

28. Cranfield, *Romans*, 2:577; F. Godet, *Commentary on St. Paul's Epistle to the Romans* (Edinburgh: T&T Clark, 1881), 257.

29. Moo, *Romans*, 728; Cranfield, *Romans*, 2:577–78; Jewett, *Romans*, 704; Bird, *Romans*, 393; Käsemann, *Romans*, 313–14.

24:14: "this gospel of the kingdom will be proclaimed through-out the whole world as a testimony to all nations, and then the end will come." Paul may have that promise in mind.

A final time-frame indicator rises from the expected consequence of Israel's coming "inclusion" and "acceptance" (vv. 12, 15). Israel's "full inclusion" (v. 12) and "acceptance" (v. 15), as we have argued, most likely refer to its future conversion. Bird takes "life from the dead" (v. 15) as an equivalent metaphorical expression.[30] But most understand "life from the dead" (1) to refer to a subsequent period of world-wide gospel advance[31] or (2) as a more literal reference to the end-time resurrection.[32] The logic of v. 12 may favor the former (#1), but we are not convinced. More importantly, our argument does not hinge on a decision—either understanding would again point to a time frame that is beyond the present day and associated with the return of Christ.

At this point what we want to establish is that the apostle associates the salvation of "all Israel" with the culmination of this age.

The Meaning of "All Israel" (11:26)

Differences regarding the interpretation of Romans 9–11 culminate in the question of the identity of "all Israel" in 11:26. Despite its long and esteemed heritage among Reformed inter-preters especially, the understanding of "all Israel" as a reference to the Jew-Gentile church[33] has more recently fallen on bad times. Such a view would seem to undermine Paul's cautions

30. Bird, *Romans*, 386.

31. E.g., Murray, *Romans*, 2:79, 81–84, 94–96; S. Lewis Johnson Jr., *Discovering Romans: Spiritual Revival for the Soul* (Grand Rapids: Zondervan, 2014), 178–79; Warfield, "Prophecies," 623–24; Godet, *Romans*, 243; Longenecker seems to favor this view also (*Romans*, 888).

32. Moo, *Romans*, 694–96; Jewett, *Romans*, 681; Cranfield, *Romans*, 2:562–63; Colin G. Kruse, *Paul's Letter to the Romans*, Pillar New Testament Commentary (Grand Rapids: Eerdmans, 2012), 431.

33. This was the view of Calvin and many in the Reformed tradition, as well as some in the early church. Robertson has more recently argued (against his own previous position) in favor of this view (*Israel of God*, 187).

against Gentile pride in the previous verses[34] and would be inconsistent with the meaning of the term "Israel" through-out this passage—even in the previous verse (v. 25). Even in 9:6, where Paul uses the term in a spiritualized sense, the focus remains ethnic Israel.[35] Afterward Paul uses the term only in its broader ethnic sense. His climactic point in 11:26 "is not so much that all *Israel* will be saved [as though he were intending to redefine the term], but that *all* Israel will be saved."[36] The apostle does want to emphasize God's global saving purpose, and he does so by tracing the advance of the gospel from Israel to the Gentiles and then back to Israel again. But the question he answers here is what he raised at the outset regarding his "kinsmen according to the flesh" who at present have fallen away in unbelief. Nanos summarizes more broadly,

> It is difficult to imagine in a letter that maintains throughout the distinction between Jews and gentiles (whether they be Christians or not), particularly in this context of explaining the destiny of empirical Israel to Christian gentiles so that they will realize the current state of the "stumbling" of Israel is not as it appears, that Paul would suddenly shift his meaning of "Israel" to that of "true" or "spiritual" Israel (by which most really mean to say that the "church" has supplanted Israel, the very point Paul is arguing against).[37]

Finally, Paul's theological argument in 11:29 regarding the immutability of God's decree and promise, has bearing here also: once God has made a promise that promise could never

---

34. Moo, *Romans*, 721.
35. Cf. A. Andrew Das, *Paul and the Jews*, Library of Pauline Studies (Peabody, MA: Hendrickson, 2003), 106.
36. Bruce W. Longenecker, "Different Answers to Different Issues: Israel, the Gentiles, and Salvation History in Romans 9–11," *JSNT* 36 (1989): 96–97.
37. Mark D. Nanos, *The Mystery of Romans: The Jewish Context of Paul's Letter* (Minneapolis: Augsburg Fortress, 1996), 275–76.

be annulled or transferred to another party. Thus, as with all God's promises, his promise to Israel stands.[38]

The question remains whether "all Israel" refers to (1) Israel as a people considered as existing at a given point in time[39] or (2) merely the cumulative total of the "remnant," believing Israelites across the centuries.[40] We hold with the majority of interpreters that "all Israel" refers to corporate Israel who in a coming day will *en masse* come to faith in Christ.[41] The factors determining this decision include the following.

First, since "all Israel" in the OT regularly carries a corporate significance—referring to the nation that exists at a given point in time—it would be unprecedented for "all Israel" to refer to the remnant.[42] As Dunn comments,

> There is now a strong consensus that πᾶς Ἰσραήλ must mean Israel as a whole, as a people whose corporate identity and wholeness would not be lost even if in the event there were some (or indeed many) individual exceptions (see, e.g., Luz, *Geschichtsverständnis*, 292 and n. 114; Mayer, 287–89; Kümmel, *Theology*, 244; Hofius, "Evangelium," 316–18; against the older view that

---

38. The "Israel = church" view in 11:26 is not a view this book represents, so we do not labor the point here, although many of the arguments in the following paragraphs also weigh against that position.

39. Only a relative few have held that "all Israel" must be absolutely inclusive, referring to a final salvation of every Israelite living at some future point (e.g., Warfield, "Prophecies," 624; Hoehner, "Israel in Romans 9–11," 155; Jewett, *Romans*, 701–2).

40. E.g., Kruse, *Romans*, 442–44; Ben L. Merkle, "Romans 11 and the Future of Ethnic Israel," *JETS* 43 (2000): 709–21.

41. Seifrid, "Romans," 673; cf. Murray, *Romans*, 2:96–100; Dunn, *Romans 9–16*, 681; Moo, *Romans*, 723; Bird, *Romans*, 391–93; Warfield, "Prophecies," 623–24; Cranfield, *Romans*, 2:577; Bruce, *Romans*, 218; Longenecker, *Romans*, 895, 897; Schreiner, *Romans*, 615–17; Käsemann, *Romans*, 313; Grant Osborne, *Romans*, IVP New Testament Commentary Series 6 (Downers Grove, IL: InterVarsity Press, 2004), 307; Leon Morris, *The Epistle to the Romans*, Pillar New Testament Commentary (Grand Rapids: Eerdmans, 1987), 421; Charles Hodge, *A Commentary on the Epistle to the Romans* (Philadelphia: Perkins, 1836), 278–79; Godet, *Romans*, 256; John R. W. Stott, *The Message of Romans: God's Good News for the World*, Bible Speaks Today (Downers Grove, IL: InterVarsity Press, 1994), 303.

42. Moo, *Romans*, 722. Cf. Exod. 18:25; Deut. 1:1; 5:1; 31:1; Josh. 3:7; 1 Sam. 7:5; 17:11; Dan. 9:7.

Paul means "all spiritual Israel," still maintained by Ponsot, and Refoulé's consistent attempt to argue that "all" here can only mean "all the remnant"). The idiom is well enough known and should not cause confusion (cf. 1 Sam 25:1; 1 Kgs 12:1; 2 Chron 12:1; Dan 9:11; *Jub.* 50.9; T. Levi 17.5; T. Jos. 20.5; T. Benj. 10.11; Ps. Philo 22.1; 23.1; etc.; and the much-quoted *m. Sanh.* 10.1; see also Plag, 46–47, 58; Hübner, *Israel*, notes particularly Isa 45:25, not to mention the typical hyperbolic description of other Christian writers—e.g., Mark 1:5; Luke 3:21; and Acts 13:24).[43]

Second, at issue in Romans 9–11 is that "Israel" itself is lost while only a remnant believes; merely to affirm the salvation of the remnant would leave this problem unanswered. Paul is "struggling to show that God remains faithful to all Israel even though Israel has to a great extent become hardened and disobedient," so he argues that "a people currently characterized by 'rejection' will be characterized by their 'acceptance.'"[44] Announcing the eventual salvation of all the remnant would in this discussion be "stunningly anticlimactic" indeed. "The salvation of the remnant is partial, but Paul expects the 'fullness' (πλήρωμα, v. 12) of salvation for Israel and an 'acceptance' (πρόσλημψις, v. 15) that outstrips anything that has occurred thus far."[45]

Third, throughout this passage Israel *contrasts* with the remnant (cf. 10:21; 11:1, 5, 7, 25–26). "All Israel" (v. 26) and Israel's "fullness" (v. 12) explicitly stand in contrast to the "remnant" (v. 5; cf. v. 7) and "some" (v. 14) as a "broad characterization" of Israel as a people.[46] Identifying the remnant with the "Israel" to whom the promise was made confuses what Paul contrasts. There is the remnant who believes, and over against this remnant is Israel itself—"the rest" of Israel (v. 7), presently in unbelief ("they," v. 11; "their," vv. 11, 12)—who will

---

43. Dunn, *Romans 9–16*, 681.
44. Das, *Paul and the Jews*, 108.
45. Schreiner, *Romans*, 616–17; cf. Murray, *Romans*, 2:97–98.
46. Dunn, *Romans 9–16*, 681.

be made jealous so as to be saved. The remnant of "the present time" (v. 5) is not coextensive with, but in contrast to, the "all Israel" who will be saved. "The sum of a remnant is still a remnant, and this would not advance the argument beyond the point Paul initially makes in chapter 9 and again in chapter 10 and again at the beginning of chapter 11."[47] In keeping with this, Paul repeatedly speaks in terms of a *reversal* of corporate Israel's present fortunes (11:11–12, 15, 23–24, 26), a reversal from unbelief to faith. The salvation of "all Israel" "must be conceived of on a scale that is commensurate with their trespass, their loss, their casting away, their breaking off, and their hardening, commensurate, of course, in the opposite direction."[48]

Fourth, the "remnant only" interpretation overlooks the role of the remnant as embodying Israel's larger hope (cf. Isa. 11:11–12, 16; 37:31–32; Mic. 2:12; 4:7; 5:7–8; Zech. 8:12).[49] "In OT prophecy the remnant of the old Israel was at the same time the nucleus of the new Israel. So it is here: the existence of the believing remnant is the earnest of the final salvation of 'all Israel.'"[50] Paul argues in 11:1–10 that the remnant's continued existence demonstrates God's continued commitment to Israel as a people. This provides the "necessary connection" to 11:11–32, which promises that God will spiritually renew the larger body of Israel: "the remnant serves as both the current expression of God's irrevocable love for the nation of Israel and as the anticipation of the fuller, future expression of God's irrevocable calling of ethnic Israel."[51] In 10:19 Paul's citation of Moses has corporate Israel in view also. The reference in its original setting (Deut. 32:21) was not merely individual but corporate.

Fifth, the contrasting events of vv. 12 and 15 concern corporate Israel. It is Israel as a people who have "trespassed," and it

47. Cornelis P. Venema, "'In This Way All Israel Will Be Saved': A Study of Romans 11:26," *Mid-America Journal of Theology* 22 (2011): 37.

48. Murray, *Romans*, 2:96.

49. Das, *Paul and the Jews*, 108–9; Sanday and Headlam, *Romans*, 317.

50. Bruce, *Romans*, 217.

51. Meyer, *End of the Law*, 202–3.

is Israel as a people who will reach "full inclusion." Indeed, the reversal of Israel's present misfortune is the basis of Paul's "from the lesser to the greater" argument:

> "Full number" [v. 12] and "acceptance" [v. 15] have clear escha-
> tological significance. Both concepts here define each other
> reciprocally. . . . "Full number" stands over against Israel's pres-
> ent "reduction." . . . The entire argument of Romans 11:15–32
> is intended to throw light not only on the possibility, but also
> on the certainty of this "acceptance" and "fulness" of Israel.[52]

This succession of events remains in view in v. 23: Paul's point is not that the remnant will continue until completion—a point that would hardly deserve extended argument. His point is that Israel will be grafted in "again" (v. 23). Paul's affirmation in v. 25 that Israel's present failure is only partial and temporary anticipates the same reversal from "partial hardness" to "all Israel saved" (vv. 25–26).

Sixth, the "mystery" revealed to the apostle (v. 25) concerns this succession of events—Jewish failure, Gentile inclusion, then Jewish regathering. It was no mystery that the remnant would be saved—the OT spoke plainly of it. Nor was the salvation of Israel itself a mystery—the OT plainly prophesied that also, and vv. 12, 15, 16, 23, 24 presuppose it. The mystery Paul reveals is the *manner* in which Israel's salvation would come about through this swinging pendulum of grace away from Israel to the Gentiles and then back again to Israel.[53]

Seventh, it is difficult to understand the "Israel" of v. 25 differently from the "Israel" of v. 26. The position advocated here holds that just as corporate Israel is now hardened in unbelief, so in the future corporate Israel will be saved. In

---

52. Herman N. Ridderbos, *Paul: An Outline of His Theology*, trans. John Richard de Witt (Grand Rapids: Eerdmans, 1975), 357–58.
53. Günter Wagner, "The Future of Israel: Reflections on Romans 9–11," in *Eschatology and the New Testament: Essays in Honor of George Raymond Beasley-Murray*, ed. W. Hulitt Gloer (Peabody, MA: Hendrickson, 1988), 77–112.

this way the problem of v. 25 finds its resolution in v. 26: the unbelief of Israel as a people will be reversed. In both cases (vv. 25 and 26) Paul refers to Israel as a people, not the believing remnant. A shift in meaning, midstream, required by the remnant interpretation seems unnatural.[54] Vos argues more fully:

> It only leads to confusion not to distinguish between the single conversions spoken of in such statements and this comprehensive eschatological recovering of the unbelieving Jews. The "pleroma" held in prospect for them stands in contrast to the "ἥττημα" and "παράπτωμα" of vs. 12. Both words, taken together with the question of vs. 11, leave no doubt but the general, national apostasy of Israel is referred to, and consequently the recovery from this must bear the same collective interpretation. Just as the "riches of the world," and the "riches of the Gentiles" take the pagan world in its organic, collective sense, so the other term in the antithesis requires the same understanding.[55]

The Israel who is partially and temporarily hardened (v. 25) is the Israel who will be saved (v. 26), whose sins will be forgiven (v. 27), and who are presently enemies of the gospel yet beloved (v. 28).

Eighth, it seems that the apostle is echoing and interpreting familiar OT promises: Jeremiah 24:5–7, Jeremiah 31:31–37, and Ezekiel 16:60, for example.[56] The OT passages Paul holds in view in vv. 26–27 (Isa. 27:9; 59:20–21; Jer. 31:31–34) speak explicitly of a time of national conversion for Israel (whatever one makes of the attending "land" promise), a turnaround for blessing to Israel corporately, and that "*after*

---

54. Bruce, *Romans*, 218; cf. Köstenberger and O'Brien, *Salvation to the Ends of the Earth*, 188–89.

55. Geerhardus Vos, *The Pauline Eschatology* (Princeton: Princeton University Press, 1930), 89.

56. John Piper, "If the Root Is Holy, the Branches Are Holy," *Desiring God*, 14 December 2003, www.desiringgod.org/messages/if-the-root-is-holy-the-branches-are-holy.

the nation has suffered indignity because of its sin."[57] The new covenant promise of conversion (11:27), moreover, never concerned the mere remnant but the nation itself. Now if the apostle anchors his argument for the salvation of "all Israel" in prophecies that anticipate a corporate reversal from rejection to blessing, it would be difficult to know why those passages refer to the remnant only. In short, "If the eschatological dimension is removed by this reductionism, the whole chapter is tautological. What would excite Paul about the evident fact that the present 'remnant' will be saved?"[58]

Ninth, Godet's observation that "Jacob" designates "the whole nation collectively"[59] is worth noticing. It would be difficult to find any occurrence of "Jacob" in the Psalms or the Prophets that should be understood in reference to the remnant. The term refers to Jacob himself, the patriarch, or to the whole of Israel, and sometimes "Jacob" is *distinguished from* the remnant (e.g., Isa. 10:21). But understanding Jacob as the remnant seems unprecedented.

Tenth, in reference to the tree metaphor of vv. 16–24 Richardson remarks, "The obvious feature of the olive tree figure, sometimes overlooked, is that a pruned Israel retains its place in God's activity."[60] The "remnant only" interpretation fails to do justice to this important—and, as Richardson describes it, "obvious"—feature of Paul's olive tree illustration and the sequence of events it is intended to convey. What is presently stripped away (corporate Israel) will yet be grafted in again. This, in turn, informs (γάρ, v. 25) Paul's future hope for "all Israel" in vv. 25–27. Not the remnant but Israel itself remains in view.

Finally, in v. 28 Paul summarizes both the problem and the solution in a way that anticipates the future reversal we have

57. Schreiner, *Romans*, 619; cf. Murray, *Romans*, 2:99.
58. Bruce Corley, "The Jews, the Future, and God," *SwJT* 19 (1976): 54.
59. Godet, *Romans*, 257.
60. Peter Richardson, *Israel in the Apostolic Church*, SNTSMS 10 (New York: Cambridge University Press, 1969), 129.

observed throughout the passage: at present Israel is a gospel enemy, but at the same time it is beloved because of God's promise to its fathers. Its majority enmity and unbelief will not continue forever.

Paul's summary statement in vv. 30–31 again depicts a process and succession of events that entail a reversal of fortune for Israel: the historical process will unfold successively from Israel's disobedience to mercy to the Gentiles to mercy shown once again to Israel (cf. vv. 11, 12, 15, 16, 17–24, 25–27).

In brief, the promised remnant indeed features prominently in one part of Paul's argument in Romans 11: it stands as proof that Israel's failure is not total, that God has not rejected Israel altogether. But Paul's argument goes beyond the remnant to Israel as a whole, who in the end times will be restored in faith to divine favor. Israel itself, now lapsed in unbelief, will turn back—from rejection to acceptance, from cut off to re-grafted, from disobedience to obedience, and from partial and temporary hardening to faith: "all Israel will be saved."

The Relation of the Church to Israel and Its Promises
Selected Reflections on Romans 9–11

In the broad-sweeping view of God's purpose in redemptive history that Paul gives us in Romans 9–11 he provides also some glimpse of the ever-debated question of the relation of Israel and the church. Some factors that may help inform our understanding on this score include the following.

1. In 9:24–26, Paul includes believing Gentiles as referents of Hosea's prophecy concerning Israel.
2. In 11:1, Paul refers to unbelieving Israel yet as "his [God's] people."
3. In 11:11–24, Paul explores the connection between believing Gentiles and (as yet) unbelieving Israel.

4. In 11:11–24, Paul also expresses the "essential oneness that exists between 'the remnant within Israel' and 'the remnant from among the Gentiles.'"[61]

5. In 11:11–32, Paul affirms that Israel will yet inherit its promised blessing.

6. In 11:28, Paul affirms that Israel, though still in unbelief, is beloved of God.

7. In 11:16–24, Paul illustrates both the unity and the distinction between Israel and believing Gentiles.

8. As we have argued, Paul does not see Israel's promise "transferred" to the Gentiles; he sees both Jews and Gentiles enjoying the Abrahamic promise together.

9. Paul does not quite equate Israel and the church or identify one with the other, but he does see the church as heir of Israel's promises.

10. In the end, Paul seems clearly to have *one* universal redeemed people of God in view: there is just one olive tree of blessing.

It appears that the relationship of Israel and the church entails elements both of continuity and discontinuity—unity there is, yet there is some distinction also. But before we conclude further, a glance at the larger biblical picture will be helpful. We begin with what Moses said to Israel before moving to the patterns and prophecies that we see in the Prophets and the Writings.

Biblical-Theological Overview

On the plains of Moab, Moses warned Israel that if they went into the land and broke the covenant, God would exile them from the land (Deut. 4:25–31; cf. 28–32). At various points in these passages, Moses begins by saying, "If you do this," and then ends with words about "when all this happens" (see, e.g., Deut. 4:25, 30; 29:4, 20; 30:1). Moses is prophesying Israel's

---

61. Longenecker, *Romans*, 886.

future. He is telling them that they will go into the land, break
the covenant, be exiled, but seek the Lord from exile, at which
point God will restore them. Moses repeatedly prophesies this
restoration (Lev. 26:41–45; Deut. 4:29–30; 30:1–10).

This basic plotline (covenant-breaking disobedience, exile,
repentance, restoration) informs all that Moses says to Israel in
Deuteronomy. The poetry of Deuteronomy 32 itself witnesses
to Israel about what their future holds (Deut. 31:28–30). Moses
celebrates God's greatness and records Israel's unworthiness
(32:1–9), emphasizing the merciful love that God chose to
place on Israel (32:10–14), recording the way that Israel became
complacent and disobedient (32:15–18), bringing upon themselves God's judgment (32:18–20). The ESV renders these statements in the past tense, but throughout the OT the past is a
paradigm for what we can expect in the future, and that seems
to be the case here as well. Moses is retelling Israel's past so that
they will know their own future. This would seem to explain
the shift to the future tense in Deuteronomy 32:20–21. The
Lord says that he will hide himself (32:20), and he goes on to
assert that because Israel has made him jealous with false gods,
he will make Israel jealous by extending his kindness to "no
people" (32:21; cf. Rom. 9:25–26).[62] God will bring the disas-
ters of the curses of the covenant on Israel (32:22–25), but he
will not utterly destroy them (32:26–27).

God will not wipe Israel from human memory (32:26)
because he does not want the nations to think that they were
triumphant. He wants all to know that Israel's defeat was due
to the fact that he was disciplining them (32:27). Ultimately,
the Lord will vindicate his people (32:36), banish idolatry from
them (32:37–38), and make himself known as the giver of life,
the one who kills and makes alive (32:39). God's killing and
making alive seem to point to bodily resurrection since the killing comes first, then those who were dead are made alive.

---

62. This reference to "no people" may shade Paul's citation of Hosea's references to
those "who were not my people" (Rom. 9:25).

The prophecies of Moses informed the prophets who inter-preted the patterns they saw in Israel's history and pointed to in Israel's future. Israel's experience of judgment is likened to the floodwaters that came on Noah's generation (Ps. 124; Isa. 8:6–8), and Israel's sin makes them a kind of new Sodom (Isa. 1:9–10). The unmaking of the world at the flood and the judg-ment that fell on Sodom foreshadow what God will do when the symbol of the world, the temple, is destroyed, and Israel is exiled. Israel's bondage in Egypt parallels the exiles to Assyria and Babylon (Hos. 11:5), and the exodus from Egypt is the prototype that informs the expectation for a new exodus that will be followed by a new pilgrimage through the wilderness on the way to a new conquest of a new and better land of promise (Hos. 2:16–23).

The prophecies prompted the prophets to notice the patterns, which they were careful to record for the notice of their audiences. As the patterns were repeated, hope for more of the same in the future intensified. After Israel was exiled, the people returned to the land as the book of Ezra narrates. Ezra claims fulfillment of Jeremiah's prophecies (Ezra 1:1), and the pattern of events is similar to the exodus from Egypt: the Lord stirs up Cyrus, who enriches Israel and sets them free, at which point they return to the land to set about rebuilding the temple. This is similar to the way the Lord hardened Pharaoh's heart and liberated Israel, who then plundered Egypt and set out for the land, building the tabernacle on the way. In a sense, then, the return to the land in the book of Ezra is an installment in the new exodus pattern. That it was not the fulfillment of the pattern can be seen from the mixed marriage crisis at the end of the book (Ezra 9–10).

Fulfillment in Christ and the Church

The NT manifestly presents Jesus as the one who brings about the fulfillment of the hoped-for new exodus. He is the Pass-over lamb who has been sacrificed (1 Cor. 5:7), purchasing his people at a price (1 Cor. 6:20). When those who belong to

Jesus are baptized, they experience a fulfillment of what was typified at the Red Sea, and when they partake of the Lord's Supper, they experience fulfillment of what the manna from heaven and water from the rock typified (1 Cor. 10:1–4). They fulfill the tabernacle that the Israelites built from the plunder of Egypt since they are the temple of the Holy Spirit (1 Cor. 3:16; 6:18), built from the plunder of the enemy (Eph. 4:8–16), living under the law of Christ, which fulfills the law of Moses (1 Cor. 9:21).

The first coming of Christ fulfilled the new exodus pattern, but the book of Revelation indicates that there will be yet one more iteration of that pattern at Christ's second coming. The judgments of the trumpets and bowls recapitulate the plagues on Egypt. Just as Israel had light when all Egypt was dark, so the servants of God are sealed and protected from the plagues in Revelation. Just as God's judgment crushed Egypt, God will destroy Babylon the great in Revelation. Just as Joshua led the people to conquer the land, the rider on the white horse comes and puts all his enemies under the ban in Revelation 19. He sets up his kingdom, and after a final rebellion, the new Jerusalem comes down from God in heaven.

What, then, of the Gentiles in the inter-advent period? How do they relate to the Jews and what God promised them? This is what Paul addresses not only in Romans 11 but also in Ephesians 1–3. The plotline Moses prophesied is what Paul presupposes. Israel has been exiled, and just as Moses prophesied, God is provoking them to jealousy with those who were no people (Deut. 32:21; Rom. 9:25–26). This is exactly how Paul understands his own ministry (Rom. 11:13–14). Moses declared that God would not wipe Israel out (Deut. 32:26–27) but vindicate them when their strength was gone (Deut. 32:36). In agreement with this, Paul sees God's gifts and calling as irrevocable (Rom. 11:29) and expects all Israel to be saved when the redeemer comes from Zion (Rom. 11:26).

Jesus inaugurated the new covenant by his death and resurrection, and many Gentiles have been grafted into that olive tree, enjoying the rich root of the blessing of Abraham. God has made Jew and Gentile one new man in Christ (Eph. 2:15), who together in unity enjoy the fulfillments of OT promises (Eph. 1:3–14). God gave Paul insight into this mystery of how the Gentiles have become fellow heirs (Eph. 3:4–6), and Paul maintains that when their full number has come in, God will bring about the consummation of the new covenant through the second coming of Jesus (Rom. 11:25–27).

The problem that provokes Paul to write Romans 9–11 is that Gentiles had begun to inherit Israel's promises. Indeed, Paul does not hesitate to describe the church in Israel terminology: seed of Abraham, children of Abraham, sons, adopted, and so on. This is the problem that underlies Paul's notion of "provoking Israel to jealousy." This extension of Israel's promises to the Gentile church is owing to the church's union with Christ, who is himself the "seed of Abraham" and the "true Israel" par excellence (Gal. 3:16, 26–28).

Gentile believers, then, experience Israel's promised blessings by virtue of their union with Christ, and the NT authors interpret what Gentile believers experience as typologically fulfilling the OT's patterns and promises. This is not "replacement theology" because instances of typological fulfillment do not preclude future fulfillments. Consider the temple and exodus patterns:

Creation as a cosmic temple
  Tabernacle built at Sinai
    Temple built by David
      Second Temple built by returnees
        Church built by Jesus
          New heaven and new earth as cosmic temple

Much could be said about each of these, but our point is that what Jesus is doing in building the church typologically fulfills the building of the tabernacle at Sinai and the two temples in the OT, and the building of the church by the King Messiah

Jesus does not preclude the future fulfillment John narrates in Revelation 21–22:

Exodus foreshadowed in Abraham's experience
  Exodus from Egypt
    Conquest of the land presented as a new exodus
      Prophesied return from exile as a new exodus
        Return from exile as a new exodus
          Salvation Christ accomplishes as a new exodus
            Revelation's trumpets and bowls as a new exodus

Here again the point under consideration is that typologically fulfilling the OT exodus pattern in the salvation accomplished by Jesus the Messiah does not preclude John in Revelation pointing to yet future fulfillment through another installment of the exodus pattern at the end of all things.

Along these lines, we can suggest a pattern for the people of God:

Promises made to Abraham and his seed
  Seed of Abraham, ethnic Israel, enjoy old covenant realization of promises
    OT indications that Gentiles too will be included in the promises
      Jesus comes in fulfillment of promises to Abraham
        Gospel goes first to the Jew, then to the Gentile
          Partial hardening of Israel, full number of Gentiles come in
            Hardening removed, all ethnic Israel saved

This shapes our understanding of biblical typology. The apostle understands Israel and the church as related typologically, and he *also* argues for Israel's yet-future blessing on OT grounds. That is, whatever anticipations of the church are seen in Israel, and however much the church may realize blessings promised to Israel, for Paul the *OT* expectation for Israel continues. Typological fulfillments, then, do not imply that the implications of the promises God has made or the patterns of his saving activity have been exhausted.

Approaching the big picture in this way allows us to under-stand why Paul continues to argue that ethnic Israel itself remains "the people of God" even in its unbelief (11:1–2). The Abraha-mic tree of blessing is "theirs" (v. 24). That is, Israel itself will inherit its promises and be blessed in Abraham's Seed.[63] Christ is the pivot on which all blessing turns for Israel and the nations alike. By virtue of its union with Christ, the whole church, Jew and Gentile, inherits the Abrahamic promise.

So then, what is the relation of Israel and the church?

It is clear from the olive tree metaphor that Paul intends for us to understand the unity of the one people of God: there is just one tree, and it is rooted in the patriarchal promise. So much lies simply on the surface of the text. Yet the same meta-phor also indicates a certain distinction: in this one tree there are both natural and wild branches. There is both unity and distinction within that unity, continuity and discontinuity.[64]

What about the Land?

Paul does not directly address the promise of land in Romans 9–11, but the biblical-theological lines we have sketched suggest how we should understand what Paul said about Abraham being promised that he would be heir of the world in Romans 4:13. To see exactly how these words fit requires a bit more detail in the pencil drawing.

When God blessed the first man and woman, he commanded them to be fruitful and multiply that they might

---

63. See further Jason S. DeRouchie, "Counting Stars with Abraham and the Prophets: New Covenant Ecclesiology in OT Perspective." *JETS* 58 (2015): 445–85.

64. So also Walter C. Kaiser, "Israel as the People of God," in *The People of God: Essays on the Believer's Church*, ed. Paul A. Basden and David S. Dockery (Nashville: Broadman & Holman, 1991), 106: "Few illustrations are as decisive as the olive tree in Romans 11 in demonstrating that there is a unity and oneness to the people of God, while both Israel and the church retain their identities." See also Philip Edgcumbe Hughes, *Interpreting Prophecy* (Grand Rapids: Eerdmans, 1980), 84. Cf. Keith Mathison, *From Age to Age: The Unfolding of Biblical Eschatology* (Phillipsburg, NJ: Presbyterian & Reformed, 2009), 578: "Throughout verses 11–25, Paul has not denied that there is only one people of God, but he has consistently distinguished between the Jews and the Gentiles who are part of that one people of God."

fill the earth and subdue it, exercising dominion over all the animals (Gen. 1:28). This command suggests that God's intention was for Adam and his seed to make all the dry lands like the garden of Eden, a place full of the knowledge of the glory of the Lord, as those made in God's image and likeness brought God's authority and character to bear on all creation. God's plan from the beginning, then, was what he asserted would indeed come to pass in Numbers 14:21—all the earth will be full of his glory.

We have seen installments in patterns above relating to temple, exodus, and God's people, and to these patterns we can add that of the exile. When Adam sinned, he and Eve were exiled from the garden of Eden. The promises that God made to Abraham in Genesis 12 answer the words of judgment in Genesis 3 point for point.[65] This suggests that what God sets out to accomplish through Abraham is what he had set out to accomplish through Adam—the filling of the world with his glory.

Just as Adam was exiled from the garden, the law stipulated that those made unclean by sin or death were to go outside the camp. Eventually, the people's sin and uncleanness resulted in the exile of the descendants of Abraham from the land.

These various exiles (from Eden, from the camp, from the land) are pictures of the way that sin separates people from God: because of sin people are banished from the realm of life. This is also depicted when unrepentant sinners are disciplined and put out of the church, and the final expression of this reality is the casting of the wicked into the lake of fire.

Exile from Eden
    Exiled from camp for sin/uncleanness
        Exiled from land
            Separated from God through sin
                Church discipline
                    Lake of fire/hell

---

65. James M. Hamilton, "The Seed of the Woman and the Blessing of Abraham," *TynBul* 58 (2007): 253–73.

God's purpose is to bring about reconciliation through cleansing, justification, and resurrection from the dead. This means that when God promised land to Abraham, he was promising a beachhead for the reclamation of the whole world. Adam sinned and was driven from the land of life. God promised Abraham a plot of ground that was the symbolic starting point from which his authority would emanate out to fill the whole world. God intended the land of promise as the first step toward reestablishing his reign over the whole world. The people of Israel, God's firstborn son (Exod. 4:22–23), failed and were exiled from the land, but Jesus *the* Son of God recapitulated Israel's history and succeeded everywhere the people had failed, setting in motion the fulfillment of God's promises and purposes, accomplishing reconciliation and restoration.

God gave Adam the world, and he forfeited it. God promised Abraham land, and his descendants were exiled from it. But Jesus came to establish Adamic dominion in fulfilment of the Abrahamic covenant through the Davidic kingship by inaugurating the new covenant in his blood. When Jesus comes, he will fill the world with God's glory.

Thus the Millennium

Adam entered a pure world where he was to image God, multiply, and fill creation with the knowledge of God's ways, authority, and character. Adam sinned, defiled the world, and was driven from God's presence.

Jesus came into the world defiled by sin, cast out its ruler (John 12:31) through his death on the cross, making the sacrifice for atonement and cleansing, inaugurating the new covenant. He rose from the dead, and the good news of his conquest of sin, death, and hell is now being proclaimed to the Gentiles. When their full number has come in, Christ will return to bring about a mass-conversion of ethnic Israelites, because the gifts and calling of God are irrevocable (Rom. 11:29).

When he returns, the risen Christ will enter and liberate the world in bondage to corruption because of what Adam did.

At the trumpet blast the ultimate jubilee will be fulfilled (Lev. 25:9; Isa. 27:13; 1 Thess. 4:16). He will set the captives free for the glorious liberty of the children of God. Jesus will accomplish what God put Adam in the garden to do: he will fill the world with the knowledge of the ways, authority, and character of the one whose image he perfectly reflects.

Understood this way, the millennium becomes a necessary step toward the new heaven and new earth, the completion of God's creation project before the purging renewal. Before God makes all things new, he will accomplish his purpose for the present heavens and earth through the reign of Christ during the millennium.

Summary Conclusion

Returning to the issues raised by Romans 9–11, we turn our thoughts to the olive tree metaphor Paul employs in Romans 11. From this metaphor we see that Paul does not conceive of Israel and the church in terms of identity. Indeed, he does not say that the tree is Israel. The tree, rooted as it is in the Abrahamic promise, is the place of blessing, salvation. It is the privileged people who inherit the promise of Abraham, the people of God of whom both Jews and Gentiles have a part. And so there is unity but not identity, both continuity and discontinuity.

As Moo writes,

> Paul's [tree] metaphor warns us not to view this transition as a transition from one people of God to another. . . . Perhaps a better word to describe the movement from OT Israel to NT church is the same word that the NT so often uses to denote such relationships: "fulfillment." We thereby capture the necessary note of continuity—the church is the continuation of Israel into the new age—and discontinuity—the church, not Israel, is now the locus of God's work in the world.[66]

---

66. Moo, *Romans*, 709. See also George Eldon Ladd, *The Gospel of the Kingdom: Scriptural Studies in the Kingdom of God* (Grand Rapids: Eerdmans, 1959), 117–18:

Paul thus maintains a focus on the place of believing ethnic Israel within the people of God and emphasizes the eschatological blessings the nation itself will experience. There is organic unity between Jew and Gentile in Christ, and yet there is distinction: one tree of promised blessing, but a tree on which both natural and wild branches grow. At this stage of redemptive history the wild branches are most prominent; in a later day the natural branches will be grafted in again.

"There is therefore but one people of God. This is not to say that the OT saints belonged to the Church and that we must speak of the Church in the OT. . . . While we must therefore speak of Israel and the Church, we must speak of only one people of God. This is vividly clear in Paul's illustration of the olive tree in Romans 11. There is one olive tree; it is the people of God."

RESPONSE TO ZASPEL AND HAMILTON

Michael J. Vlach

I appreciate Fred Zaspel and James Hamilton's presentation on the typological future-mass-conversion view of Romans 9–11. They have made my task difficult since they make several good points, and my agreements with their chapter outweigh my disagreements. The beginning sections dealing with Romans 9–11 were mostly accurate. Also, their exegesis of Romans 11:26 in particular was excellent and the high point of their essay.

Not surprisingly, as a representative of a non-typological approach to Romans 9–11, I am less positive about their sections concerning typology that came after their exegesis of Romans 9–11. I did not have stark disagreements with their findings there, but I think their typological assertions concerning temple, exodus, and people of God patterns were complicated and largely removed from Paul's message in Romans 9–11. I also don't think they connected national Israel's relationship to these matters enough. Thus, I found the later sections dealing with typology to be less helpful. In my estimation, a non-typological approach more simply and accurately connects OT promises and patterns with NT fulfillment. I was glad, however, to see that their belief in typological fulfillments does not rule out literal fulfillments of OT prophecies for Israel.

That is not always the case for those who affirm a typological approach.

Also, while rightly grasping a coming salvation of the mass of Israel, I do not think their essay captured the importance of Israel's restoration as a nation. But on a fundamental point that God's purposes for Israel include the salvation of the mass of corporate Israel at a coming point in the future, Zaspel and Hamilton are spot on. And they accurately explain that the "all Israel" destined to be saved in 11:26 is not the trickle of believing Jews throughout history, nor is it the church of believing Jews and Gentiles.

Concerning key points of their presentation, I particularly appreciate Zaspel and Hamilton's beliefs on the following:

- Paul is not expanding the meaning of "Israel" in Romans 9–11; he is "narrowing it." This is important since some wrongly believe the concept of Israel expands to include Gentiles. But as the authors show, "Israel" refers exclusively to ethnic descendants of Abraham, Isaac, and Jacob in Romans 9–11.

- Concerning Romans 9:24–26 and its quotations of Hosea 2:23 and 1:10, Zaspel and Hamilton accurately note that Paul is not identifying believing Gentiles as Israel. Instead, Paul is showing that "the same God who sovereignly called Israel to be his people has sovereignly called Gentiles also." Thus, the application of God's calling purposes applies to Israel and Gentiles. This is rooted in OT statements that both Israel and Gentiles would be blessed by the Abrahamic covenant.

- Paul's emphasis in 11:1–10 is on the remnant of believing Israelites, but "vv. 11–31, however, point to a shift in his thought, a new stage of his argument" (p. 109). This shift, as they show, involves the coming salvation of corporate Israel. Thus, Zaspel and Hamilton rightly understand the importance of both the present believing remnant of Israel *and* the coming salvation of the mass of Israel.

- Concerning Paul's olive tree analogy, I also like Zaspel and Hamilton's insistence that Paul "does not say that the tree is Israel" and that the olive tree is connected with the "Abrahamic promise" and "the place of blessing." This is important because some scholars wrongly conclude that the olive tree of 11:17–24 is Israel. But the olive tree must be broader than Israel since it includes both Israel and Gentiles. Israel in Paul's analogy corresponds to the natural branches specifically, not the tree itself.
- Paul's use of "until" in v. 25 is not meant in a terminative sense but involves a reversal of corporate Israel's current state of unbelief. As they say, "This flow of argument also informs the significance of 'until' in v. 25, which likewise retains its usual force, highlighting the temporary nature of Israel's partial hardness" (p. 119).
- If Paul uses *kai houtōs* ("and so") in a modal sense, this involves a sequential aspect in which corporate Israel's salvation follows the fullness of the Gentiles.
- The "all Israel" in 11:26 "refers to corporate Israel who in a coming day will *en masse* come to faith in Christ." Their eleven points showing why "all Israel" refers to corporate Israel at a future point in time are very helpful.

So there is much to commend in their essay. Concerning their exegesis of Romans 11, I have some minor differences. For example, I believe their understanding of *plērōma* as "full number" in 11:12 and 11:25 is too narrow. As I argue in my essay, Israel's *plērōma* in 11:12 is most likely qualitative and refers to the completeness and fullness of everything God intended for Israel, including full participation in the blessings of 9:4–5 (i.e., covenants, promises, temple service, etc.). Likewise, the *plērōma* of 11:25 is probably qualitative and refers to everything God intends for Gentiles in this age, including their provoking Israel to jealousy. So more than a quantity is in view. I also take the "first-fruits" or "first piece of dough" in 11:16a as a reference to the remnant of believing Israel, while Zaspel and Hamilton say the patriarchs are in view. But even here I acknowledge the possibility of their understanding, and this does not affect a proper grasping of Paul's overall argument. In addition, I also understand the "Zion" of 11:26b to be earthly Zion, while Zaspel and Hamilton believe heavenly Zion is in view.

Salvation and Restoration

The differences I have with their essay mostly concern broader issues. My essay often explicitly refers to corporate Israel as "national Israel" to emphasize the historical and biblical significance of Israel as a national entity among other nations.[1] Just as Israel was a corporate national entity in the OT, so too Israel's future involves a national aspect.

I also speak more explicitly of a "restoration" of Israel. The concepts of salvation and restoration concerning Israel are closely related, but they are not the same. Affirming that a mass of believing Israel will be *saved* in the future is not the same as grasping that Israel as a whole is headed for national *restoration* as a political entity with a role to other nations when Jesus returns to rule the nations of the earth ("He will rule them" [Rev. 19:15; cf. 5:10]). Since Jesus is coming to rule literal nations, it should be no surprise that national Israel will have a role during this time, as the prophets predicted (Isa. 2:2–4; 11; Zech. 14). In addition to several other passages that teach the restoration idea, the restoration of Israel concept is found in Romans 9:4–5 with Paul's words concerning promises, covenants, and temple service still belonging to Israel. I was hoping to see their essay address Romans 9:4–5 in more detail. I do not think this section was adequately addressed in their essay.

In my estimation, those who affirm a coming salvation of corporate Israel should be consistent and also accept Israel's coming restoration. If one acknowledges that Israel as

---

1. It is understood that for most of church history Israel has been dispersed from its homeland. But the Bible predicts the restoration of Israel to her land (see Lev. 26:40–45; Ezek. 36–37).

nation will be saved in line with the OT expectation, then why wouldn't Israel's restoration take place as the OT prophets predicted? In other words, if Israel's salvation will occur in line with OT promises, why wouldn't OT expectations about a restoration of Israel as a nation be fulfilled too? So I emphasize these twin truths of salvation and restoration in my essay more explicitly. Israel's restoration must happen if Israel is to experience the complete fulfillment of all dimensions of the covenants, promises, and temple service mentioned in the OT prophets and Romans 9:4–5.

Typology

The later sections of their essay, starting with "Biblical-Theological Overview," address typology and how typology relates to Jesus, Israel, Gentiles, and the church. I did not find the claims here wrong as much as I found them less helpful and somewhat disconnected from Paul's message in Romans 9–11. Also, although the authors reference typological language nearly a dozen times in their essay, they do not explicitly define *type* or *typology*. This would have been helpful.

The common view is that a *type* refers to a person, place, event, institution, or other entity in the OT that points toward or anticipates a superior NT reality, often called an *antitype*. In some cases, once the NT antitype or reality arrives, the OT type fades away in significance. Most Christian theologians, myself included, acknowledge the existence of types and antitypes in Scripture that show divinely intended correspondences between the two Testaments. For example, Adam is a type of Jesus (see Rom. 5:14). The Mosaic covenant and its Levitical priesthood were shadows of the superior new covenant and Jesus's better priesthood (see Heb. 10:1). Typological connections certainly exist in Scripture, and their significance must be considered.

Zaspel and Hamilton are not specific on what they mean by "type" and "typical." But whatever their specific understanding is, to their credit they seem to avoid an unbiblical typological approach that often leads to the spiritualizing or transcending of Israel's promises. So, even though they affirm a typological approach, I was glad to see Zaspel and Hamilton state, "whatever anticipations of the church are seen in Israel, and however much the church may realize blessings promised to Israel, for Paul the *OT* expectation for Israel continues" (p. 135).

Such a cautious typological approach is not always found. Sometimes a typological approach brings a reality shift to the Bible's storyline by reinterpreting OT promises concerning Israel and replacing national Israel with the church.[2] A skewed understanding of types has led some to erroneously adopt "typological interpretation," which sees the NT redefining or reinterpreting the storyline begun in the OT. Matters such as Israel, Israel's land, Jerusalem, and the temple, which all seem important to the Bible's narrative, are allegedly redefined and transcended by Jesus and the church.[3]

A non-typological approach, such as the one I advocate, affirms continuity in the Bible's storyline and does not see the NT transcending OT themes and passages. There is no typological trajectory that overturns explicit national and physical promises in the OT concerning Israel. A non-typological approach sees literal fulfillment of the covenants and promises over the course of Jesus's two comings. In addition, this posi-

---

2. For Bruce K. Waltke, the New Testament teaches the "hard fact that national Israel and its law have been permanently *replaced* by the church and the New Covenant." Bruce K. Waltke, "Kingdom Promises as Spiritual," in *Continuity and Discontinuity: Perspectives on the Relationship Between the Old and New Testaments,* ed. John S. Feinberg (Wheaton, IL: Crossway, 1988), 274 (emphasis added).

3. One example of someone using such a "reinterpretation" approach is found with George Ladd who stated, "The Old Testament must be interpreted by the New Testament. In principle it is quite possible that the prophecies addressed originally to literal Israel describing physical blessings have their fulfillment exclusively in the spiritual blessings enjoyed by the church. It is also possible that the Old Testament expectation of a kingdom on earth could be *reinterpreted* by the New Testament altogether of blessings in the spiritual realm." George E. Ladd, "Revelation 20 and the Millennium," *RevExp* 57 (1960): 167 (emphasis added). Kim Riddlebarger also says, "But eschatological themes are *reinterpreted* in the New Testament, where we are told these Old Testament images are types and shadows of the glorious realities that are fulfilled in Jesus Christ." Kim Riddlebarger, *A Case for Amillennialism: Understanding the End Times* (Grand Rapids: Baker, 2003), 37 (emphasis added).

tion argues that Israel is a specific people group who received eternal and unconditional promises from God in the OT. Since God cannot lie, and Paul said that changes to covenants cannot occur once they are made (Gal. 3:15), we should expect a literal fulfillment of what God promised in the OT.

Unconditional and eternal covenants and promises to Israel are not types that lose their significance. Furthermore, promises to Israel are reaffirmed in the NT (see Matt. 19:28; Luke 1:32–33; Acts 1:6; Rom. 9:4–5). While passages like Hebrews 10:1 indicate that the Mosaic covenant is a shadow or type, national Israel and its land, temple, and role are not transcended types. *In sum, the temporary conditional Mosaic covenant, including its Levitical priesthood and sacrifices, is transcended by the new covenant and Jesus's superior priesthood and sacrifice (see Heb. 10:1). But national Israel and the promises of the Abrahamic, Davidic, and new covenants, which are eternal unconditional covenants, are not transcended.* Their significance continues and is reaffirmed in the NT.

Jesus, Temple, and Fulfillment

Concerning the central role of Jesus, Zaspel and Hamilton note, "Christ is the pivot on which all blessing turns for Israel and the nations alike. By virtue of its union with Christ, the whole church, Jew and Gentile, inherits the Abrahamic promise" (p. 136). I agree that Jesus is the "pivot" and that Jews and Gentiles experience covenant blessings only by being in union with Jesus.

In regard to those who belong to Jesus and their relationship to the tabernacle and temple, Zaspel and Hamilton say, "They fulfill the tabernacle that the Israelites built from the plunder of Egypt since they are the temple of the Holy Spirit (1 Cor. 3:16; 6:18)" (p. 133). They also illustrate how "creation as a cosmic temple" leads eventually to "New heaven and new earth as cosmic temple" (p. 134). The authors then state, "our point is that what Jesus is doing in building the church typologically fulfills the building of the tabernacle at Sinai and the two temples in the OT, and the building of the church by the

King Messiah Jesus does not preclude the future fulfillment John narrates in Revelation 21–22" (p. 134). Thus, it seems they are saying Jesus and the church fulfill the tabernacle-temple concept although a future dimension in the new earth also awaits.

I agree that believers in Jesus are connected to the tabernacle and temple concept, as 1 Corinthians 3:16 and Ephesians 2:21 indicate. But I would add that corporate Israel is still connected to the "temple service" idea that Paul refers to in Romans 9:4.[4] So a proper theology of "temple," including what Paul says about it in 9:4, should take into account Israel's relationship to it. The significance of the Jewish temple in Jerusalem for the future is affirmed by Jesus (Matt. 24:15; Luke 21:24), Paul (2 Thess. 2:4), and John (Rev. 11:1–2). A full and multi-dimensional theology of the temple grasps three related truths: (1) Jesus's role as true temple (John 2:19–21), (2) believers in Jesus functioning like a temple, and (3) the future significance of a Jerusalem temple. All three senses are important. In sum, I am not entirely disagreeing with what the authors are saying, but I believe Israel's relationship to the temple must also be considered.

Land and Millennium

In their essay, Zaspel and Hamilton affirm the significance of land and a coming millennial kingdom. They rightly link these with the mandate for Adam to rule and subdue the earth (Gen. 1:26–28). They also connect the land with Abraham: "God promised Abraham a plot of ground that was the symbolic starting point from which his authority would emanate out to fill the whole world." (p. 138). Concerning the millennium they are correct that "the millennium becomes a necessary step toward the new heaven and new earth, the completion of God's

---

4. Since A.D. 70 there has been no Jewish temple in Jerusalem and thus no temple service. But Scripture foretells a future temple in Jerusalem (see Ezek. 40–48; Matt. 24:15; 2 Thess. 2:4; Rev. 11:1–2).

creation project before the purging renewal. Before God makes all things new, he will accomplish his purpose for the present heavens and earth through the reign of Christ during the millennium" (p. 139). I agree. While Romans 9–11 does not explicitly mention the millennium, there are implications for a future millennial kingdom in Romans 11:12, 15. These verses discuss better conditions for the world with national Israel's fullness that are best fulfilled in a coming millennial kingdom (see Rev. 20:1–6).

One thing, though, that is missing or not clear from their discussion of land and a millennium is the role of a restored national Israel during this millennium (Isa. 2:2–4; Matt. 19:28). In the coming millennial kingdom Israel will be a microcosm of what God will do for all nations and their lands (Isa. 27:6). So a comprehensive discussion of the coming millennial kingdom should include national Israel's role in the kingdom.

Conclusion

In sum, Zaspel and Hamilton do a fine job of explaining and defending the position that there will be a salvation of corporate Israel on a future day. Their exegesis of Romans 11:26 in particular is excellent, although I do not think they give enough justice to the restoration of Israel idea found in Romans 9–11. However, when the discussion moves to typology, I find their arguments complicated and less helpful. As an adherent of a non-typological view of Romans 9–11, I think a typological approach is not as useful for understanding Romans 9–11 and the Bible's storyline. Paul's argument for a future salvation and restoration of national Israel can be grasped best from Paul's explicit statements and his contextual reliance on many OT texts. Thus, a non-typological approach is simpler and clearer.

One final point. All contributors to this book, including Zaspel and Hamilton, have concluded that Paul's discussion of Israel in Romans 9–11 focuses on ethnic Israelites. The contributors to this book might disagree on whether the "all Israel" to be saved refers to the cumulative believing remnant of

ethnic Israelites or the mass of corporate Israel in the future and
what this salvation means. But we all agree that Romans 9–11,
specifically, is not teaching that the concept of "Israel" refers
to believing Gentiles. This is important since Romans 9–11 is
the most detailed section in the NT concerning the relationship between Israel and Gentiles in Christ. Believing Gentiles
are saved through faith alone and participate in the covenants
of promise along with believing Israelites, but they do so as
Gentiles, just as the prophets predicted (cf. Gen. 12:3 with Gal.
3:7–9 and Amos 9:11–12 with Acts 15:14–18). Paul's argument
makes clear the wonderful beauty of both unity and diversity:
Jews and Gentiles are saved the same way, through faith alone
in Jesus (unity), yet they still retain their ethnic identities so
that equality in salvation does not mean sameness in identity
(diversity). This glorious situation even extends into the new
earth where we see the various nations and their kings bringing
their glory into the New Jerusalem (Rev. 21:24, 26).

RESPONSE TO ZASPEL
AND HAMILTON

Benjamin L. Merkle

I would like to begin by commending Zaspel and Hamilton on presenting a solid defense of their position. I have no doubt that many who already hold their position will be pleased with their exegesis and argumentation. Most of the ways I critically respond to Vlach's view could also apply Zaspel and Hamilton's view. In fact, I was surprised that their views are so similar. In this response, I limit my critique almost entirely to their exegesis of Romans 9–11 since I have more solidarity with their affirmation that Israel and Christ are related typologically.[1] Specifically, I address seven weaknesses in their essay.

First, Zaspel and Hamilton insufficiently consider the significance of Paul's statement in 9:6 ("But it is not as though the word of God has failed. For not all who are descended from Israel belong to Israel"). Perhaps most notable is their claim that Paul's initial answer to the question of God's faithfulness is incomplete: "There is more to be said since God did make great sweeping promises to the nation, as Paul will recall in due course" (p. 101). They

---

1. Though I should note that our views of typology differ at points. For example, in their diagrams showing biblical "patterns" (pp. 134–137), they seem to miss Christ as the key to fulfilling the temple, the exodus, and the people of God.

further maintain that Paul's argument in chapter 11 is "climactic" and therefore more fully explains what he stated in 9:6 (p. 107). In addition, they affirmingly cite Moo, who states, "[Paul's] point seems to be that the present situation in salvation history, in which so few Jews are being saved, cannot finally do full justice to the scriptural expectations about Israel's future."[2]

They are not the only ones who find Paul's argumentation incomplete or insufficient in chapter 9. For example, Das suggests that Romans 9:6 is only Paul's "first attempt" at resolving the problem of God's elect people not benefiting from their elect status.[3] He states that in Romans 11:25–32 Paul "reaches a very different conclusion," a "sudden and powerful reversal of the course of [his] argument."[4] Even Schreiner admits, "Paul was unsatisfied that the answer given thus far was a complete solution to the problem."[5]

But does Paul really advance his initial argument in 9:6 only to change and improve it later in chapter 11? I contend that Paul does not move in a new explanatory direction that seems to conflict with his initial reasoning. The primary issue involves misperceiving the *nature* of God's promise of salvation for Israel and not merely a misunderstanding of God's *timeframe and instrumental means* for saving Israel. In other words, my critique of their position is not merely that it views Paul as giving a two-part answer, but that the parts of the answer (as explained by Zaspel and Hamilton) seem to contradict each other. Zaspel and Hamilton claim that if Paul is merely affirming the salvation of the remnant, such a statement would not answer his dilemma (p. 124). But the dilemma is not so much about Israel as how Israel's response relates to God's faithfulness. Is God unfaithful even if only a remnant believes? Paul's answer is No, because

---

2. Douglas J. Moo, *The Epistle to the Romans*, NICNT (Grand Rapids: Eerdmans, 1996), 724.

3. A. Andrew Das, *Paul and the Jews*, Library of Pauline Studies (Peabody, MA: Hendrickson, 2003), 88.

4. Ibid., 89, 96.

5. Thomas R. Schreiner, *Romans*, BECNT (Grand Rapids: Baker Academic, 1998), 474.

God never promised to save every individual Israelite, but only those elected according to his sovereign purpose. Or, in his own words, his answer is "not all are children of Abraham because they are his offspring" (9:7). Does Paul then change his position in chapter 11 by claiming that the promises that God made do apply to all of Abraham's offspring (or at least to those alive at the time of the second coming)? By implication, the view of Zaspel and Hamilton has Paul begin his argument in one direction, only later to jettison that argument in favor of a contradictory claim. Do the promises apply to all the children of Abraham, or do they *not* apply to all the children of Abraham? Romans 9:6–13 is the single greatest argument against the future mass-conversion view. Unfortunately, in an effort to quickly demonstrate a "reversal" in Israel's future, Zaspel and Hamilton do not adequately consider the implications of this passage. If Paul's point is that God is not, and has ever been, obligated to save every individual Israelite (or even the majority of Israelites), but only those he elects according to sovereign grace, how is it consistent to also maintain that God will (indeed must) also save all (or the majority) of ethnic Jews in the future?

Second, Zaspel and Hamilton seem to misunderstand how Paul's concept of the remnant relates to Israel. They claim, "throughout this passage Israel *contrasts* with the remnant" (p. 124). They add, "Identifying the remnant with the 'Israel' to whom the promise was made confuses what Paul contrasts. There is the remnant who believes, and over against this remnant is Israel itself" (p. 124). But they wrongly conceive of how Paul is relating the remnant to Israel. The remnant does not stand outside of Israel but is within Israel. In fact, Paul declares in 9:6, "For not all who are descended from Israel belong to Israel." Clearly, the second use of "Israel" refers to the remnant. Thus, Zaspel and Hamilton do not seem to rightly conceive of how Paul uses the term "Israel." Within the larger group of ethnic Israel (Israel[1]) is the subset that contains the remnant (Israel[2]). Indeed, the remnant *is* the true Israel. They are the children of the promise. The blessings of the "promises" (9:4) are limited to those who are the true Israel and not for those who are merely physical descendants of Abraham.

Furthermore, Zaspel and Hamilton argue that the presence of a remnant anticipates a fuller harvest in the future (p. 125). Indeed, the texts they cite to bolster their position that "the existence of the believing remnant is the earnest of the final salvation of 'all Israel'" (p. 125) do not support their claim (see, e.g., Isa. 11–12, 16; 37:31–32; Mic. 2:12; 4:17; 5:7–8; Zech. 8:12). These texts indicate merely that God will save a remnant but do not explicitly (or even implicitly) identify the remnant as the representative sign that God will save all of ethnic Israel in the future (especially at one point in time). Instead, the presence of a remnant in Romans 9–11 demonstrates that God has not completely forsaken or abandoned his people. To be fair, Zaspel and Hamilton acknowledge this when they state, "the remnant's continued existence demonstrates God's continued commitment to Israel as a people" (p. 125). In order to justify a future mass-conversion of Israel, however, they claim that the remnant also secures the final salvation of all Israel. But Paul appeals to the remnant in order to demonstrate that God never intended to save the entire nation and that God is faithful *even though* he does not save the entire nation.

Third, Zaspel and Hamilton misconstrue the questions in 11:1 ("has God rejected his people?") and 11:11 ("did they stumble in order that they might fall?"). They maintain that the two are "very different questions" (p. 108), suggesting that v. 1 is asking "Is God's rejection of Israel complete?" or "Is Israel's failure total?" whereas v. 11 is asking "Is Israel's rejection and present state of failure permanent or final?" They maintain that when the questions are construed this way, the second question implies reversal. That is, Israel's current situation of stumbling will someday be reversed so that they embrace the Messiah and receive salvation. But one must notice the lack of exegetical evidence. Paul asks merely if Israel's stumbling (rejection of Christ) will lead to them falling (being utterly rejected by God). In this context there is *no* indication of a future reversal.

What is more, Zaspel and Hamilton have betrayed their own exegesis in order to prove their point. That is, after first declaring that the answer to Paul's question in v. 11 is an emphatic "No!" ("[Israel] did not stumble so as to fall," NASB), they go on to declare that Israel has indeed fallen (but that their fall is not final). They state, "Israel has fallen, but not forever" (p. 108) and "Israel has fallen, but God's ultimate purpose for it is not its fall but its recovery" (p. 112). Yet, quoting Moo and Beasley-Murray, Zaspel and Hamilton admit that "fall" denotes "irretrievable spiritual ruin" or a "complete downfall, never to rise again" (p. 111). So has Israel fallen or not? And if they have fallen (which they claim more than once), by their own explanation Israel's downfall should be permanent. But Paul's point is that Israel has *not* (*mē genoito*) fallen.

Again, the question Paul is asking is *not* "Will this present status of failure continue?" (p. 111). Rather, the question asks what exactly their status is, and Paul answers that they have not fallen. They are not out of the race. There may be some who are stumbling (even a large majority), but they have not completely been removed from God's saving purpose. He will continue to save a remnant. He did it in the past. He was doing it in Paul's day. And he will continue to do it in the future until the very last elect Israelite is saved. That is how God is faithful to his promises, and that is why his word has not failed.

Fourth, Zaspel and Hamilton insist that Israel as a nation will be grafted into the Abrahamic tree of salvation. For example, they claim that God "will graft the natural branches in again" since he is both able to do so and has purposed to do so (p. 114). Surprisingly, they also assert, "the restoration of Israel to its promised blessing is more likely than the Gentile salvation already under way" (p. 114). Perhaps they mean that if God is able to graft in unnatural branches, he can certainly graft in natural branches. But as I argue in my essay and in my response to Vlach, Paul is not predicting what will happen to corporate Israel but indicating what God will do whenever individual Israelites believe. Furthermore, his main thrust is to warn his Gentile readers of pride since they are unnatural branches. God is able and willing to graft into the tree all those natural branches who believe in Jesus the Messiah.

Fifth, Zaspel and Hamilton sometimes apply inconsistent reasoning. For example, in 11:25 they argue that the term "until" (*achris hou*) indicates a reversal of Israel's destiny. That is, Israel is currently partially hardened, but that will last only *until* the full number of Gentiles is saved, at which time Israel will no longer be hardened but will embrace the Messiah. At one point they declare that "the 'until' of v. 25 signals . . . the eventual reversal of Israel's fortune" (p. 120n27). But they also claim that it is the "flow of argument" that "informs the significance of 'until' in v. 25," which is needed since they admit that *houtos* is "not explicitly temporal in meaning" (p. 119). On one hand, it is *achris hou* ("until") that suggests a reversal is in view in the context, but it is the context that determines that the phrase implies a reversal. But I demonstrate in my essay that the context does not imply a reversal of Israel's fortune. Israel has not been forsaken by God and will continue to have a remnant who believe until the end.

Sixth, Zaspel and Hamilton maintain that the phrase "all Israel" (11:26) can't refer merely to a remnant because of OT expectations (p. 128). But one of the main functions of Romans 9–11 is to correct misunderstandings regarding God's promises to the nation of Israel in the OT. Because of Israel's vast unbelief some may have wondered if God's promises had failed. Did God not make certain promises to Israel? He adopted them, gave them his covenants, law, temple service, and promises. Do these blessings guarantee that a majority of the nation will have faith in God and his Messiah? Paul's answer is no, and his reasoning is that God *never* promised to save every Israelite (or even Israel as a nation). Therefore, Paul is not merely affirming the status quo regarding OT expectations of Israel, but is correcting a particular (mis)understanding about what God *must* do in order to be faithful to his promises. Paul's answer is that God is completely faithful to *all* that he has promised since he never promised to save all.

So, to claim that God is *not* faithful unless there is a future mass-conversion of Israel is contrary to Paul's argument beginning in chapter 9 and concluding in chapter 11.

Furthermore, Zaspel and Hamilton state, "it is difficult to understand the 'Israel' of v. 25 differently from the 'Israel' of v. 26" (p. 126). That is, when Paul declares that "a partial hardening has come upon *Israel*," the referent must be the same as in the subsequent verse when he announces that "all *Israel* will be saved" (emphasis added). There are several problems with their statement.

First, it is grammatically possible for the same word to have two different referents. If the first instance of "Israel" includes the entire Jewish nation, can the second refer to the remnant within Israel, or must it be the same? I often tell my Greek students that the same word in the same context must mean the same thing—unless it doesn't (or can't). In Romans 3 Paul uses the word "law" (*nomos*) with two different referents in the same sentence: "But now the righteousness of God has been manifested apart from the *law*, although the *Law* and the Prophets bear witness to it" (v. 21, emphasis added). The first use of "law" refers to the Mosaic covenant, whereas the second use refers to the Torah.

Second, it is contextually possible (I would argue probable) that Paul uses the term "Israel" with two different referents (Israel as a nation and the remnant within Israel) in the space of two sentences. There is no reason why Paul could not shift the meaning, especially when we consider the key text of this passage—9:6. In this text Paul undoubtedly uses the term "Israel" with two different (but overlapping) referents: within the larger ethnic group called "Israel" (Israel[1]) is the smaller remnant also called "Israel" (Israel[2]).[6] I argue that this is precisely the pattern in 11:25–26. This is also the position of N. T. Wright:

---

6. Terms are frequently delimited by their relationship to other elements in the context. For example, the "fullness" of the Gentiles does not mean "all the Gentiles," but "all within the set of Gentiles who will be saved." The same is true for the "fullness" of the Jews. "All Israel," then, denotes all of Israel[1] who is *also* a part of or included in Israel[2].

It is impermissible to argue that 'Israel' cannot change its referent within the space of two verses, so that 'Israel' in v.25 must
mean the same as 'Israel' in v.26: Paul actually began the whole
section (9.6) with just such a programmatic distinction of two
'Israels', and throughout the letter (e.g. 2.25–9) as well as elsewhere (e.g. Philippians 3.2–11) he has systematically transferred the privileges and attributes of 'Israel' to the Messiah
and his people.[7]

In addition, a similar pattern occurs in 11:7, where Paul
describes two groups: "the elect" and "the rest."

Third, in their view, "Israel" has two different referents
even if they do not explicitly acknowledge it. Those who
hold to a future-mass-conversion view are not as consistent as
they claim since the first mention of "Israel" refers to all Jews
between the first and second comings of Christ, whereas the
second "Israel" is limited to a single generation living at the
time of Jesus's return! Thus, they do not actually believe that
the Israel of v. 25 and the Israel of v. 26 are the same because in
their view the first concerns corporate Israel *through time* (i.e.,
many generations), and the other concerns corporate Israel *at
one point in time* (i.e., one generation).

Finally, like Vlach, Zaspel and Hamilton incorrectly interpret the meaning of the Isaiah 59:20–21 citation in 11:26 ("The
Deliverer will come from Zion") to refer to Jesus's second
coming (p. 120). Unlike Vlach, however, they claim that
"Zion" refers to the "heavenly" Zion (cf. Heb. 12:22) and not
the earthly Zion (or Jerusalem). But if Isaiah's citation refers to
the second coming, it is unclear how Jesus's return relates to
the "mystery" and the modal sense of *houtos* in the immediate
context. The mystery is the provoking-to-jealousy-through-
Gentile-blessings method by which God plans to save Jews, not
a *parousia* salvation of Jews. Furthermore, banishing ungodli-

---

7. N. T. Wright, *The Climax of the Covenant* (Minneapolis: Augsburg Fortress,
    1991), 250.

ness from "Jacob" fits better with the ideas of "covenant" and "taking away sins" (v. 27) that happened at Christ's first coming. As Das explains,

> Nowhere in Romans 11 does Paul connect the salvation of all Israel to Christ's Parousia or second coming. Paul does not even refer to the Parousia of Christ in Romans 9–11. In 11:26–27 he certainly speaks of a Deliverer who "will come" out of Zion . . . but for Paul those prophecies have already been fulfilled. Christ came from Zion as the Jewish Messiah (9:5). God has already placed in Zion the stumbling stone (9:33). . . . The prophecies Paul cites in 11:26–27 were therefore fulfilled in Christ's *first* coming.[8]

In conclusion, Zaspel and Hamilton present a respectable case for their position. Although they differ from Vlach's view in regard to the typological function of Israel in relation to the church, their exegesis of Romans 9–11 is substantially the same. In the end, their exegesis is not persuasive because it finds a future mass-conversion of the Jewish nation in texts that do not support such a reading. Specifically, (1) Romans 9:6 is not given its full weight as a programmatic statement for chapters 9–11 and instead is viewed as the first stage in Paul's argument. The problem with such a view is that the supposed second stage of Paul's argument (future mass-conversion of Abraham's physical seed) runs contrary to his initial response about why God's word has not failed (God never promised to save all of Abraham's physical seed). In addition, Zaspel and Hamilton (2) misunderstand how Paul's concept of the remnant relates to Israel, (3) misconstrue the questions in 11:1 and 11:11, wrongly claiming that Israel had fallen, (4) insist that Israel as a nation will be grafted in to the tree of salvation, (5) apply inconsistent reasoning, (6) assume OT expectations demand a future mass-conversion of Israel, and (7) incorrectly

---

8. Das, *Paul and the Jews*, 110.

interpret the citation of Isaiah 59:20–21 in Romans 11:26 to refer to the second coming. Instead, Paul carefully and consistently demonstrates that God is faithful and that his word has not failed because Israel has not been cut off from God's promises since he will continue to save a remnant of Israel until the fullness of the Gentiles has come in.

A TYPOLOGICAL NON-FUTURE-MASS-CONVERSION VIEW

Benjamin L. Merkle

Although Romans 9–11 is a well-known passage and the center of discussion for many important doctrines, it is not an easy passage. In fact, N. T. Wright claims, "Everything about Romans 9–11 is controversial."[1] But its controversial status signifies that this passage lies at the heart of many key doctrines as various schools of thought seek to interpret the passage consistently within the larger framework of their beliefs. There are at least three main doctrines that Romans 9–11 illuminates perhaps better than any other passage in the Bible:

(1) *Predestination.* Romans 9 (and some of Rom. 11) presents a sustained treatment of God's sovereignty in salvation that is difficult to overlook or deny. Theologians such as Augustine and Calvin have emphasized God's sovereign grace that this passage highlights.

---

1. N. T. Wright, "The Letter to the Romans: Introduction, Commentary, and Reflections," in *The New Interpreter's Bible*, 12 vols. (Nashville: Abingdon, 2002), 10:620.

(2) *The New Testament Use of the Old Testament*. Longenecker notes, "Out of the 45 explicit biblical quotations in Romans, with 55 to 60 OT passages being quoted, . . . about 30 of these biblical quotations appear in twenty-five or so places in 9:1–11:36."[2] That is, about two thirds of the OT quotations in Romans occur in chapters 9–11.

(3) *The Place of Israel in God's Plan*. Paul's explication of God's sovereignty and his citation of OT passages both serve to illustrate his main point: God's faithfulness in relation to the nation of Israel. Indeed, "The themes relating to 'Israel' . . . take us to the heart of biblical theology."[3] This statement rings true because God's purpose of redemption as recorded in the Bible is about primarily the story of Israel. In the OT God chose Abraham and made a covenant with him, which included making him a great nation, granting him the land of Canaan, and blessing the nations through him. Subsequently, God formed the nation of Israel and made a covenant with it through his servant Moses. He later anointed David as king and made a covenant with him that established an everlasting kingdom. Along the way, God made certain promises to Israel, with some of these promises considered *irrevocable* (unconditional) in the sense that God would ensure that the promises would come to fruition (especially those related to the Abrahamic, Davidic, and new covenants).[4] With the coming of the long-awaited Messiah, many of these promises have been fulfilled. But questions remain as to the status of the nation of

---

2. Richard N. Longenecker, *The Epistle to the Romans*, NIGTC (Grand Rapids: Eerdmans, 2016), 775.

3. Stephen Motyer, "Israel (Nation)," in *New Dictionary of Biblical Theology*, eds. T. Desmond Alexander and Brian S. Rosner (Downers Grove, IL: InterVarsity Press, 2000), 581.

4. I understand Gentry and Wellum's concern for refraining from labeling certain covenants as unconditional or conditional (Peter J. Gentry and Stephen J. Wellum, *Kingdom through Covenant: A Biblical Theological Understanding of the Covenants* [Wheaton, IL: Crossway, 2012], 120, 608–11). In using the label "unconditional," I am not denying the need for conditions to be met (either by Christ or the believer), but because God has promised something, it is certain to happen because God will ensure that the conditions will be met.

Israel in redemptive history. Is the nation of Israel still the chosen (favored) people of God? Are there prophecies that are yet to be fulfilled regarding Israel? How does the church relate to Israel? Will there be a mass-conversion of Jewish people near or at the second coming? Romans 9–11 certainly does not answer all these questions with the same degree of clarity, but there is no other passage of Scripture that treats all these issues with as much detail.

Before I get into the heart of this essay, let me say a few things about the title of the position that I am defending. First, by "typological" I mean that the nation of Israel is a "type" that points to a greater reality. A *type* can be defined as "a biblical event, person or institution which serves as an example or pattern for other events, persons or institutions,"[5] and *typology* is "the study of analogical correspondences among revealed truths about persons, events, institutions, and other things within the historical framework of God's special revelation, which, from a retrospective view, are of a prophetic nature and are escalated in their meaning."[6] In other words, an initial event (or person or institution) foreshadows a corresponding event (or person or institution) that occurs at a later time in salvation history. The earlier divine intervention is called the "type," and the corresponding figure is called the "antitype." Typology is often viewed as a type of prophecy that lacks an overt verbal prediction. John Currid lists four characteristics found in typology:

- It must be grounded in history; both type and antitype must be actual historical events, persons, or institutions.

---

5. David L. Baker, *Two Testaments, One Bible: The Theological Relationship between the Old and New Testaments,* 3rd ed. (Downers Grove, IL: InterVarsity Press, 2010), 180. See also A. Berkeley Mickelsen, *Interpreting the Bible* (Grand Rapids: Eerdmans, 1963), 336–64; Richard M. Davidson, *Typology in Scripture: A Study of Hermeneutical τύπος Structures* (Berrien Springs, MI: Andrews University Press, 1981); Leonhard Goppelt, *Typos: The Typological Interpretation of the Old Testament in the New,* trans. Donald H. Madvig (Grand Rapids: Eerdmans, 1982).

6. G. K. Beale, *Handbook on the New Testament Use of the Old Testament: Exegesis and Interpretation* (Grand Rapids: Baker Academic, 2012), 14. Based on this definition, Beale lists five essential characteristics of a type: (1) analogical correspondence, (2) historicity, (3) a pointing-forwardness, (4) escalation, and (5) retrospection.

- There must be a historical and theological correspondence between type and antitype.
- There must be an intensification of the antitype from the type.[7]
- Some evidence that the type is ordained by God to foreshadow the antitype must be present.[8]

Because one of the key features of typology is *intensification* or *escalation*, this signifies that the antitype is greater than the type that preceded it. Furthermore, when the antitype arrives, the divine purpose of the type is completed.

If Israel is the *type*, then what is the *antitype*? *Jesus* is the antitype since he is the fulfillment of Israel. That is, Jesus is the "true Israel" because he fulfills (typologically) all that the nation of Israel was to accomplish as well as all that they hoped for and anticipated. Parker summarizes,

> The NT presents Jesus as the fulfillment of Israel and all the OT covenant mediators, for he ushers in the promises to Israel (restoration and return from exile, the land, etc.), embodies their identity, and completes Israel's role, calling and vocation. All the institutions (the sacrificial system, tabernacle, temple, Sabbath, feasts, the law), identity markers (e.g., circumcision), offices (prophet, priest, king), and key events (e.g., the exodus) of Israel find their culmination in the life, death, resurrection, and ascension of Christ.[9]

---

7. Hebrews 8:5 seems to reverse the order so that Moses patterns the earthly things (such as the tabernacle), which are merely a "copy and shadow of the heavenly things" (= antitype), after the heavenly things, which are the type (τύπος). Lane rightly adds, "The fact that it was only a copy of the heavenly reality consigns the earthly sanctuary to the realm of the changing and transitory, which has only limited validity because it must ultimately pass away" (William L. Lane, *Hebrews 1–8*, WBC 47A [Dallas: Word, 1991], 206).

8. John Currid, "Recognition and Use of Typology in Preaching," *RTR* 53 (1994): 121.

9. Brent E. Parker, "The Israel-Christ-Church Relationship," in *Progressive Covenantalism: Charting a Course between Dispensational and Covenant Theologies*, eds.

This means, however, that the church is only *indirectly* related to Israel. Jesus is the *direct* fulfillment, and the church is related to Israel only through the mediatorial work of Jesus. Therefore, the church is not the replacement of Israel but is a new redemptive-historical reality based on the completed work of the Messiah. The church is "the heavenly, eschatological, Spirit-empowered, new covenant community, which is the new creation (2 Cor 5:17; Gal 6:15) and new humanity in Christ (Eph 2:15)."[10] Thus, the church, based on its relationship with Christ, has continuity with OT Israel since both are the people of God. And yet, there is also some discontinuity since the church is a new, eschatological people of God. Consequently, the church is connected to Israel through its union with Christ. The church does not *replace* Israel, but it does *fulfill* certain promises made to Israel.

This reality is affirmed throughout the NT and especially in Paul's writings. He states that "God shows no partiality" (Rom. 2:11) and that "no one is a Jew who is merely one outwardly, nor is circumcision outward and physical. But a Jew is one inwardly, and circumcision is a matter of the heart" (Rom. 2:28–29). He affirms that Abraham is "the father of all who believe without being circumcised" (Rom. 4:11) and that "if you are Christ's, then you are Abraham's offspring, heirs according to promise" (Gal. 3:29). He calls the church at Galatia, consisting of primarily Gentiles, "the Israel of God" (Gal. 6:16).[11] In Ephesians he explains how Christ

---

Stephen J. Wellum and Brent E. Parker (Nashville: Broadman & Holman, 2016), 44–45.

10. Ibid., 45.

11. Moo calls this interpretation "the most common interpretation of the verse" (Douglas J. Moo, *Galatians*, BECNT [Grand Rapids: Baker Academic, 2013], 401). See, e.g., Ronald Y. K. Fung, *The Epistle to the Galatians*, NICNT (Grand Rapids: Eerdmans, 1988), 311; Andreas J. Köstenberger, "The Identity of the ΊΣΡΑΗΛ ΤΟΥ ΘΕΟΥ (Israel of God) in Galatians 6:16," *Faith and Mission* 19, no. 1 (2001): 12–18, 586; Richard N. Longenecker, *Galatians*, WBC 41 (Dallas: Word, 1990), 298–99; Moo, *Galatians*, 403; Motyer, "Israel (Nation)," 586; Thomas R. Schreiner, *Galatians*, Zondervan Exegetical Commentary on the New Testament (Grand Rapids: Zondervan, 2010), 381–83.

has broken down the dividing wall so that Jew and Gentile have become "one new man" (Eph. 2:15). In his first epistle, Peter unashamedly applies the terminology typically used to describe Israel in the OT to the church, which now is called God's "temple" (1 Peter 2:5, NLT), "holy/royal priesthood" (2:5, 9), "chosen race" (2:9), "holy nation" (2:9), and "God's people" who have "received mercy" (2:10).

Even in Romans 9–11, which focuses on the destiny of Israel, Paul affirms the Gentiles as part of God's purpose and plan of redemption. In chapter 9 Paul claims that those whom God has called to experience the riches of his glory are "not from the Jews only but also from the Gentiles" (v. 24). In support of this claim Paul cites Hosea 2:23 and 1:10: "Those who were not my people I will call 'my people,' and her who was not beloved I will call 'beloved'" (Rom. 9:25); "And in the very place where it was said to them, 'You are not my people,' there they will be called 'sons of the living God'" (Rom. 9:26). Regarding this passage Moo rightly states, "OT predictions of a renewed Israel find their fulfillment in the church."[12] In chapter 10 Paul adds, "For there is no distinction between Jew and Greek" (v. 12). He also quotes Isaiah 65:1 in reference to the Gentiles: "I have been found by those who did not seek me; I have shown myself to those who did not ask for me" (Rom. 10:20). This citation demonstrates that it was God's desire all along to include the Gentiles into his plan of redemption.[13]

But many wrongly understand this to mean that Israel is now "out" and that the church (consisting of mostly Gentiles) is

---

12. Moo, *Romans*, 613. In a footnote he adds, "It is not that Paul's convictions about Christ have blinded him to the meaning of the OT text . . . , but that God's final revelation in Christ gives to him a new hermeneutical key by which to interpret and apply the OT" (ibid., 613n13).

13. Many commentators insist that the original citation in Isaiah refers to Israel. For example, Moo claims that in the original context this passage "refers to God's making himself known to the people of Israel" but that Paul takes the Old Testament that speaks "of Israel" and applies it "on the principle of analogy, to the Gentiles" (ibid., 669).

now "in." I believe this understanding is altogether wrong. The privileged status of Israel is not now transferred to the church. Instead, we must approach this issue with a Christ-centered (or gospel-centered) hermeneutic that insists that the promises to Israel are fulfilled *first* in Christ and not the church. Christ is the blameless Israelite who perfectly kept God's laws. He is the one who provided the perfect atoning sacrifice to purify a people for his own possession. He is the one who secures the new covenant benefits for his people. Therefore, I do not affirm replacement theology because the church does not replace Israel but continues and fulfills the promises God made to Israel—and all these promises are fulfilled in Jesus the Messiah, the perfect Israelite. In Romans 11:16–24, Paul describes some natural branches (Jews) who are broken off so that some wild branches (Gentiles) could be grafted in. And yet, if the natural branches believe in Christ, they will be grafted back in. Both branches are grafted into the same tree. There is only one people of God—those who trust in Jesus Christ.[14]

But just because Paul *can* use the term "Israel" (or terms associated with Israel) as a designation for the church, this does not mean he *always* uses the term in this way. In fact, in this essay I propose that when Paul speaks of "Israel" in Romans 9–11, he is referring to ethnic Jews. This includes Romans 11:26: "all Israel will be saved."

Second, my view represents a non-future-mass-conversion view of ethnic Israel.[15] That is, when Paul writes that "all Israel will be saved" (Rom. 11:26), he is not predicting a future time

---

14. Based on the illustration of the olive tree, Hoekema notes, "Every thought of a separate future, a separate kind of salvation, or a separate spiritual organism for saved Jews is here excluded. Their salvation is here pictured in terms of becoming one with the saved totality of God's people, not in terms of a separate program for Jews!" (Anthony A. Hoekema, *The Bible and the Future* [Grand Rapids: Eerdmans, 1979], 143).

15. Although I disagree with those who affirm that "Israel" in Romans 11:26 represents the church (e.g., Calvin, Wright, Irons), we do agree that there is no future-mass-conversion. Furthermore, we agree that elsewhere in the New Testament "Israel" (Gal. 6:16) is a reference to the church and is thus used typologically.

when the majority of ethnic Jews will embrace Jesus as the Messiah and be saved. Instead, Paul's point is that God will never completely forsake the nation of Israel, but there will always be a remnant of believing Jews throughout history until Christ returns. Israel will experience only a *partial* hardening until the end of time (i.e., until the fullness of the Gentiles comes in). They will never be *fully* hardened and rejected from the salvation offered in the Messiah. Thus, the sum-total of all the elect remnant throughout history represents the salvation of "all Israel." Although not a majority view, there continues to be a (growing) remnant who embraces it.[16]

---

16. Those who hold this view include Herman Bavinck, *The Last Things*, trans. John Vriend (Grand Rapids: Baker Books, 1996), 104–7; G. K. Beale, *A New Testament Biblical Theology: The Unfolding of the Old Testament in the New* (Grand Rapids: Baker Academic, 2011), 710; Louis Berkhof, *Systematic Theology* (Grand Rapids: Eerdmans, 1994), 699–700; G. C. Berkouwer, *The Return of Christ*, trans. James Van Oosterom (Grand Rapids: Eerdmans, 1972), 323–58; Christopher R. Bruno, "The Deliverer from Zion: The Source(s) and Function of Paul's Citation in Romans 11:26–27," *TynBul* 59 (2008): 119–34; William Hendriksen, *Israel in Prophecy* (Grand Rapids: Baker Books, 1974), 39–52; Hendriksen, *Exposition of Paul's Letter to the Romans* (Grand Rapids: Baker Academic, 1981), 359–85; Hoekema, *Bible and the Future*, 139–47; Herman Hoeksema, *God's Eternal Good Pleasure* (Grand Rapids: Reformed Free Publishing Association, 1979), 327–41; Charles Horne, "The Meaning of the Phrase 'And Thus All Israel Will Be Saved' (Romans 11:26)," *JETS* 21 (1978): 329–34; Colin G. Kruse, *Paul's Letter to the Romans*, Pillar New Testament Commentary (Grand Rapids: Eerdmans, 2012), 441–44, 448–51; Robert L. Reymond, *Paul: Missionary Theologian* (Fearn, Scotland: Mentor, 2000), 539–48; Herman Ridderbos, *Paul: An Outline of His Theology*, trans. John R. De Witt (Grand Rapids: Eerdmans, 1975), 354–61; O. Palmer Robertson, "Is There a Distinctive Future for Ethnic Israel in Romans 11?" in *Perspectives on Evangelical Theology: Papers from the Thirtieth Annual Meeting of the Evangelical Theological Society*, ed. Kenneth Kantzer and Stanley Gundry (Grand Rapids: Baker Academic, 1979), 209–27 (a revised version of this article can now be found in Robertson's *The Israel of God: Yesterday, Today, and Tomorrow* [Phillipsburg, NJ: Presbyterian & Reformed, 2000], 167–92); Sam Storms, *Kingdom Come: An Amillennial Alternative* (Fearn, Scotland: Mentor, 2013), 303–34. For example, Bavinck states, "All Israel (*pas Israël*) in 11:26 is not, therefore, the people of Israel that at the end of time will be converted in mass. Nor is it the church of the Jews and the Gentiles together. But it is the *plērōma* that in the course of centuries will be brought in from Israel" (*The Last Things*, 106). Berkhof writes, "'All Israel' is to be understood as a designation not of the whole nation but of the whole number of the elect out of the ancient covenant people" (*Systematic Theology*, 699).

Although the focus of this book is Romans 9–11, there is little doubt that 11:26 is the key verse.[17] More specifically, how one understands the phrase "And in this way all Israel will be saved" is central to how one interprets the rest of the passage, and vice-versa, one's understanding of the rest of the passage will influence how one interprets 11:26. Instead of providing a sustained interpretation of every verse of Romans 9–11, I highlight particular portions that are central to understanding Paul's meaning in 11:26. Thus, in the following section, I offer five reasons why the salvation of "all Israel" refers to the elect Jews throughout history: (1) the context of Romans 9–11; (2) the meaning(s) of "Israel" in 9:6; (3) the nature of the questions in 11:1 and 11:11; (4) the emphasis on the present situation in chapter 11; and (5) the nature of the "mystery" in 11:25. Then I respond to five common objections. Finally, I offer several implications of this view in relation to biblical theology.

Support for a Typological Non-Future-Mass-Conversion View of Israel[18]
The Context of Romans 9–11

All acknowledge that Romans 9–11 forms a unit in Paul's thought. Therefore, any interpretation of Romans 11 must also be consistent with Romans 9 and 10. There is some debate over the function of these three chapters, which have been interpreted as (1) an excursus[19] or (2) the climax of the book of Romans.[20] It is best, however, to view Romans 9–11 as neither a tangent (excursus) to Paul's main argument nor the heart

---

17. Moo comments, "The first clause of v. 26 is the storm center in the interpretation of Romans 9–11 and of NT teaching about the Jews and their future" (Moo, *Romans*, 719).

18. This section is a revision and expansion of my earlier work, "Romans 11 and the Future of Ethnic Israel," *JETS* 43 (2000): 709–21.

19. E.g., C. H. Dodd, *The Epistle of Paul to the Romans* (London: Hodder & Stoughton, 1949), 148–50.

20. E.g., James D. G. Dunn, *Romans 1–8*, WBC 38A (Dallas: Word, 1988), lxii; N. T. Wright, *The Climax of the Covenant* (Minneapolis: Augsburg Fortress, 1991), 246; A. Andrew Das, *Paul and the Jews*, Library of Pauline Studies (Peabody, MA: Hendrickson, 2003), 86.

(climax) of his argument but as an integral step that continues his argument. At the end of Romans 8, Paul unequivocally
affirms God's sovereignty and benevolence as he proclaims that
God will work all things for the good of those who love him
and are called by him (v. 28). Those whom God predestined
he will also call, justify, and glorify (v. 30). He encourages his
readers by telling them that if God is for them, there is nothing
that can stand against them (v. 31) and that God will graciously
give them all things (v. 32). He then ends with the promise
that nothing in all creation is able to separate them from God's
love for them (vv. 35–39). But all these grandiose promises are
called into question if God is not able or willing to deliver on
them. In addition, many of the appellations that were showered
upon Christians were previously applied to the chosen people
of Israel. Das rightly identifies the problem: "If God is so faithful to the elect in Christ, of what value is God's prior election to
ethnic Israel? Were not all these blessings originally Israel's? . . .
How can Christians find solace in their special place of election
by God when God's historic, elect people are not benefiting
from their blessings?"[21]

Thus, beginning in chapter 9 Paul addresses the question
of God's faithfulness to his promises. If God made promises
to the people of Israel but did not deliver on those promises,
what kind of assurance do believers have regarding his promises
to them? Romans 9–11, then, vindicates God's righteousness

---

21. Das, *Paul and the Jews*, 82. See also Paul J. Achtemeier, *Romans*, IBC (Louisville:
Westminster John Knox, 1985), 153–54; James D. G. Dunn, *Romans 9–16*, WBC
38B (Dallas: Word, 1988), 530. But, as N. T. Wright has persuasively argued,
the relation of chapter 9 to chapter 8 is more than simply answering a possible
objection to God's faithfulness. Indeed, it was always God's plan to bless the
world through Israel: "Israel was and is . . . the people through whom God would
bless the world. This section is where Paul shows how, in the Messiah, God *has*
done that, and *will* do it, and what that strange new fulfillment means for Israel
itself" (*Paul and the Faithfulness of God*, Christian Origins and the Question of God
[Minneapolis: Augsburg Fortress, 2013], 4:1186). See also Barclay, who notes,
"God's faithfulness to Israel does not just *support* Paul's independent assurance
that 'nothing can separate us from the love of God in Christ' (Rom. 8:31–39)
but *grounds* that assurance" (John M. G. Barclay, *Paul and the Gift* [Grand Rapids:
Eerdmans, 2015], 522).

and faithfulness regarding his covenantal promises to Israel.[22]
I agree with Hafemann that God's faithfulness is the central
theme of Romans 9–11:

> The main theme of Romans 9–11 . . . is not the relationship
> between Jews and Gentiles, the nature of Paul's mission in the
> plan of God, the future of Israel, the scheme of salvation history,
> the identity of true Israel, nor even the nature of God's election
> or predestination, *per se*. These are all penultimate concerns.
> The central issue in Romans 9–11 is whether God's faithfulness
> to himself and to his promised redemptive, saving activity can
> be maintained in spite of Israel's rejection of Jesus.[23]

In Romans 9:1–5, Paul declares his personal anguish and
sorrow regarding his fellow Israelites because of their rejection of the Messiah. Their rejection is all the more difficult to
accept since they are the beneficiaries of God's special blessings
(the adoption, the glory, the covenants, the law, the worship,
the promises, the patriarchs, and the Messiah). With all these
unique privileges, as a whole Israel was still under God's judgment. Consequently, Paul's readers might wonder if God has
reneged on his promises to Israel, and if so, if he might also do
the same with his promises to them.[24]

In 9:6–29, Paul explains that although Israel has rejected the
Messiah despite their covenantal privileges, God is not unfaithful

---

22. So Wright, *Climax of the Covenant*, 234, 236; Joseph A. Fitzmyer, *Romans*,
    AB 33 (New York: Doubleday, 1993), 559. Holwerda comments, "Without
    a satisfactory answer to the unbelief of Jewish Israel, the certainty expressed in
    Romans 8 stands in jeopardy. Consequently, Paul necessarily raises the question
    of the status and destiny of Jewish Israel in the light of its prior election. The
    validity of his gospel depends on the answer" (David E. Holwerda, *Jesus and Israel:
    One Covenant or Two?* [Grand Rapids: Eerdmans, 1995], 153).
23. Scott Hafemann, "The Salvation of Israel in Romans 11:25–32: A Response to
    Krister Stendahl," *ExAud* 4 (1988): 43. See also Thomas R. Schreiner, *Romans*,
    BECNT (Grand Rapids: Baker Academic, 1998), 471.
24. It is important to note here that Paul's anguish over most of Israel's rejection of
    the Messiah is not the main point of Romans 9–11 (contra Das, *Paul and the Jews*,
    108). Paul is concerned primarily with defending God's faithfulness.

or unrighteous because his promises to Israel never included the salvation of every ethnic Israelite. That is, Paul demonstrates how God is indeed faithful to his promises ("But it is not as though the word of God has failed," v. 6a) although most of Israel has rejected the Messiah. Paul then gives the reason why God's word has not failed: "For not all who are descended from Israel belong to Israel" (v. 6b). God never promised Abraham that all his descendants would be saved based on their ethnic identity. True Israel consists of those who are the children of promise, not the children of the flesh. God never promised that every individual Jew would be saved but only those he unconditionally elected within Israel. Paul then presents two examples of God's sovereign discrimination between Abraham's descendants. In Isaac, not in Ishmael, Abraham's descendants were named (v. 7); and it was Jacob, not Esau, who was chosen to perpetuate the covenant lineage, and in whom the covenant promises were to be fulfilled (vv. 10–13). Therefore, Paul refutes the notion that God's word has failed by pointing out that God's promises apply to only the spiritual offspring within ethnic Israel.

Furthermore, the particular Israelites whom God has elected are chosen not because of anything in them but "in order that God's purpose of election might continue" (v. 11). As the sovereign Lord, God has the right to do what he wants with his creation, including electing some and hardening others (vv. 14–23). This selective election of God is true not only of Israel, but also of Gentiles (vv. 24–26). Paul also quotes from Isaiah 10:22–23: "Though the number of the sons of Israel be as the sand of the sea, only a remnant of them will be saved" (v. 27). In the OT it is clear that God never promises to save the majority of Israel, but he does promise to save a remnant. God chooses to save some from among ethnic Israel to be the true, spiritual Israel.[25] It is important to note the terms Paul uses: God chooses some according to the purpose of his "election" (ἐκλογήν, *eklogēn*; v. 11), that is, those whom he "has called"

---

25. See Dunn, *Romans 9–16*, 575; Moo, *Romans*, 615.

(ἐκάλεσεν, *ekalesen*; v. 24), so that as a result only a "remnant" (ὑπόλειμμα, *hypoleimma*) will be saved (v. 27, quoting Isa. 10:22–23). The theme of remnant continues throughout this section, especially in chapter 11.[26]

In 9:30–10:21, Paul addresses the question of Israel's current rejection of the Messiah. The answer he provides is not that God failed to elect them but that they failed to pursue God's righteousness by faith. They "stumbled over the stumbling stone" (9:32) and tried to establish a righteousness according to the law. Consequently, they are accountable for their own unbelief. Paul reiterates his desire for his fellow Israelites to be saved (10:1) and acknowledges that they have a zeal for God (v. 2) but sought to establish their own righteousness. Israel's unbelief in the Messiah was not due to lack of opportunity. They heard the message (v. 18), and their rebellion against God is therefore inexcusable. Because of their obstinacy, God is taking the good news to the Gentiles. Furthermore, "There is no distinction between Jew and Greek; for the same Lord is Lord of all, bestowing his riches on all who call on him" (v. 12). As for obtaining salvation, there is no distinction between Jew and Gentile. If God has a special dispensation for saving Israel in the future, that would seem to contradict v. 12.

In chapter 11, Paul opens with a question: "Has God rejected his people?" (v. 1). This question *in no way* anticipates a future restoration of Israel. Rather, Paul is asking whether God has *completely* rejected his covenant people. His answer, of course, is "By no means!" (μὴ γένοιτο, *mē genoito*; v. 1). God has not totally rejected his people because God always has an elect remnant, even when it appears that all have forsaken him. Thus, Paul uses himself (v. 1b) and Elijah (vv. 2–4) as exam-

---

26. Longenecker maintains that 9:6–11:32 "is best understood when seen in terms of a Jewish and/or Jewish Christian remnant theology" (*Romans*, 767). See also his excursus "On the Terms for 'Remnant' in the OT Scriptures (MT and LXX), as Well as the Use of 'Remnant' in the Rabbinic Tractates of Formative Judaism and the Jewish Nonconformist Writings of the First Two Centuries B.C." (ibid., 803–10).

ples to explain to his readers that "at the present time there
is a remnant [λεῖμμα, *leimma*], chosen by grace" (v. 5). Once
again Paul divides "Israel" into two groups: (1) "the elect" (ἡ
ἐκλογή, *hē eklogē*), who obtain God's promises, and (2) "the
rest" (οἱ λοιποί, *hoi loipoi*), who are hardened (v. 7). *The elect*
represent the remnant, those earlier described as the children of
the promise (9:8), whereas *the rest* are the majority of Israelites,
those earlier described as the children of the flesh (9:8).

In 11:11, Paul rephrases the question in v. 1: "So I ask, did
they stumble in order that they might fall?" His answer is the
same, "By no means!" Again, this question does not presuppose the reversal of Israel's fortune in the future. Paul is merely
asking if God has *utterly* rejected his covenant people. To read
the question as if Israel is now fallen but will later be redeemed
is to misread the question. Through Israel's (partial) rejection of
the Messiah, God is bringing salvation to the Gentiles, which
will in turn make Israel jealous. God is able to graft in those
Israelites who turn to Christ since they are the natural branches
(v. 23). We must be careful not to read in the idea that God
will graft in Israel *as a nation* (see exegesis below). Paul's point
is simply that he *can* graft in those who believe the gospel. Paul
then elaborates on this mysterious interdependence between
Jews and Gentiles: God has not utterly forsaken Israel since they
will be hardened only partially, and this condition will continue
until all the Gentiles are saved—that is, until Christ returns (v.
25). And this is precisely how God will save "all Israel" (v. 26).
There will always be a remnant of elect Israelites who are saved,
until the end of time.[27] Because "the gifts and the calling of
God are irrevocable" (v. 29), he will not fail to show mercy
to those whom he has chosen and elected (vv. 30–32). At this

---

27. Arguing for a non-future-mass-conversion view, Wright correctly notes problems
with the future-mass-conversion view: "If v. 26*a* does indeed teach a special
kind of salvation for all or most Jews, with or without Christian faith, awaiting
them at the end of time, then it is exegetically out of step with the passage before
it (11:1–24) and . . . with the one that follows (11:28–34); it is theologically
incompatible with the entire argument of 9:6–10:21; and it undermines what
Paul has emphasized again and again in Romans 1–8" ("Romans," 689).

point Paul erupts with praise when he considers the unsearchable wisdom, knowledge, judgments, and ways of God (v. 33). Because all things are "from him and through him and to him," to him belongs "glory forever" (v. 36).

The Meaning(s) of "Israel" in 9:6

Correctly understanding the meaning of 9:6 is the key to correctly interpreting 11:26.[28] In this passage Paul clarifies why God is not unfaithful to his promises to Israel regarding their salvation:[29] "For not all who are descended from Israel belong to Israel" (οὐ γὰρ πάντες οἱ ἐξ Ἰσραὴλ οὗτοι Ἰσραήλ, *ou gar pantes hoi ex Israēl houtoi Israēl*; 9:6). That is, not every physical Israelite receives God's promises. It is crucial to recognize that throughout Romans 9–11, Paul uses the term "Israel" in at least two ways. For simplicity, I use *Israel*[1] to refer to all of ethnic Israel and *Israel*[2] to refer to believing ethnic Israel (the remnant) as a subset of all of ethnic Israel.

In Romans 9:6, the first use of "Israel" *must* be different than the second use. The first group refers to all physical Israelites (Israel[1]), whereas the second group denotes a smaller subgroup of Israelites who are heirs of God's promises (Israel[2]). The first group is described as "the descendants" or "seed" (σπέρμα, *sperma*) of Abraham (v. 7)[30] and "the children of the flesh" (τὰ τέκνα τῆς σαρκός, *ta tekna tēs sarkos*; v. 8). The second group is described as "the children" (τέκνα, *tekna*) of

---

28. Many correctly note that the statement that God's word has not failed (i.e., the faithfulness of God) is the thesis of chapter 9 and even chapters 9–11 (so Dunn, *Romans 9–16*, 539; Fitzmyer, *Romans*, 609; Jason C. Meyer, *The End of the Law: Mosaic Covenant in Pauline Theology*, NAC Studies in Bible and Theology [Nashville: Broadman & Holman, 2009], 204; Schreiner, *Romans*, 472; Wright, "Romans," 635). Jewett helpfully clarifies, "The focus of the denial is not on the impossibility of God's word failing but on avoiding a potential misunderstanding of Paul's grief as justifying the inference that God's word had in fact failed" (Robert Jewett, *Romans*, Hermeneia [Minneapolis: Augsburg Fortress, 2007], 573).

29. When Paul states that "the word of God" (ὁ λόγος τοῦ θεοῦ, *ho logos tou theou*) has not failed, he is referring to the blessings and advantages in 9:4–5 (cf. 3:1–2).

30. Note that the next reference ("Through Isaac shall your offspring [σπέρμα] be named") uses the term "offspring" in the more narrow sense.

Abraham (v. 7), "the children God" (τέκνα τοῦ θεοῦ, *tekna tou theou*; v. 8), and "the children of the promise" (τὰ τέκνα τῆς ἐπαγγελίας, *ta tekna tēs epangelias*; v. 8).

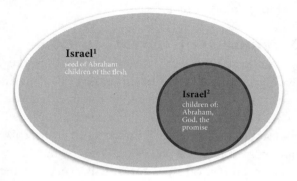

Later Paul uses different terms to make the same division. In 11:7 he declares that "Israel" as a whole "failed to obtain what it was seeking." But then he makes a division within Israel when he states, "The elect obtained it, but the rest were hardened." Those who are described as "the rest" (οἱ λοιποί, *hoi loipoi*) represent the majority of "Israel," whereas "the elect" (ἡ ἐκλογή, *hē eklogē*) represent the faithful "remnant" (λεῖμμα, *leimma*, 11:5).[31]

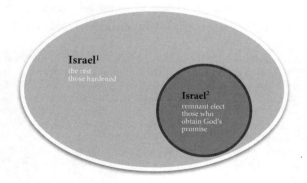

---

31. The term "remnant" (λεῖμμα, *leimma*) is a cognate of the verb "kept/left" (καταλείπω, *kataleipō*) in 11:4.

It is important to stress Paul's reasoning here. He states that God is not unfaithful to his promises. Why? God never promised to save every ethnic Jew but only an elect remnant. But if that is the answer to this apparent dilemma, then why do some feel that such an answer is insufficient?[32] If God never promised to save all ethnic Jews or at least all ethnic Jews living at one time, then why would Paul change his initial response and state that God will indeed save all ethnic Jews in the future (even though such an approach has never been God's modus operandi)? Bavinck rightly concludes,

> It is a priori very unlikely that Paul later reconsidered this reasoning, supplementing and improving it in the sense that the promises of God are not fully realized in the salvation of spiritual Israel but will be fully realized only when in the last days a national conversion of Israel takes place.[33]

Charles Horne similarly states the dilemma for those claiming a special future for Israel.

> If Paul is speaking in 11:26 of a future mass-conversion of the nation of Israel, then he is destroying the entire development of his argument in chaps. 9–11. For the one important point that he is trying to establish constantly is exactly this: that God's promises attain fulfillment not in the nation as such (that is, all of ethnic Israel) but rather in the remnant according to the election of grace.[34]

---

32. For example, Das maintains that Romans 9:6 is only Paul's "first attempt" at resolving the problem of God's elect people not benefiting from their elect status (*Paul and the Jews*, 88). He states that in Romans 11:25–32 Paul "reaches a very different conclusion" (89). He later calls Paul's conclusion a "sudden and powerful reversal of the course of [his] argument" (96). Even Schreiner maintains that "Paul was unsatisfied that the answer given thus far was a complete solution to the problem" (*Romans*, 474).

33. Bavinck, *Last Things*, 105.

34. Horne, "Meaning of the Phrase 'And Thus All Israel Will Be Saved,'" 333.

Wright addresses the same dilemma: "The problem about the content of Romans 9–11 then becomes one of *integration*. Put simply, the issue is this: if Paul rejects the possibility of a status of special privilege for Jews in chs. 9 and 10, how does he manage, apparently, to reinstate such a position in ch. 11?"[35]

This question represents a serious flaw in the future-mass-conversion view. All along Paul's main point has been that God is not, and has ever been, obligated to save every individual Israelite (Israel[1]) or even the majority of Israelites.[36] He has promised to save only those who receive his sovereign grace. To argue that God must save all (or the majority) of ethnic Jews at one period of time (because of his OT promises) is to claim something more than the apostle Paul argues.

The Nature of the Questions in 11:1 and 11:11

In 11:1 Paul asks the question, "Has God rejected his people?" This question is dealing not with the future but with the past and the present. Paul is asking whether the ethnic people of Israel, although they received special blessings (3:1–2; 9:4–5), are cut off from God's promises because they have rejected the Messiah. Thus, the question is whether God has *completely* or *utterly* rejected them because of the hardness of their hearts. Again, the question is *not,* "Has God cast off ethnic Israel with respect to his special plan for their future?" It seems, however, that people often subconsciously read the question that way, but that misses Paul's real question and prejudices one toward interpreting the rest of the chapter as advocating a special future for Israel. The nature of the question does not anticipate a future mass-conversion. The question Paul asks is, "Has God cut off ethnic Israel *altogether*?" or, "Is there any

---

35. Wright, *Climax of the Covenant*, 236.
36. Schreiner writes, "The substance of the argument is that salvation was never promised to every ethnic Israelite" (*Romans*, 472).

hope that God will continue to save Israelites?"[37] O. Palmer Robertson explains,

> Ethnic Israel had rejected their Messiah. They had crucified the Christ. Would it not therefore be quite logical to conclude that God would reject ethnic Israel? If a Gentile rejects Christ, he is lost. Israel as a nation rejected Christ; so should the nation be lost? Why should God continue to act savingly among the Jews? They received all the special favors of the Lord (Rom. 9:4–5), and yet rejected his Christ. Why should they not be cast off completely?[38]

Paul's response to the question of whether God has rejected his people is "By no means!" (v. 1).[39] He then identifies himself as proof that God still is working his sovereign plan through his people. It is instructive that Paul does not answer, "May it never be! For you know that in the Millennium God will restore Israel to its former glory."[40] Paul then directly answers the question in v. 2: "God has not rejected his people whom he foreknew."[41] God did not in the past, did not in the present (of Paul's day), and will not in the future completely reject his chosen covenant people.

The same could be said of the question in 11:11: "Have they stumbled so as to fall?" (NRSV). Again, the question Paul poses

---

37. Dunn rephrases the question: "Has God rejected his covenant people once and for all?" (*Romans 9–16*, 644). See also Robertson, *Israel of God*, 172; Storms, *Kingdom Come*, 308.

38. Robertson, *Israel of God*, 172.

39. This negative answer is also anticipated by the use of the negative particle μή (*mē*, "not").

40. Lee Irons, "Paul's Theology of Israel's Future: A Nonmillennial Interpretation of Romans 11," *Reformation and Revival* 6, no. 2 (1997): 105.

41. Holwerda seems to miss Paul's answer when he comments that "the burden of the apostle's concern throughout Romans 11" is regarding Israel who "has been hardened and cut off" (*Jesus and Israel*, 169). But the very point Paul has been making in Romans 11 is that Israel is only partially hardened and *not* cut off or rejected by God. Paul's statement ("God has not rejected his people") is identical to both 1 Samuel 12:22 and Psalm 94:14 (93:14 LXX) except that Paul changes κύριος (*kurios*, "Lord") to ὁ θεός (*ho theos*, "God").

has to do with whether Israel is totally out of the race.[42] Paul is not asking if there is going to be a future mass-conversion of Israel. Rather, he is asking if Israel has completely forfeited their past privilege and is now an utterly rejected people. Dunn uses a running metaphor to describe Israel's predicament: "their stumble is not so serious as it at first sounds. It is not a complete fall, as, for example, the sprawling on one's face which puts a runner completely out of the race."[43]

Romans 11:11 does not mean that Israel has indeed fallen, but its fall is only temporary and not permanent.[44] That is, they have fallen from God's favor now, but sometime in the future, prior to or at the return of Christ, their status will change when the vast majority of ethnic Jews embrace Christ as Savior. Although such a scenario is possible (and even hoped for), it is not what Paul is saying. Israel has *not* fallen: "they did not stumble so as to fall, did they? May it never be!" (11:11 NASB). There is still a remnant of believing Jews, and there will always be such until Christ returns.

The Emphasis on the Present Situation

Romans 9–11 (especially ch. 11) focuses on the present, not the future.[45] In answer to the question in 11:1, Paul offers himself as proof that God has not rejected his people: "For I myself am an Israelite, a descendant of Abraham, a member of the tribe of

---

42. Das wrongly suggests that Paul's argument "has finally taken a new turn" (*Paul and the Jews*, 96). Actually, Paul's question in 11:11 is essentially the same as his question in 11:1.

43. James D. G. Dunn, *The Theology of Paul the Apostle* (Grand Rapids: Eerdmans, 1998), 522–23. See also Dunn, *Romans 9–16*, 653, 666.

44. Unfortunately, some English versions read this particular interpretation into the text. For example, the NIV reads, "Did they stumble so as to fall beyond recovery?" The words "beyond recovery" are not in the Greek text but are unnecessarily added. Consequently, the reader is biased to read a future mass-conversion into the text. The same is true for Schreiner's translation: "Israel has not stumbled so as to fall permanently, has it?" (*Romans*, 593). Again, the term "permanently" has been added to the text. The fact that there is a remnant demonstrates that Israel has *not* fallen. That is, God has not completely rejected them.

45. Cf. Barclay, *Paul and the Gift*, 544; Hafemann, "Salvation of Israel in Romans 11:25–32," 49–50, 53.

Benjamin" (v. 1). Hendriksen paraphrases Paul's question and answer: "Does anyone need proof that God fulfills his promise and has not rejected Israel? Well, then look at me. God did not reject me, and I am an Israelite."[46] Paul's immediate answer to the question he raises in v. 1 involves the present, not the future.

Several authors contend that Paul's point is not simply that God is presently saving a remnant but that the small remnant is a pledge or firstfruits of a greater harvest.[47] That is, since God took Paul, a person who was hardened to God and rejecting his will, and made him an apostle to the Gentiles, he can also take Israel, who is currently rebelling against his will, and make it into an obedient people.[48] Holwerda notes, "Paul himself is the hopeful sign that God has not rejected his disobedient people because Paul also was in an active state of disobedience when God's grace was given to him."[49] But as Storms rightly points out, "The appeal to the remnant in Romans 9–11 is to demonstrate or prove that God *never* intended to save the nation as a whole."[50] The reason Paul appeals to the principle of a remnant is not to imply that God will save the entire nation of Israel, but to show that God is faithful *even though* he does not save the entire nation. Thus, "to suggest that Paul's appeal to the remnant is to prove that God saves a part as a pledge of his intention to save the whole, is . . . utterly antithetical to the purpose for which Romans 9–11 was written."[51]

Verse 5 gives further evidence that the present is at the forefront of Paul's reasoning: "So too at the present time there is

---

46. Hendriksen, *Romans*, 361. Cranfield argues that Paul's argument is more than that he, a Jew, is part of the saved remnant but that he as a Jew is God's apostle to the Gentiles: "God would hardly have chosen a Jew to be His special apostle to the Gentiles, had He cast off His people, the Jews" (C. E. B. Cranfield, *A Critical and Exegetical Commentary on the Epistle to the Romans*, 2 vols., ICC [Edinburgh: T&T Clark, 1975–1979], 2:543).

47. E.g., Das, *Paul and the Jews*, 109.

48. So Cranfield, *Romans*, 2:544; Kim Riddlebarger, *A Case for Amillennialism: Understanding the End Times*, 2nd ed. (Grand Rapids: Baker Books, 2013), 213–14.

49. Holwerda, *Jesus and Israel*, 164.

50. Storms, *Kingdom Come*, 310.

51. Ibid.

a remnant, chosen by grace." Paul specifically emphasizes the present situation of Israel by using the phrase "at the present time" (ἐν τῷ νῦν καιρῷ, *en tō nyn kairō*). In the preceding verses Paul illustrates his point with the example of Elijah. Just as in Elijah's day there was a remnant, so now there is a remnant within Israel. God did not reject his people during the days of Elijah and has not done so now.[52] Horne contends that the import of Paul's argument in using the situation in Elijah's day "is simply that the salvation of a small remnant from the total mass is ample proof that God's true people have not been, are not now, nor will be cast off."[53] Paul's point is *not* that God has rejected his people temporarily but in the future he will once again show mercy to them. Rather, his point is that just as God did not reject Israel in the past (but preserved a faithful remnant as in the days of Elijah), so too (οὕτως, *houtōs*) God has not rejected his people during Paul's day.

Furthermore, vv. 13–14 support this conclusion: "Now I am speaking to you Gentiles. Inasmuch then as I am an apostle to the Gentiles, I magnify my ministry in order somehow to make my fellow Jews jealous, and thus save some of them." Does Paul's hope of provoking the Jews to jealousy imply a future mass-conversion? The answer to this question must be "no" since Paul uses his own ministry as the means of provocation. That is, Paul's hope for the salvation of "some of them" comes through his own ministry.[54] G. C. Berkouwer notes this emphasis:

> From our perspective, centuries after Paul, there is a danger of looking at his concern for Israel as the unveiling of a chilias-tic secret, and seeing it as some kind of apocalyptic schema

---

52. Scott states, "Paul's main point in citing this text is that now as always God has preserved a remnant in Israel" (James Scott, "Restoration of Israel," *DPL* 803).

53. Horne, "Meaning of the Phrase 'And Thus All Israel Will Be Saved,'" 330.

54. Wright maintains that Paul's comment "I magnify my ministry" "need not refer only to things still unaccomplished. It refers more naturally to things he *has* already done, as in 15.15–21" (*Paul and the Faithfulness of God*, 1203 [emphasis original]).

or narrative. Such an interpretation raises a peculiar dilemma: either the "last" generation (as "all Israel") shall return, or Paul was mistaken. This position, however, ignores the extent to which Paul, convinced by the evidence of salvation among the Gentiles, concentrated his attention on the *maximum* possibilities *in his own time*. This expectation is not that of apocalyptic, but something that generates tremendous apostolic activity.[55]

The principle that a "remnant" will remain throughout every age is the basis for Paul's hope that "some" would be saved during his ministry.

Finally, vv. 30–31 support the thesis that Paul is concerned with the present more than with the future: "For just as you [Gentiles] were at one time disobedient to God but *now* have received mercy because of their [Israel[1]] disobedience, so they [Israel[1]] too have *now* been disobedient in order that by the mercy shown to you [Gentiles] they [Israel[2]] also may *now* receive mercy" (emphasis added). The threefold "now" (νῦν, *nyn*) emphasizes Israel's present situation. Although the final "now" is textually debated, most commentators favor its inclusion.[56] Wright asserts, "It seems to be the case that not all the scholars who favour the addition of the extra *nyn* appreciate the weight it gives to the reading of the whole passage in which Paul envisages the salvation of 'all Israel' as something to be achieved within the present dispensation, rather as something to be accomplished in a sudden last-minute divine action, perhaps at the *parousia*."[57] Romans 11 focuses on the present, not the future.

---

55. Berkouwer, *Return of Christ*, 349 (emphasis original).
56. Jewett comments, "The inclusion of νῦν is therefore the more difficult reading that should be accepted" (*Romans*, 694). See Richard Bell, who cites various scholars who include the third νῦν (*nyn*) as authentic (*Provoked to Jealousy: The Origin and Purpose of the Jealousy Motif in Romans 9–11* [Tübingen: Mohr Siebeck, 1994], 149n233). The inclusion of the third νῦν (*nyn*) is supported by א, B, and D*,c. For a more neutral opinion, see Bruce M. Metzger, *A Textual Commentary on the Greek New Testament*, 2nd ed. (Stuttgart: United Bible Societies, 1994), 465.
57. Wright, *Paul and the Faithfulness of God*, 1252n714.

The Nature of the "Mystery" (11:25–26a)

Paul writes in 11:25–26a, "Lest you be wise in your own sight,
I do not want you to be unaware of this mystery, brothers: a
partial hardening has come upon Israel, until the fullness of the
Gentiles has come in. And in this way all Israel will be saved."
The "mystery" includes a threefold schema: (1) the hardening
of part of Israel, (2) the coming in of the fullness of the Gentiles,
and (3) the salvation of all Israel.

What does Paul mean when he states that Israel is experiencing a "partial hardening" (πώρωσις ἀπὸ μέρους, *pōrōsis
apo merous*)? The noun "hardening" (πώρωσις, *pōrōsis*) corresponds to the verb "were hardened" (from πωρόω, *pōroō*) in
v. 7, where Paul contrasts "the elect" of Israel, who obtain
salvation, with "the rest," who were hardened (ἐπωρώθησαν,
epōrōthēsan). As in v. 7, in v. 25 Paul is speaking quantitatively
("in part") and not temporally ("for a while"). In other words,
this verse does *not* mean "for a while hardening has happened
to Israel" but "a partial hardening (or 'a hardening in part') has
happened to Israel."[58] Also, by a "partial hardening" Paul does
not mean that all of Israel is only partially hardened, but that
some are fully hardened while the elect remnant is being saved.
In no way does the phrase suggest that God intends to initiate a
special dispensation for Israel in the future.

The meaning of "until the fullness of the Gentiles has come
in" is also debated. Those who affirm a future mass-conversion of Jews naturally interpret this phrase to mean that Israel is
currently hardened, but their hardened status will change when
God turns from saving the Gentiles to saving Israel. When this
shift takes place, an unprecedented number of Jews will put
their faith in Christ. Moo paraphrases the verse, "Israel's partial
hardening will last only *until* the fullness of the Gentiles comes

---

58. Excluding this occurrence, ἀπὸ μέρους (*apo merous*, "in part") occurs three times
    in the quantitative sense (Rom. 15:15; 2 Cor. 1:14; 2:5) and once in the temporal
    sense (Rom. 15:24). Even if Paul is using the phrase in a temporal sense, such a
    view is not incompatible with my overall interpretation (so Kruse, *Romans*, 442–
    43; Wright, *Paul and the Faithfulness of God*, 1236–37).

in—and then it will be removed."[59] But is that the most natural way to read this phrase?[60]

This question can be answered only by examining "until" (ἄχρις οὖ, *achris hou*). This phrase is essentially terminative in its significance, implying the end of something. Yet only the context can determine where the emphasis lies after the termination. Often the phrase occurs in an eschatological context where the termination envisioned contains a finalization aspect that makes questions concerning the reversal of the circumstance irrelevant. In other words, what is important is not what will take place *after* the event is completed, but *that* the event is eschatologically fulfilled.[61]

For example, in 1 Corinthians 11:26 Paul states that the church is to partake of the Lord's Supper and thus proclaim the Lord's death "until" (ἄχρις οὖ, *achris hou*) he comes. Paul's purpose is not to stress that one day the church will not celebrate the Lord's Supper. Instead, his point is that this celebration will continue "until" the end of time. Also, 1 Corinthians 15:25 states that Christ must reign "until" (ἄχρις οὖ, *achris hou*) he has put all enemies under his feet. The intended stress is not that a time will come when Christ will no longer reign, but that he must continue to reign until the last enemy is conquered at the final judgment.[62] Likewise, the hardening of Israel that will occur "until" the fullness of the Gentiles comes in refers to an eschatological termination.[63] A hardening will occur through-

---

59. Moo, *Romans*, 717; see also Schreiner, *Romans*, 618.

60. Hafemann maintains that with his interpretation of 11:1–24, "the 'until' of 11:25 is itself enough to posit the future salvation of ethnic Israel!" ("Salvation of Israel in Romans 11:25–32," 53).

61. So Robertson, *Israel of God*, 178–80; Reymond, *Paul*, 546; Marten H. Woudstra, "Israel and the Church: A Case for Continuity," in *Continuity and Discontinuity: Perspectives on the Relationship between the Old and New Testaments*, ed. John S. Feinberg (Wheaton, IL: Crossway, 1988), 236.

62. See also Luke 21:4, Acts 7:18, Acts 27:33, Galatians 3:19, Hebrews 3:13, and Revelation 2:25, where ἄχρι(ς) οὖ (*achri[s] hou*) occurs, and Matthew 24:38, Acts 22:4, and Hebrews 4:12, where only ἄχρι (*achri*) occurs.

63. Joachim Jeremias states, "Actually, in the New Testament ἄχρι οὖ with the aorist subjunctive without ἄν regularly introduces a reference to reaching the

out the whole of the present age until the return of Christ. Paul is not suggesting a time when the hardening will be reversed but a time when the hardening will be eschatologically fulfilled (i.e., it will have served its full, God-ordained purpose).[64]

The climax of the mystery is v. 26a: "And in this way all Israel will be saved." The question under consideration is whether God has forsaken Israel *altogether*—not whether there is a special future for Israel. Much of the discussion surrounding the phrase "and in this way all Israel will be saved" centers on the meaning of "in this way" (οὕτως, *houtōs*). There are at least three possibilities:

(1) *Temporal:* "and *then* all Israel will be saved."[65] Hardening has happened to part of Israel "until" the fullness of the Gentiles has come in; but *then after that*, all Israel will be saved. Such a rendering naturally leads one to suppose a special time of grace for ethnic Israel. But *houtōs* rarely, if ever, has temporal significance.[66]

(2) *Logical:* "and *in consequence of this process* [v. 25b] all Israel will be saved."[67] There are a few cases in Paul where *houtōs* has a logical sense,[68] but most scholars opt for the third usage.

---

eschatological goal, Rom 11.25; 1 Cor 15.25; Luke 21.24" (*The Eucharistic Words of Jesus* [New York: Charles Scribner's Sons, 1966], 253).

64. Robertson comments, "The phrase implies not a new beginning after a termination, but the continuation of a circumstance until the end of time" (*Israel of God*, 180).

65. The NEB apparently follows this popular, but little supported, rendering by translating it, "when that has happened, all Israel will be saved."

66. BDAG does not even list a temporal use. For an attempt to justify the temporal meaning, see Pieter W. van der Horst, "'Only Then Will All Israel Be Saved': A Short Note on the Meaning of καὶ οὕτως in Romans 11:26," *JBL* 119 (2000): 521–39. He suggests that Acts 7:8, Acts 20:11, Acts 27:17, and 1 Thessalonians 4:16–17 support the temporal usage of *houtōs*. Those four examples are debated (see Wright, *Paul and the Faithfulness of God*, 1240n677). In addition, the term *houtōs* occurs 208 times in the NT, and therefore, his four debated examples are far from convincing. Thus, Das incorrectly claims that the temporal interpretation "is equally plausible" as the modal interpretation (*Paul and the Jews*, 117).

67. So Otfried Hofius, "'All Israel Will Be Saved': Divine Salvation and Israel's Deliverance in Romans 9–11," *PSB 11*, Suppl 1 (1990): 35.

68. Moo lists Romans 1:15, 6:11, 1 Corinthians 14:25, and 1 Thessalonians 4:17 (*Romans*, 720).

(3) *Modal:* "and *in this manner* all Israel will be saved." But this reading does not settle the interpretative debate. Moo (rightly) argues that the "manner" comes from vv. 11–24, which v. 25 summarizes.[69] His interpretation of these earlier verses, however, leads him to the wrong conclusion: "God imposes a hardening on most of Israel while Gentiles come into the messianic salvation, with the Gentiles' salvation leading in turn to Israel's jealousy and its own salvation. But this means that *houtōs*, while not having a temporal *meaning*, has a temporal *reference*."[70]

But in its context does *houtōs* have a (future) temporal reference? (1) Is Paul looking prospectively into the future beyond the fullness of the Gentiles, or (2) is he looking retrospectively into the past as well as considering the present?[71] The first option (i.e., the future-mass-conversion view) has at least three additional problems:

(1) If *houtōs* has a (future) temporal reference, then Paul is claiming that the salvation of "all Israel" takes place after the salvation of every elect Gentile.[72] That is, Israel's salvation takes place after the partial hardening is removed, which will only take place once "the fullness of the Gentiles has come in" (11:25). As such, this view must maintain that when the Jewish people turn to Christ in droves, *not one single Gentile will be converted.* Although such a view is possible, it is unlikely: "Is there, then, a lapse of time between the coming of the *plērōma* from the Gentile world and the end of the ages? If so, are there

---

69. Although it is possible that the manner is found in what follows (i.e., the quote from Isa. 59:20–21), this interpretation is not likely because the pairing of *houtōs* with "as it is written" (καθὼς γέγραπται, *kathōs gegraptai*) is never found in Paul (see Moo, *Romans*, 720). The position that *houtōs* refers to what follows is held by BDAG 742; Peter Stuhlmacher, *Paul's Letter to the Romans: A Commentary*, trans. Scott J. Hafemann (Louisville: Westminster John Knox, 1994), 172.

70. Moo, *Romans*, 720; see also Bell, *Provoked to Jealousy*, 136; Cranfield, *Romans*, 2:576; Schreiner, *Romans*, 621.

71. Wright (correctly) argues for the latter view: "Paul gives no indication that he is talking about a *further* event, but rather gives every indication that this process in 11.25 . . . *is the means by which* God is saving 'all Israel'" (*Paul and the Faithfulness of God*, 1241 [emphasis original]).

72. Schreiner states, "Paul argues that the salvation of Israel will *follow* the salvation of the Gentiles" (*Romans*, 599).

still Gentile nations in that period and is there not a single person from among them that turns to the Lord?"[73]

(2) If "all" means a great number of Jews at the end of time, does that interpretation do justice to the meaning of all?[74] It would in fact include only a small fraction of Jews, which is not as climactic as it might first appear.[75]

(3) A future mass-conversion of Israel is completely absent, not only in the rest of Paul's writings, but in the rest of the NT.

Robertson summarizes the meaning of the "mystery" based on the context of Romans 11.

> First the promises and the Messiah were given to Israel. Then in God's mysterious plan, Israel rejected its Messiah and was cut off from its position of distinctive privilege. As a result, the coming of the Messiah was announced to the Gentiles. The nations then obtained by faith what Israel could not find by seeking in the strength of their own flesh. Frustrated over seeing the blessings of their messianic kingdom heaped on the Gentiles, individual Jews are moved to jealousy. Consequently, they too repent, believe, and share in the promises originally made to them. "And in this manner" (*kai houtōs*), by such a fantastic process which shall continue throughout the present age "up to" (*achris*

---

73. Bavinck, *Last Things*, 107.
74. For an in-depth study of "all Israel" in the OT and Jewish literature, see James M. Scott, "'And Then All Israel Will Be Saved' (Rom 11:26)," in *Restoration: Old Testament, Jewish, and Christian Perspectives*, ed. James M. Scott (Leiden: Brill, 2001), 498–515.
75. Kruse comments, "It is unlikely that Paul means that there will be a last minute national turning to Christ on the part of the last generation, something that would have no significance for those many generations of Jews who had come and gone in the meantime" (*Romans*, 443). Robertson argues that if one takes "all Israel" to refer to the nation of Israel, it must further refer to every individual and not merely a majority of the nation: "the hardening in verse 25 refers to the historical outworking of reprobation. . . . If a day is coming when the principle of reprobation is lifted from Israel, then every single Israelite living at that time will be saved. If even one Israelite of that period is to be lost, then the principle of hardening or reprobation would still be active" (*Israel of God*, 183). See also Irons, "Paul's Theology of Israel's Future," 121; Wright, "Romans," 689.

hou) the point where the full number of the Gentiles is brought in, all Israel is saved.[76]

Thus, it is best to take "all Israel" as referring to the elect of ethnic Israel throughout history.[77]

Defense of a Typological Non-Future-Mass-Conversion View of Israel
11:12 and 11:15 Do Not *Suggest a Future Mass-Conversion of Israel*

In 11:12 Paul declares, "Now if their [Israel[1]] trespass means riches for the world, and if their [Israel[1]] failure means riches for the Gentiles, how much more will their [Israel[2]] full inclusion mean!" Verse 15 parallels v. 12: "For if their [Israel[1]] rejection means the reconciliation of the world, what will their [Israel[2]] acceptance mean but life from the dead?"

Those who interpret 11:26a as referring to a future mass-conversion of ethnic Israel state that Israel's "trespass," "failure," and "rejection" refer to the present time, whereas their "full inclusion" and "acceptance" refer to a time yet to come. Currently, Israel is rejecting Christ, but the time will come when they accept Christ and will be saved. Therefore, the "full inclusion" and "acceptance" of Israel refer to a time, after the present age of gospel proclamation, when Israel again turns to God.[78]

---

76. Robertson, *Israel of God*, 182.
77. Horne comments, "When Paul states that 'all Israel shall be saved' he means to refer to the full number of elect Jews whom it pleases God to bring into his kingdom throughout the ages until the very day when the full number of Gentiles also shall have been brought in" ("Meaning of the Phrase 'And Thus All Israel Will Be Saved,'" 334). Likewise Hendriksen writes, "It is evident . . . that the salvation of 'all Israel' was being progressively realized in Paul's own day and age, and that it will continue to be progressively realized until 'all Israel' shall have been saved. When the full number of elect Gentiles will have been gathered in, then the full number of elect Jews will also have been gathered in. . . . In Elijah's day there was a remnant. In Paul's day there was a remnant. In the years to come there would be a remnant. These remnants of all the ages taken together constitute 'all Israel'" (Hendriksen, *Israel in Prophecy*, 48–49, 50–51).
78. See Cranfield, *Romans*, 2:577; Dunn, *Romans 9–16*, 668; Schreiner, *Romans*, 597–99.

The above interpretation is not without its difficulties. First, the ESV cited above is somewhat biased. A more form-based translation of v. 12 is "how much more their fullness [πλήρωμα, plērōma]." To translate plērōma as "full inclusion" biases one to the future-mass-conversion view.[79] Second, there is no clear evidence in this passage that "fullness" refers to a future event when Israel returns to their God. One clue to the meaning of "fullness" is in v. 25 where Paul speaks of the "fullness" of the Gentiles. Since virtually every scholar interprets "the fullness of the Gentiles" as the full number of elect Gentiles throughout history,[80] is it not also likely that the "fullness" of Israel refers to the full number of elect Jews throughout history?[81]

Because of the parallel structure, the "acceptance" of v. 15 correlates to "fullness" in v. 12.[82] Paul argues from the lesser to the greater. If the failure of Jews meant gospel-blessings for the Gentiles, then their acceptance (i.e., the coming in of the full number of the elect Jews) will mean nothing less than the resurrection itself ("life from the dead").[83] Of course, their

---

79. So also NIV, RSV, NRSV. Interestingly, the ESV never translates the word πλήρωμα (plērōma) as "full inclusion" in any other verse, including Romans 11:25. Demonstrating even more bias, the NLT translates the phrase, "when they finally accept it [i.e., God's offer of salvation]."

80. For example, Cranfield comments that the phrase *fullness of the Gentiles* "is probably to be explained as the meaning of the full number of the elect from among the Gentiles" (*Romans*, 2:575). See also Moo, *Romans*, 719; Schreiner, *Romans*, 598–99; Kruse, *Romans*, 428, 443; Richard J. Lucas, "The Dispensational Appeal to Romans 11 and the Nature of Israel's Future Salvation," in *Progressive Covenantalism: Charting a Course between Dispensational and Covenant Theologies*, ed. Stephen J. Wellum and Brent E. Parker (Nashville: Broadman & Holman, 2016), 246.

81. Kruse writes, "In light of the use of 'fullness' in respect to the Gentiles in 11:25 we are justified in concluding that Israel's 'full inclusion' means the full number of believing Jews, which will be made up when those yet to believe are added to the remnant that already believe" (*Romans*, 428–29). Wright maintains, "There is no reason to suppose that 'the fullness' of Israel will mean anything more than this: the complete number of Jews, many more than at present, who likewise come to faith in the gospel" ("Romans," 681).

82. The "acceptance" here is most likely God accepting Israel as opposed to Israel accepting God, though the former implies the latter (see, e.g., Schreiner, *Romans*, 598).

83. So Schreiner, *Romans*, 599; Robert B. Strimple, "Amillennialism," in *Three Views on the Millennium and Beyond*, ed. Darrell L. Bock, Counterpoints (Grand Rapids:

"acceptance" by God based on their belief could occur at any stage in the process, at which point they are grafted back in (see vv. 13–14, 23–24). Therefore, the "fullness" refers to the full number of the elect Israelites, not just the salvation of a large number of Jews at the end of time.[84]

Again, there is a potential problem here for those who hold to a future-mass-conversion view. If the salvation of "all Israel" occurs *after* the fullness of the Gentiles is saved ("has come in," v. 25), how can there be a subsequent time of salvation for the Gentiles? Indeed, that is how some interpret Paul's statements in v. 12. For example, Murray states, "The fullness of Israel will involve for the Gentiles a much greater enjoyment of gospel blessing than that occasioned by Israel's unbelief. Thus there awaits the Gentiles . . . gospel blessings far surpassing anything experienced during the period of Israel's apostasy, and this unprecedented enrichment will be occasioned by the conversion of Israel on a scale commensurate with that of their earlier disobedience."[85] But it contradicts vv. 25–26 to interpret v. 12 to mean that now the Gentiles are blessed ("riches"), but after the majority of Jews turn to Christ, even more Gentiles will be saved. As Storms notes, "If *all* elect Gentiles are to be saved *before* Israel is restored (and according to the [future-mass-conversion] view, that is what vv. 25–26 assert), how can Israel's restoration yield *subsequent*, additional, indeed unprecedented, Gentile salvation?"[86] Instead, both the fullness of Israel (11:12) and the fullness of the Gentiles (11:25) refer to the full number of the elect throughout the ages.

Zondervan, 1999), 118; Riddlebarger, *Case for Amillennialism*, 188. For the view that "life from the dead" does not refer to the final bodily resurrection but to salvation, see Storms, *Kingdom Come*, 317–20.

84. Robertson comments, "The 'full number' in Israel will be realized by the same process in which Jews are currently being received and added to the number" (*Israel of God*, 175).

85. John Murray, *The Epistle to the Romans*, 2 vols., NICNT (Grand Rapids: Eerdmans, 1959–1965), 2:79. See also Robert L. Saucy, *The Case for Progressive Dispensationalism: The Interface between Dispensational and Non-Dispensational Theology* (Grand Rapids: Zondervan, 1993), 260–61.

86. Storms, *Kingdom Come*, 324.

Paul Does Not Imply That Israel as a Nation Will Be Grafted In (11:23–24)

Paul states in 11:23–24,

> And even they [Israel²], if they do not continue in their [Israel²] unbelief, will be grafted in, for God has the power to graft them [Israel²] in again. For if you [Gentiles] were cut from what is by nature a wild olive tree, and grafted, contrary to nature, into a cultivated olive tree, how much more will these [Israel²], the natural branches, be grafted back into their [Israel²] own olive tree.

Those who affirm a special future for Israel claim that Paul teaches that a great majority of ethnic Israelites will be grafted into the tree of salvation.[87] There are at least three difficulties with such an interpretation. First, Paul's primary purpose for using this metaphor is to warn the Gentiles of pride; they are not the natural branches. In other words, this metaphor does not demonstrate that in the future Israel will be grafted back into the olive tree; it cautions the Gentiles not to become arrogant. Second, nowhere does Paul state or imply that God is going to graft *all* unbelieving Jews back into the tree. Rather, he states that those who believe will be grafted into the olive tree. In fact, Paul prefaces his statement with a conditional clause ("if [ἐάν, *ean*] they do not continue in their unbelief, will be grafted in," 11:23). Third, the focus is not only on the future but also on the present. Robertson notes, "This participation by being 'grafted in' cannot be postponed to some future time, while Gentile believers immediately experience the blessing of the covenant. Just like every present Gentile believer, every present Jewish believer will be grafted in."[88] Paul is not predicting or

---

87. See Barclay, *Paul and the Gift*, 554; Cranfield, *Romans*, 2:577; Das, *Paul and the Jews*, 109; Meyer, *End of the Law*, 175, 179; Schreiner, *Romans*, 617.

88. Robertson, *Israel of God*, 170. Wright likewise explains that "the gentile mission itself will make Jews 'jealous' and so save some of them *in the present time*. . . . But his postponement of the 'grafting back in' to the *parousia* hardly fits with the point Paul is eager to ram home throughout the chapter. Such a postponement would

prophesying that Israel *as a nation* will be grafted back into the tree of salvation. Rather, his point is that when *individual* Jews believe in Christ, they will be grafted back in.

The "Mystery" Need Not Be Mysterious (11:25)

For Paul, "mystery" (μυστήριον, *mystērion*) is not something that remains concealed but something that was hidden and now is revealed.[89] In 16:25–26 Paul declares, "Now to him who is able to strengthen you according to my gospel and the preaching of Jesus Christ, according to the revelation of the mystery that was kept secret for long ages but has now been disclosed. . . ."[90]

Those who reject the position that "all Israel" in 11:26 refers to the elect Jews throughout history often state that the mystery Paul speaks of is no longer a mystery if Paul is only declaring that all the elect Jews will be saved.[91] But Paul is not simply asserting *that* all elect Israel will be saved; he is speaking of the *manner* ("and in this manner") in which God will save them. What then is the nature of this mystery?[92] It likely involves the

---

not relate to his specific warning to the gentile Christians in Rome" (*Paul and the Faithfulness of God*, 1221).

89. Bockmuehl argues that the term "mystery" does not necessarily indicate that Paul is basing the authority of his doctrine on a private vision but suggests that it is more likely "that we are dealing with 'revelation by exegesis': a dynamic inter-reaction of Scripture, [exegetical] tradition, and religious experience (which may or may not *include* a vision)" (Markus N. A. Bockmuehl, *Revelation and Mystery in Ancient Judaism and Pauline Christianity* [Grand Rapids: Eerdmans, 1997], 174 [emphasis original]).

90. See also Ephesians 3:4–6 and Colossians 1:26–27. Other uses of *mysterion* (μυστήριον, "mystery") are found in the NT (1 Corinthians 2:1, 7; 4:1; 13:2; 14:2; 15:51; Ephesians 1:9; 3:9; 5:32; 6:19, Colossians 2:2; 4:3; 2 Thessalonians 2:7; 1 Timothy 3:9, 16).

91. E.g., Murray argues, "That all the elect will be saved does not have the particularity that 'mystery' in this instance involves" (*Romans*, 2:97). Michael Vanlaningham argues, "If 'all Israel' is simply the elect from ethnic Israel who are saved along with the Gentiles throughout the age, special revelation to Paul in the form of a *mysterion* (v. 25) is pointless" ("Romans 11:25–27 and the Future of Israel in Paul's Thought," *MSJ* 3 [1992]: 160). See also Cranfield, *Romans*, 2:576; Schreiner, *Romans*, 617.

92. Wright claims that when Paul uses the term "mystery," it "does not of itself indicate that this is a new point introduced here for the first time, different to what has been said before. . . . Rather, referring to his summary statement here as a 'mystery' simply indicates that it is part of God's previously hidden plan that

interdependence of the salvation of the Gentiles and Israel.[93] Ridderbos explains, "The mystery (v. 25) is thus situated in the manner in which this fullness of Israel is to be saved: in the strange interdependence of the salvation of Israel and that of the gentiles. . . . God grants no mercy to Israel without the gentiles, but neither does he do so to the gentiles without Israel."[94]

"Israel" in 11:25 and 26 Can Have Different Referents

Some are convinced that it is not probable that Paul uses "Israel" with two different referents in the space of two sentences. Cranfield comments, "It is not feasible to understand [Israel] in v. 26 in a different sense from that which it has in v. 25."[95] Paul's first reference to Israel in v. 25 ("a partial hardening has

---

Paul wants his readers to understand" ("Romans," 687; see also 690). Wright argues that the "mystery" is the entire sequence of thought from 11:11 onwards (*Paul and the Faithfulness of God*, 1232–33).

93. Beale and Gladd argue that the mystery is the reversal of the order of salvation from Jew first, then Gentile to Gentile first, then Jew: "That there would be two stages of fulfillment of Jewish and Gentile redemption was not clearly foreseen by the Old Testament: (1) an initial salvation of Jews consisting of the majority of the redeemed, then Gentiles [i.e., as recorded in Acts], and then (2) a second longer stage of Gentiles composing the majority of the saved, which would spark off a remnant of Jews being saved [i.e., the present era]. This is a mystery because such an *explicit* chronological two-stage salvation cannot be found in the Old Testament" (G. K. Beale and Benjamin L. Gladd, *Hidden but Now Revealed: A Biblical Theology of Mystery* [Downers Grove, IL: InterVarsity Press, 2014], 89).

94. Ridderbos, *Paul*, 359–60; see also Hendriksen, *Romans*, 378; Robertson, *Israel of God*, 182n9. Wright states, "The 'mystery' consists of this: that, instead of immediately judging the people that rejected his Son, God has allowed a period of hardening, within which his salvation will spread to the ends of the earth, but at the end of which there will be judgment (this is always the point of 'hardening' within the apocalyptic context). During this period of time, the Gentiles are to come in to the people of God: and *that is how* God is saving 'all Israel'" (*Climax of the Covenant*, 249). Storms likewise writes, "Paul is not simply asserting *that* all elect Israel will be saved but is describing the mysterious *manner* in which it will occur. That is, *it is not so much the fact as it is the fashion in which they will be saved.* It is by means of nothing less than the incredible scenario of Jewish unbelief → Gentile salvation → Jewish jealousy and salvation → Gentile blessing" (*Kingdom Come*, 329–30, emphasis in original).

95. Cranfield, *Romans*, 2:576. Moo similarly states that a major objection to the view I am defending is "that it requires a shift in the meaning of 'Israel' from v. 25b to v. 26a" (*Romans*, 722). See also Schreiner, *Romans*, 615.

come upon Israel") refers to the entire Jewish nation (Israel[1]). By stating that only part of Israel is hardened, he is also implicitly referencing those who are not hardened (i.e., the remnant or the elect). In the next sentence Paul states that "all Israel will be saved." Is it likely that "Israel" now refers only to the elect remnant from within the nation (Israel[2])?[96]

Cranfield's objection, however, bears very little weight. There is no reason why Paul could not shift the meaning of Israel within two sentences—the first reference to the nation of Israel as a whole (Israel[1]) and the second to the elect within the nation of Israel (Israel[2]). In 9:6 Paul unambiguously uses the term "Israel" with two different (but overlapping) referents: "Not all who are descended from Israel [Israel[1]] belong to Israel [Israel[2]]." That is, not all of ethnic Israel are part of the elect remnant of ethnic Israel. In the *same sentence* Paul uses Israel to refer to both all ethnic Israelites and a subset. That is precisely the pattern in 11:25–26.[97] Furthermore, there is a similar pattern in chapter 11 itself. In v. 7 Paul declares, "What then? Israel failed to obtain what it was seeking. The elect obtained it, but the rest were hardened." Within Israel Paul describes two groups: "the elect" and "the rest." There is the Israel who is "currently missing out and the Israel which is already experiencing the eschatological grace in Christ through faith."[98]

---

96. Even though Moo affirms that both references to Israel are the same, he later qualifies, "We must note, however, that the interpretation that takes the phrase to refer to the elect among Israel throughout time deserves consideration as a serious alternative" (*Romans*, 723). Unfortunately, his commentary does not consider it.

97. Wright agrees: "It is impermissible to argue that 'Israel' cannot change its referent within the space of two verses, so that 'Israel' in v.25 must mean the same as 'Israel' in v.26: Paul actually began the whole section (9.6) with just a programmatic distinction of two 'Israels', and throughout the letter (e.g. 2.25–9) as well as elsewhere (e.g. Philippians 3.2–11) he has systematically transferred the privileges and attributes of 'Israel' to the Messiah and his people" (Wright, *Climax of the Covenant*, 250; see also Wright, "Romans," 690). Robertson likewise states, "The fact that in this view the term *Israel* is used in two different ways in consecutive verses (Rom. 11:25–26) should not be disturbing. When Paul says in Romans 9:6 that 'they are not all Israel that are Israel,' he is using the term *Israel* with two different meanings in a single verse" (*Israel of God*, 186).

98. Dunn, *Theology of Paul*, 522.

Furthermore, those who hold to a future-mass-conversion view are not as consistent as they claim since they too use "Israel" in two different ways. As Storms notes, "According to the [future-mass-conversion] view, 'Israel' in verse 25 refers to the ethnic nation as a whole during the inter-advent period, whereas 'Israel' in verse 26 is restricted to one generation of ethnic Jews living at the time of the parousia."[99]

It is also important to distinguish my view from the view of others such as Calvin, Wright, and Irons, who maintain that "all Israel" refers to all of God's people, Jews and Gentiles.[100] This view is similar to the view I am supporting in that both affirm a typological function of Israel, and both reject the view that 11:26 refers to a future mass-conversion of ethnic Jews. But I disagree with them that when Paul states, "And in this way all Israel will be saved," he is offering a "polemical redefinition" of the term so that "Israel" also includes believing Gentiles (i.e., the church).[101]

From my perspective, the reference to "Israel" in v. 26 must refer to ethnic Israel (Israel²) and not a spiritual Israel consisting of both Jews and Gentiles. The main reason for this position is that in Romans 9–11 the terms "Israel" (9:6 [2×], 27 [2×], 31; 10:19, 21; 11:2, 7, 25) and "Israelite(s)" (9:4; 11:1) consistently

---

99. Storms, *Kingdom Come*, 328.

100. See John Calvin, *Commentary on the Epistle to the Romans*, trans. John King (repr., Grand Rapids: Baker Books, 1993), 437; Wright, *Climax of the Covenant*, 249–50; Wright, "Romans," 689; Wright, *Paul and the Faithfulness of God*, 1242–43; Irons, "Paul's Theology of Israel's Future," 101–26. See also Philip E. Hughes, "The Olive Tree of Romans XI," *EvQ* 20 (1948): 44–45; Karl Barth, *The Epistle to the Romans*, trans. Edwyn C. Hoskyns (London: Oxford University Press, 1968), 415–16; Ralph P. Martin, *Reconciliation: A Study of Paul's Theology* (Atlanta: John Knox, 1981), 134; Hervé Ponsot, "Et Ainsi Tout Israel Sera Sauvé: Rom., XI, 26a," *RB* 89 (1982): 406–17. Robertson later endorsed this view in *Israel of God*, 187–92.

101. Wright calls Paul's use of "Israel" a "polemical redefinition" consistent with Paul's redefinition of "Jew" (Rom. 2:29), "circumcision" (Rom. 2:29; Phil. 3:3), and "seed of Abraham" (Rom. 4; 9:6–9; Gal. 3) ("Romans," 690; Wright, *Paul and the Faithfulness of God*, 1242–43). Irons similarly maintains that "the reference in verse 26 to 'all Israel' should be interpreted as a Pauline redefinition of the concept of 'Israel' in light of the great mystery that has been revealed in the person and work of the Lord Jesus Christ" ("Paul's Theology of Israel's Future," 102).

refer to an ethnic group. Paul wishes he could be accursed for the sake of his "brothers," his "kinsmen according to the flesh" (9:3). Israel is "beloved for the sake of their forefathers" (11:28). Thus, the entire purpose of Paul's discussion centers on the fate of his fellow Jews. It would be altogether unexpected at this point in Romans 9–11 for Paul to introduce the same term with a different referent. Furthermore, one wonders if Gentiles would misuse such a redefinition. Moo explains, "For Paul in this context to call the church 'Israel' would be to fuel the fire of the Gentiles' arrogance by giving them grounds to brag that '*we* are the true Israel.'"[102] Thus, the context of Romans 9–11 strongly argues against the view that "Israel" is a designation for the church.[103] Rather, Paul is referring to the elect throughout history of his fellow Jews.

The Deliverer Coming from Zion Does Not Refer to Christ's Second Coming (11:26–27)

After Paul states "And in this way all Israel will be saved," he quotes Isaiah 59:20–21a in vv. 26–27a and Isaiah 27:9 in v. 27b: "The Deliverer will come from Zion, he will banish ungodliness from Jacob; and this will be my covenant with them when I take away their sins."[104]

Some argue that Paul is referring to the second coming of Christ because he uses the future tense: "The Deliverer *will come* [ἥξει, *hēxei*] from Zion."[105] For example, Horner

---

102. Moo, *Romans*, 721.

103. Reidar Hvalvik notes, "As to the meaning of 'all Israel', there is today almost general agreement that 'Israel' here refers to the Jewish people" ("A 'Sonderweg' for Israel: A Critical Examination of a Current Interpretation of Romans 11.25–27," *JSNT* 38 [1990]: 100; see also Jewett, *Romans*, 701).

104. Paul's citation of Isaiah does not exactly follow the LXX. The most notable difference is that in Isaiah the Deliverer will come "for the sake of" Zion (ἕνεκεν, *heneken*; Heb. "to Zion" [לְצִיּוֹן]), but Paul writes that the Deliverer will come "out of" or "from" (ἐκ, *ek*) Zion. Bruno suggests that Paul is intentionally alluding to Isaiah 2:3 ("For out of Zion [ἐκ Σιων, LXX] shall go the law, and the word of the LORD from Jerusalem") together with Isaiah 59:20–21 and Isaiah 27:9 ("Deliverer from Zion," 119–34).

105. See Cranfield, *Romans*, 2:578; Dunn, *Romans 9–16*, 682–83, 692; Meyer, *End of the Law*, 179, 183; Moo, *Romans*, 724, 728; Schreiner, *Romans*, 619–20;

remarks, "The future tense here suggests the return of Jesus Christ, having come from the heavenly Zion and his throne of intercession (Heb 12:22–24)."[106] But the question is whether or not *Paul* understood it as future.[107] Certainly it was future from the perspective of *Isaiah*, but when Paul quotes the passage, he is quoting it because he sees it as past. As Hvalvik notes,

> For Paul the Deliverer has already come from Zion (cf. 9:33). This is clearly seen if one compares Rom. 11.28 with 15.8. In 11.26–28 the salvation of 'all Israel' is linked with the promises to the fathers (cf. also 9.5), and in 15.8 Paul tells how these promises have been confirmed when 'Christ became a servant to the circumcised'. This means that God's truthfulness toward his promises are seen in Christ's first coming.[108]

Those who maintain that Paul is referring to the second coming often insist that "Zion" means "heavenly Zion."[109] But in Isaiah's context, Zion is earthly, not heavenly.[110] It is also assumed that Paul's reference to Christ as the "Deliverer" (ὁ ῥυόμενος, *ho rhuomenos*) presupposes the second coming since

---

Stuhlmacher, *Romans*, 172–73; Hofius, "'All Israel Will Be Saved,'" 36; George Eldon Ladd, "Israel and the Church," *EvQ* 36 (1964): 212–13 (tentatively).

106. Barry E. Horner, *Future Israel: Why Christian Anti-Judaism Must Be Challenged*, NAC Studies in Bible and Theology (Nashville: Broadman & Holman, 2007), 261. See also Dunn, *Romans 9–16*, 692.

107. Fitzmyer rightly admits, "Not even the future *hēxei* necessarily implies the second coming." He adds, "reference to the parousia is nowhere made in chaps. 9–11" (*Romans*, 627). Wright similarly notes, "The complex of quotations in verses 26 and 27 thus have no specific reference to the *parousia*" (*Paul and the Faithfulness of God*, 1251).

108. Hvalvik, "'Sonderweg' for Israel," 93. Bruno adds, "For Paul, the coming of Christ marked the beginning of the eschatological era" ("Deliverer from Zion," 127).

109. See, e.g., Horner, *Future Israel*, 261; Meyer, *End of the Law*, 183.

110. Bruno comments, "Throughout the book of Isaiah, Zion, although transformed from an immoral city, is consistently an *earthly* location. Paul's quotation reflects the original Isaiah context, and the original context of Zion in Isaiah 59 is clearly not an ethereal heavenly city, but a more tangible earthly location" ("Deliverer from Zion," 127 [emphasis original]).

that term is associated with Christ's return in 1 Thessalonians 1:10 ("Jesus who delivers [τὸν ῥυόμενον, *ton rhuomenon*] us from the wrath to come"). But this connection is not convincing since the term appears in a number of Pauline texts that do not refer to the second coming (Rom. 7:24; 15:31; 2 Cor. 1:10; Col. 1:13).[111] Therefore, Romans 11:26 refers to Christ's first coming.[112] The climax of redemptive history is the cross and resurrection of Christ. Storms explains,

> It was by virtue of Christ's atoning death and resurrection that the new covenant has been inaugurated and the foundation laid for the removal of ungodliness from Jacob (i.e., from elect Israel). The forgiveness of sins is available to both ethnic Gentiles and Jews because of what Jesus did at his *first* coming when he ratified the new covenant in his blood. . . . It is therefore by means of this which the Deliverer accomplished at his first advent that all elect Gentiles ("the fullness of the Gentiles") and all elect Israelites ("all Israel") will be saved.[113]

---

111. So ibid.; Fitzmyer, *Romans*, 625.
112. So Bruno, "Deliverer from Zion," 119–34; Das, *Paul and the Jews*, 110; Hendriksen, *Romans*, 383; Hoekema, *Bible and the Future*, 146; Holwerda, *Jesus and Israel*, 172–73; Hvalvik, "'Sonderweg' for Israel," 92–95; Marten, "Israel and the Church," 236; Riddlebarger, *Case for Amillennialism*, 220–21; Reymond, *Paul*, 547; Robertson, "Is There a Distinctive Future for Ethnic Israel in Romans 11?" 226; Storms, *Kingdom Come*, 331; Wright, *Climax of the Covenant*, 250–51. Das comments, "Nowhere in Romans 11 does Paul connect the salvation of all Israel to Christ's Parousia or second coming. Paul does not even refer to the Parousia of Christ in Romans 9–11. In 11:26–27 he certainly speaks of a Deliverer who 'will come' out of Zion . . . but for Paul those prophecies have already been fulfilled. Christ came from Zion as the Jewish Messiah (9:5). God has already placed in Zion the stumbling stone (9:33). . . . The prophecies Paul cites in 11:26–27 were therefore fulfilled in Christ's *first* coming" (*Paul and the Jews*, 110).
113. Storms, *Kingdom Come*, 331–32. Bruno likewise states, "The OT promises of salvation have been fulfilled through Christ; therefore, Paul views Isaiah 59 as an already fulfilled prophecy that is continuing to be applied to the people of God during his ministry (and beyond). Furthermore, the decisive removal of sin in Pauline theology was clearly accomplished in the death and resurrection of Christ" ("Deliverer from Zion," 128).

Romans 9–11 and Biblical Theology

In this final section I consider three main implications that my view of Romans 9–11 has on biblical theology, especially in relation to the place of Israel in redemptive history.

God Is Faithful to All His Promises to Israel

Paul emphatically declares that the word of God has not failed (9:6). God fulfills what he promised according to his plan and his timeline. But sometimes the fulfillment of God's promises is different from what might have been *expected* (though not different from what was *predicted*). Such was the case with the coming of Jesus where the Jews were expecting one type of Messiah based on certain OT prophecies, but because of the veiled nature of prophecy and the hardness of their hearts, they misunderstood them. Even John the Baptist was uncertain at one point as to whether Jesus was truly the Messiah (Matt. 11:3). In the NT, however, we discover that Christ was the promised Messiah and that he fulfills what God promised in the OT to ethnic Israel. Thus, although the people of Israel were God's chosen people in the OT, now these promises are expanded to all who place their faith in Christ. There are at least four reasons that testify to this reality:[114]

Redemptive History Is Progressive

The new covenant fulfills God's plan, and a return to the shadows and images (Col. 2:17; Heb. 8:5) of the OT is therefore unwarranted. For example, although some prophecies, such as Amos 9:11–15, picture the nation of Israel with restored cities, defeated enemies, and abundant crops, the fulfillment of these prophecies has an even greater significance. God will never give less than he has promised, but he certainly has the prerogative to give more.

---

114. See Benjamin L. Merkle, "Old Testament Restoration Promises regarding the Nation of Israel: Literal or Symbolic," *The Southern Baptist Journal of Theology* 14, no. 1 (2010): 14–25; Alan S. Bandy and Benjamin L. Merkle, *Understanding Prophecy: A Biblical-Theological Approach* (Grand Rapids: Kregel, 2015), 107–23.

Biblical Prophecy Is a Unique Genre

That is, prophecy concerning the end of time or the coming of God's kingdom uses metaphorical or figurative language. The prophets often employed earthly imagery to describe a heavenly reality because they spoke and wrote in terms that both they and their audience would understand. They described the messianic kingdom in terms of concepts and imagery that were meaningful to the people of that day. It would be a mistake to claim that the fulfillment of all prophecies will be fulfilled in precisely the manner they were recorded. For example, the Gospels testify that John the Baptist fulfilled Isaiah's prophecy: "Prepare the way of the Lord, make his paths straight. Every valley shall be filled, and every mountain and hill shall be made low, and the crooked shall become straight, and the rough places shall become level ways, and all flesh shall see the salvation of God" (Luke 3:4–6). Isaiah says the forerunner of the Messiah will make physical changes to the landscape of Israel. But John was involved in changing people's hearts rather than changing the geography of Palestine. That is, he prepared their hearts spiritually by calling them to repentance. We must be careful, then, not to force an overly literal hermeneutic upon OT prophecies.

New Testament Authors Interpret Old Testament Prophecies Symbolically

One of the principles of sound hermeneutics is that we should let Scripture interpret Scripture. For example, Acts 15:16–17 cites Amos 9:11–12 to justify accepting the Gentiles into the people of God without forcing them to be circumcised. Thus, God is building his people by including the Gentiles in the people of God.[115] Because James sees this occurrence as fulfill-

---

115. So John B. Polhill, *Acts*, NAC 26 (Nashville: Broadman & Holman, 1992), 330; I. Howard Marshall, *Acts*, TNTC 5 (Grand Rapids: Eerdmans, 1980), 252; John R. W. Stott, *The Message of Acts: To the Ends of the Earth*, Bible Speaks Today (Leicester: Inter-Varsity Press, 1990), 247; William W. Klein, Craig L. Blomberg, and Robert L. Hubbard, *Introduction to Biblical Interpretation*, 2nd ed. (Dallas: Word, 2004), 379.

ing an OT text, we should allow for a fulfillment that expands beyond the wording of the original prophecy but yet is consistent with the original intention.[116]

Jesus's Death and Resurrection Has a Central Role in Redemptive History

One of the problems with interpreting OT prophecies regarding the nation of Israel in a literalistic (i.e., overly wooden) manner is that it tends to minimize the work of Christ, especially his suffering, death, and resurrection. The NT teaches that the death and resurrection of Christ are the climax of God's work in redemptive history. But if we interpret the many OT restoration prophecies regarding the nation of Israel literalistically, then such prophecies do not find their fulfillment in God's greatest work.

The NT writers do not seem to expect OT prophecies about the nation of Israel to be fulfilled literalistically. Bavinck rightly notes that "even if Paul expected a national conversion of Israel at the end, he does not say a word about the return of the Jews to Palestine, about a rebuilding of the city and a temple, about a visible rule of Christ: in his picture of the future there simply is no room for all this."[117] Wright declares, "Paul nowhere gives the slightest indication that ethnic Israel will one day return to their land and set up an independent state, which

---

116. See Darrell L. Bock, "Single Meaning, Multiple Context and Referents," in *Three Views on the New Testament Use of the Old Testament*, ed. Kenneth Berding and Jonathan Lunde, Counterpoints (Grand Rapids: Zondervan, 2008), 124, 131.

117. Bavinck, *Last Things,* 107. Similarly, Berkhof comments, "It is remarkable that the New Testament, which is the fulfillment of the Old, contains no indication whatsoever of the re-establishment of the Old Testament theocracy by Jesus, nor a single undisputed positive prediction of its restoration, while it does contain abundant indications of the spiritual fulfilment of the promises given to Israel" (*Systematic Theology*, 713). Goldsworthy notes, "The New Testament seems to be completely indifferent to the restoration referred to [in the OT]" (Graeme Goldsworthy, *Gospel-Centered Hermeneutics: Foundations and Principles of Evangelical Biblical Interpretation* [Downers Grove, IL: InterVarsity Press, 2006], 170). See also Bruce K. Waltke, "Kingdom Promises as Spiritual," in *Continuity and Discontinuity: Perspectives on the Relationship between the Old and New Testaments*, ed. John S. Feinberg (Wheaton, IL: Crossway, 1988), 273.

will in the due course become a vehicle of God's blessing to the world. . . . Any attempt to give a Christian gloss to the Middle Eastern political events of 1947 and thereafter is without exegetical foundation."[118]

Jesus is the full and final revelation of God (Heb. 1:1–2), and his first coming was the climax of redemptive history. Paul explains, "All the promises of God find their Yes in him" (2 Cor. 1:20). Jesus fulfills OT prophecy by embodying and completing the expectations of the nation of Israel. As Motyer states, "Jesus appears, not just as the Saviour of Israel in fulfilment of prophetic expectation, but also as an embodiment of Israel as they should be."[119] This has massive ramifications for how we interpret the Bible and how we understand the relationship between Israel and the church. For example, in seeking to demonstrate that the new covenant is superior to the old covenant, the author of Hebrews quotes Jeremiah 31: "I will establish a new covenant with the house of Israel and with the house of Judah" (Heb. 8:8). It is incorrect to claim (without qualification) that God gave the new covenant to the church and not to Israel. No blessings come to the church that Christ did not first secure. In one sense, then, God gave the new covenant to the house of Israel and the house of Judah because Christ fulfilled it. The church has access to this covenant only because of their union with Christ. But this shows the expansive nature of the fulfillment. Christ, the perfect representative Israelite, fulfills what God originally prophesied to a single nation, and any believer from the nations is united with Christ. In this way, God is faithful to his promises. To maintain that Christ and his church cannot fulfill such OT promises denies the testimony of God's inspired apostolic witness.

---

118. Wright, "Romans," 698.
119. Motyer, "Israel (Nation)," 584. Beale similarly writes, "when gentiles believe, they do not retain an independent status as redeemed gentiles; they are seen to be gentiles converting to the faith of Israel, and although their gentile ethnicity is not erased, they gain a greater identity as part of Israel because they identify with Jesus, the summation and representative of true Israel" (*New Testament Biblical Theology*, 710).

God Has Not Rejected (Nor Will He Ever Reject) Israel

God has not (completely) rejected or abandoned ethnic Israel, nor will he ever do so (11:1, 11). Like Gomer, who was unfaithful to Hosea and left him for another lover, Israel may turn their backs on their covenant-making and covenant-keeping God, but he will not forsake them. Whenever Jewish people embrace Christ as God's anointed Messiah and believe in his atoning work on the cross, they are grafted back into the tree of God's covenant blessings (11:23). Even though elsewhere Paul can speak of the church as the Israel of God (Gal. 6:16), this in no way means that the church is *in* and ethnic Israel is *out*. After all, many members of the early church were ethnic Jews. Rather, it means that God's covenant blessings are no longer focused on Israel because the Messiah has redeemed people from every tribe, language, people, and nation (Rev. 5:9). So, although it is true that God's promises (through Christ) extend to the church, God is still concerned about ethnic Israel. That is, simply because ethnic Israel no longer has a special status before God as his chosen or elect people does not mean that as a people they are insignificant or irrelevant.

The church does not eliminate the concept of Israel so that it has no identity or significance. In fact, like Paul, Christians should weep for and evangelize Jewish unbelievers. Simply because Paul believes that God is faithful to his promises and will continue to redeem a remnant of ethnic Jews does not mean that he is content with a small number believing while the vast majority reject God's Messiah.[120] Instead, Paul worked as hard as he could to win the Gentiles so that his people would become jealous and also turn to Christ (Rom. 11:13–14). Consequently, Paul *does* anticipate a larger ingathering of the remnant in the future. But this ingathering will not occur through some apocalyptic work of God when Christ returns. Rather, it will occur as the result of Paul's ministering to the

---

120. Cf., e.g., Isaiah 11:11–12, 16; 37:31–32; Micah 2:12; 4:7.

Gentiles, which in turn makes Israel jealous. It will also occur as the result of subsequent Christians ministering to both Jews and Gentiles. Interestingly, the response to Paul's angst (9:1–5; 10:1) is *not* that God will miraculously save a large number of Jews at the *parousia*, but that he himself will continue to work harder than all his contemporaries by the grace of God (1 Cor. 15:10). This reversal of the hardening, however, is neither automatic nor guaranteed.[121]

Paul believes that those who are hardened, if they do not trust in the Messiah, will face God's judgment. That is why in Romans 9:1–5 he writes of his unceasing anguish of heart. That is why he prays for their salvation and desires for the gospel message to reach them before it is too late. In the Bible, judgment gives way to final judgment. The only hope for unbelieving Israel is not the second coming, but for them to repent and believe.[122]

My view is *not* a form of replacement theology.[123] The church does not *replace* Israel. Rather, God *incorporates* the church into his people through their union with Christ. Replacement theology states that one group is out (Jews) and another is in (Gentiles/the church). My view is that both groups can be in if they believe in Christ. Israel has not been replaced or substituted for another. Instead of replacement theology, Paul embraced remnant theol-

---

121. Wright notes that the position that the hardening will be overcome "is so firmly fixed in recent exegetical tradition that it, ironically, has itself formed such a hard crust on the reading of the passage that it may take a miracle to break through" (*Paul and the Faithfulness of God*, 1237).

122. Wright makes an excellent point: "[If] Paul really did believe that those who are 'hardened' would sooner or later be rescued by a fresh divine act (perhaps soon, if he did indeed expect the *parousia* in a short time), then why all the tears? . . . The only answer to this would be the exegetically fantastic one: that *up to the point of writing Romans* Paul has had this unceasing sorrow and anguish of heart, but *now that he has thought the matter through afresh* or perhaps indeed has received a sudden divine revelation between the writing of verses 24 and 25 of Romans 11, he sees that actually he need not have been so concerned" (ibid., 1238 [emphasis original]). He continues, "If the majority view were correct, Paul ought really to have told Tertius, his scribe, to throw away these three chapters [Romans 9–11] and start again. And, actually, with that, he should have told him to scrap the whole letter. A good deal of chapters 2, 3, and 4 would have to go as well" (ibid.).

123. So Wright, "Romans," 675, 676, 690; Wright, *Paul and the Faithfulness of God*, 1180, 1201, 1206, 1212, 1220.

ogy. God will continue to save a remnant of ethnic Jews until the return of Christ. My view is that Christ fulfills promises to Israel so that anyone (Jew or Gentile) can come into the blessings that God has promised to his people.

God Does Not Have a Special Plan for Israel That Excludes the Church

"There is one body and one Spirit . . . one Lord, one faith, one baptism, one God and Father of all" (Eph. 4:4–6). Through Christ, God has made those who were far off (Gentiles) and those who are near (Jews) "both one" (Eph. 2:13–14). There is no special future dispensation for ethnic Jews any more than there is for ethnic Gentiles: "There is no distinction between Jew and Greek" (Rom. 10:12; cf. 3:22). Indeed, "there is one God, and there is one mediator between God and men, the man Christ Jesus" (1 Tim. 2:5). Because there is one Savior and one people of God, there is also a common future for God's people. I heartily agree with Kruse, who states, "I am reluctant to embrace any of the interpretations placing the salvation of 'all Israel' at the end of the age because that involves special provision for the salvation of Jews different from that provided for Gentiles. This flies in the face of the overall argument of Romans that Jews and Gentiles are treated alike in the matters of sin, judgment, and salvation."[124] There will not be a time when God will refuse to admit any more Gentiles into his people but open the floodgates where millions of Jews will be saved. Not only is such a position contrary to Paul's teaching elsewhere, it simply does not occur in Romans 9–11. Paul does hope and even anticipate more Jews coming to faith in Christ, but he sees that as a result of his ministry, not the result of a special dispensation.

In Galatians 3:28 Paul states, "There is neither Jew nor Greek, there is neither slave nor free, there is no male and female, for you are all one in Christ Jesus." Regarding salvation and the blessings that come from salvation, there are no ethnic,

---

124. Kruse, *Romans*, 451.

socio-economic, or gender distinctions. But just as gender distinctions are still relevant today, so are ethnic distinctions. Thus, although Paul knows that one's heritage or ethnicity is irrelevant when it comes to salvation, he still yearned for the salvation of his fellow Jews. And God's promise is that they, just like every other ethnicity, can be saved if they trust in Jesus as their Lord and Savior.

Some may claim that my view of typology, as it relates to Israel and Jesus, is inconsistent. That is, if Jesus fulfills all of the promises to ethnic Israel, how is it that Paul can also state that the promises to Israel are fulfilled by the Jewish remnant? But Paul can affirm both at the same time. That is, Jesus is the fulfillment of certain OT promises to Israel, *and* Israel has a unique place in salvation history. It is unhelpful to cast Paul's theology concerning this matter as a binary choice. Paul (as well as other NT authors) undoubtedly acknowledges that Jesus's life, death, resurrection, and ascension demonstrate that he is the long-awaited Messiah who fulfills God's word in ways that Israel (and especially Israel's kings) never did. And yet, Paul affirms that Israel's distinctive place in redemptive history is still in effect. Israel's status as a nation is not dissolved because the Messiah has come. Earlier in Romans Paul writes how the message of the gospel is to go "to the Jew first and also to the Greek" (Rom. 1:16). He often directly addresses his fellow Jews (Rom. 2:1, 17; 3:9; 4:1). In some contexts, Paul still views Israel as a historical, theological, and ethnic entity. In Romans 9–11 Paul is concerned about his kinsmen according to the flesh and the faithfulness of God. Consequently, Paul does not simply dismiss the issue of the lostness of ethnic Israel by claiming that Jesus as the new Israel fulfills God's promises to his people (expanded to include Gentiles). Paul experienced pain and heartache because his fellow Jews were rejecting the Messiah. Although it is true that God is rebuilding his people by including Gentiles (see Acts 15:16–17), the issue at hand will simply not allow Paul to theologize so callously regarding the lostness of his beloved fellow Jews. Instead, he shows that

God is faithful to his promises because (1) God never promised to save all Israel, and (2) as God has done in the past, he will continue to save some of them—until the end.

Conclusion

Romans 9–11 does not teach a future mass-conversion of ethnic Israel. Rather, it teaches that there will always be a remnant of believing Jews until the end of time. Although it is possible for Paul to speak of the church as the *new* or the *true* Israel, in this context Paul's concern relates to his "brothers," his "kinsmen according to the flesh" (Rom. 9:3). The major flaw of those who hold to a future-mass-conversion view is consistency: God is not unfaithful to his promises because he never promised to save all ethnic Israelites. Instead, his promises legitimately apply only to the elect remnant. This was true before Paul's life (such as during the time of Elijah), during Paul's life (after all, he is an Israelite), and up until God saves the last Israelite. Consequently, there will always be a remnant of Israelites who are grafted into the people of God until God saves the last Gentile. Paul does not turn his initial reasoning on its head by arguing that God is not unfaithful to his promises because sometime in the future he will save the majority of Jewish people living at that time. Such a position is based primarily on a faulty understanding of OT restoration promises to the nation of Israel.

But Paul's view of Israel is noticeably different. Salvation is of the Jews. Our Messiah is a Jew. And true salvation is possible only because our Jewish Messiah atoned for sin, defeated death, conquered the grave, and reigns even now on the throne of David. Through our union with Christ, believers (including Gentiles) are adopted into God's family and become heirs to the promises first offered to Abraham but finally fulfilled in Christ. All believers belong to the same family because all have a common Savior and are grafted into the same tree. God has promised that this tree will always include ethnic Jews. And because God is faithful, it will be so.

RESPONSE TO MERKLE

Michael J. Vlach

Benjamin Merkle offers a well-written presentation and defense of the typological non-future-mass-conversion view of Romans 9–11. His essay is the best defense yet of the position that the "all Israel" who will be saved in Romans 11:26 is the believing Jewish remnant throughout history. I appreciate the clarity with which Merkle makes his specific points and overall case. While my response below reveals why I disagree with his view, his essay must be taken seriously.

Upon analysis, I do not think Merkle's view sufficiently explains Paul's argument in Romans 9–11. While rightly drawing attention to the believing Jewish remnant in God's purposes, his essay misses the importance of corporate Israel's future salvation and restoration. Merkle does not adequately account for the message of Romans 9–11 and the Bible as a whole that God's plans for the world include the strategic role of corporate national Israel,[1] who will be saved and contribute to even greater blessings for the nations (11:12, 15, 26; see Isa. 19:16–25).

Merkle's focus on the believing remnant of Jews, apart from the salvation of corporate Israel, leads to inaccurate interpretations, particularly in 11:11–32, where Paul mostly goes beyond

---

1. I use the terms "corporate" and "national" in this response. Corporate stresses Israel as a whole, a group. National emphasizes Israel as a national entity.

the Jewish remnant and addresses Israel as a whole. His view also results in a skewed understanding of the remnant. The believing Jewish remnant preserves the existence of Israel (Isa. 1:9) and functions as a "firstfruits" (HCSB), bridge, and vehicle for God's purposes for the nation (Rom. 11:16a). But the remnant is not an end in itself, nor is it the means for greater world blessings (Rom. 11:12, 15). Also, the sum of a remnant is still just a remnant and does not remedy Paul's concern for corporate Israel's unbelief (Rom. 9:3). Nor does the believing remnant throughout history qualify for Paul's "all Israel" reference in 11:26.

His essay also misses the grand nature of Paul's "mystery" concept in 11:25 and the explosion of praise Paul offers in 11:33–36. The great "mystery" Paul explains is not a small stream of believing Jews throughout history, but it involves the stunning reversal of national Israel's unbelief after a period of Gentile salvation that provokes Israel to jealousy. To hold that Israel's "partial hardening" expires at some point in the future without a reversal is anticlimactic. As Venema explains, "It would be an extraordinary anti-climax for Paul to conclude that Israel's restoration, acceptance, and life from the dead will amount to nothing other than the salvation of a small remnant."[2]

Typology, Symbolical Interpretation, Israel, and Jesus

As an adherent of a typological approach Merkle stresses the importance of typology for his views on Israel, Jesus, and the church. He sees Jesus as the fulfillment (not replacement) of Israel, and he views national Israel as a type of Jesus. He says, "the nation of Israel is a 'type' that points to a greater reality." Then he declares, "If Israel is the *type*, then what is the *antitype*? *Jesus* is the antitype since he is the fulfillment of Israel" (p. 164). This leads to the view that "Jesus is the 'true Israel' because he fulfills (typologically) all that the nation of Israel was

---

2.   Cornelis P. Venema, "'In This Way All Israel Will Be Saved': A Study of Romans 11:26," *Mid-America Journal of Theology* 22 (2011): 36.

to accomplish as well as all that they hoped for and anticipated" (p. 164). And all who are in union with Jesus, including believing Gentiles, also participate in Israel. Thus, for Merkle, the church in Jesus is Israel.

Concerning the interpretation of Bible prophecy Merkle asserts that "biblical prophecy is a unique genre" (p. 201) with significant metaphorical and figurative language. The prophets allegedly employed "earthly imagery to describe a heavenly reality" (p. 201). He also says there are times when "New Testament authors interpret Old Testament prophecies symbolically" (p. 201). For example, he believes the quotation of Amos 9:11–12 in Acts 15:16–17 is evidence for symbolical interpretation. These are some reasons to avoid being too literal with OT prophecies concerning national Israel.

These issues of typology, Jesus as the fulfillment of Israel, the church as Israel, Bible prophecy as a unique genre, and symbolical interpretation are broad topics, and I cannot respond fully to his assertions. But I found it interesting that Merkle does not anchor these ideas much within Romans 9–11. He does not offer any cases of OT prophecies being interpreted symbolically in these chapters. No case is made for national Israel as a type of Jesus in Romans 9–11. He also acknowledges that all references to "Israel" in these chapters refer only to ethnic Jews and that Paul is not identifying the church as "Israel" here. So major parts of Merkle's overall argument are not found in Romans 9–11. This is an issue since Romans 9–11 offers a large cluster of OT citations. Plus, it is the most detailed section concerning the relationship of Israel and the Gentiles in the Bible. If his assertions are true, why do they not show up in Romans 9–11?

Merkle cites other passages to make his points. This is fine since perhaps these ideas can be found outside Romans 9–11. But these appeals are not persuasive. His mention of Amos 9:11–12 in Acts 15:16–17 is not a true example of symbolical interpretation. Because of Jesus, who is the focal point of the Davidic covenant, James quotes Amos 9:11–12 contextually to show that Gentiles have become God's people without needing to be incorporated into Israel. Next, Paul's "Israel of God" reference in Galatians 6:16 is not identifying the church as Israel. Here Paul refers to believing ethnic Jews who had not fallen for the false gospel of the Judaizers. Also, 1 Peter 2:5–10 does not show the church is Israel but instead reveals that "people of God" language once used of Israel in the OT is now also applied to all believers in Jesus, just as the OT predicted (see Isa. 19:24–25).

I also disagree with his views concerning how typology relates to Jesus and Israel. I too believe correspondences and typological connections exist between national Israel and Jesus (see Hos. 11:1; Matt. 2:15), but these show that Jesus is the Messiah and corporate head of Israel who can restore national Israel and bless Gentiles. The purpose of Jesus's connection to Israel is not to transcend the significance of national Israel, but to restore Israel to be everything God intended for it, even if this awaits Jesus's second coming. So typology concerning Jesus and Israel maintains national Israel's significance. In Isaiah 49:1–6 Jesus is presented as the true servant of Israel who restores the nation Israel. In the new covenant passage of Jeremiah 31 God says "the offspring of Israel" will always be "a nation before Me forever" (Jer. 31:35–36).

A non-typological approach, on the other hand, affirms that Jesus as the "fulfillment" of Israel means the continuing theological significance of national Israel. Here we must distinguish and harmonize Jesus as a *referent* for many of Israel's prophecies and Jesus as the *means* through which promises to Israel will be fulfilled. First, Jesus is the *referent* for many specific messianic OT passages predicting a savior (Gen. 3:15; Isa. 53) and king (Gen. 49:10; Pss. 2; 110). He also embodies all that Israel was supposed to be as an obedient Son who loves God and people perfectly. There are also events in Israel's history that correspond to events in Jesus's life (see Matt. 2:15; Hos. 11:1). Yet while all promises concerning Israel are related to Jesus (see 2 Cor. 1:20), we must note that Jesus is not the only referent for all promises to Israel since some prophecies are made with Israel as a corporate group and involve entities such as land, Jerusalem, and the temple. Daniel 9:24–27, for example, specifically predicts the Messiah ("Messiah the Prince") and what his ministry will mean for the people of Israel, Jerusalem, and the temple. These distinctions are also found in Jesus's Olivet Discourse, where he mentions prophetic matters concerning himself, the people of Israel, Jerusalem, and the temple (see Matt. 24). So not all prophecies concerning Israel are absorbed into Jesus or climaxed in him in such a way that removes literal fulfillment with other entities. Jesus himself said, "not the smallest letter or stroke shall pass from the Law [i.e., OT] until all is accomplished" (Matt. 5:18). Concerning future events Jesus said, "all things which are written will be fulfilled" (Luke 21:22). If Jesus expected literal fulfillment of prophecies concerning Israel, so should we (Matt. 19:28; 23:37–39; Luke 21:24).

Jesus is also the *means* through whom promises to Israel will be fulfilled. In other words, Jesus will bring about all that God intends for Israel on every level. This includes Israel's salvation, restoration, and role and kingdom conditions under his reign (Isa. 2:2–4). With Romans 15:8 Paul says, "Christ has become a servant to the circumcision [i.e., Israelites] on behalf of the truth of God to *confirm* the promises given to the fathers" (emphasis added). Jesus actively brings everything promised concerning Israel (and the nations) to fulfillment (see Acts 3:20–21). So Jesus is also the *means* through whom promises to Israel will be fulfilled. "Fulfillment" in Jesus is multi-dimensional and does not remove or transcend literal fulfillment of OT promises to national Israel.

Significantly, Merkle acknowledges that his views on Jesus as the fulfillment of Israel and Israel's promises could be construed as an inconsistency since he also believes that certain promises will be fulfilled with the remnant of believing Israelites:

> Some may claim that my view of typology, as it relates to Israel and Jesus, is inconsistent. That is, if Jesus fulfills all of the prom-

ises to ethnic Israel, how is it that Paul can also state that the
promises to Israel are fulfilled by the Jewish remnant? But Paul
can affirm both at the same time. That is, Jesus is the fulfillment
of certain OT promises to Israel, *and* Israel has a unique place in
salvation history. It is unhelpful to cast Paul's theology concerning this matter as a binary choice. (p. 207)

I agree with what he says here, although I think it does introduce a critical contradiction for his view. He is correct that we
do not have to make a "binary choice" between fulfillment in
Jesus and fulfillment with other Israelites. That is my point too.
But here is the problem. Merkle seems to indicate that Israel's
promises are fulfilled in Jesus so we do not have to look for
literal fulfillments with national Israel, but he also says there are
promises that will be fulfilled with the Jewish remnant. It seems
that he wants to limit fulfillment concerning Israel beyond Jesus
to the believing Jewish remnant. But why make this limitation?
If God can keep his promises to the Jewish remnant, why can't
he keep his promises to the corporate entity of Israel? *My main
point here is that fulfillment in Jesus does not exclude God fulfilling
promises literally with believing Israelite individuals or the nation Israel.*
So the idea that we should not look for a literal fulfillment of
OT promises to national Israel because of typology or because
Jesus fulfills Israel does not work. Once one acknowledges that
"fulfillment" in Jesus does not mean the dissolving of Israel's
significance, as Merkle admits, one should be open to the entire
package of blessings promised to national Israel in the OT and
affirmed by Paul in Romans 9:3–5. In 9:3–5 the following are
all viewed together: (1) national Israel, (2) promises, covenants,
and temple service for Israel, and (3) Jesus the Messiah. All
three are important.

Merkle also says, "The NT writers do not seem to expect
OT prophecies about the nation of Israel to be fulfilled literal-
istically" (p. 202). I disagree. Passages like Matthew 19:28,
Matthew 23:39, Luke 1:32–33, Luke 21:24, Luke 22:29–30,
Acts 1:6, 3:19–21, 2 Thessalonians 2:1–10, and Revelation 7:4–8

reveal the NT persons and writers expected literal fulfillments of OT expectations concerning national Israel. There is no reality shift from OT expectation to NT fulfillment.

I also disagree with Merkle's statement that "one of the problems with interpreting OT prophecies regarding the nation of Israel in a literalistic (i.e., overly wooden) manner is that it tends to minimize the work of Christ, especially his suffering, death, and resurrection." This is not proven and unfortunately takes the debate to a disappointing level. We do not have to choose between the infinite value of Jesus's death and literal fulfillment of OT promises. Belief in literal fulfillment of OT prophecies affirms both the infinite value of Jesus's death and God's integrity in fulfilling everything just as he predicted. In Acts 3:18–21 the death of Jesus (v. 18) is linked with his return and the "restoration of all things" (vv. 20–21), which in this context includes the restoration of national Israel since the same term for "restoration" (*apokatastasis*) in Acts 3:21 is used in Acts 1:6 concerning the "restoring" of Israel's kingdom.

Methodology

Concerning his methodological approach to Romans 9–11, Merkle focuses mostly on 11:26 along with 9:6; 11:1; 11:11; and 11:25. Other verses like 11:12 and 11:15 also receive attention. Yet there are some gaps in his presentation that hinder it from being comprehensive.

In addition to little interaction with Paul's quotations of the OT, the strategic sections of 9:4–5 and 11:28–29 receive only brief attention. Romans 9:4–5 affirms that the covenants, promises, temple service, and more still belong to national Israel even in unbelief. Romans 11:28–29 brings 9:4–5 full circle by affirming that God's gifts to national Israel cannot be revoked. Concerning 9:4–5 and 11:28–29, Soulen notes, "It is impossible to overstate the importance of these two present-tense passages for the structure of Paul's argument. They are the iron brackets which surround Paul's argument and ultimately contain its explosive force."[3] Every view of Romans 9–11 should account for these "iron brackets" of Paul's argument.

Romans 11:28 is particularly significant since it operates like a filter that removes incorrect positions of the "all Israel" in 11:26. Romans 11:28 highlights the referent of "all Israel" (11:26) that is destined for salvation. It says, "from the standpoint of the gospel they are enemies for your sake, but from the standpoint of God's choice they are beloved for the sake of the fathers." The supplied "they" points back to the "all Israel" of 11:26 that is currently in unbelief but is also headed for salvation. Significantly, this group in 11:28 is both an *enemy* of the gospel and *beloved* by God—*at the same time*. This seems to rule out the Jewish-remnant-only view since the believing remnant of Israel is never an enemy of the gospel. Only the whole of Israel currently characterized by unbelief is simultaneously both *enemy* and *beloved*. Paul is not claiming that the "all Israel" will transition from being an enemy to being beloved. Instead, being an enemy and being beloved are concurrent truths. Only corporate Israel currently characterized by unbelief but destined for salvation by God's grace can be both enemy and beloved simultaneously. Thus, 11:28 disqualifies the view that the "all Israel" of 11:26 is the Jewish believing remnant throughout history.

Interpretive Forks in the Road

There are several occasions where I believe Merkle makes a wrong turn at important interpretive forks in the road. Individually and collectively these make his view unlikely.

First, in reference to Romans 9:6–29 and 9:7–13 in particular, Merkle says, "Paul refutes the notion that God's word has failed by pointing out that God's promises apply to only the

---

3. R. Kendall Soulen, "The Priority of the Present Tense for Jewish–Christian Relations," in *Between Gospel and Election: Explorations in the Interpretation of Romans 9–11*, eds. Florian Wilk and J. Ross Wagner (Tübingen: Mohr Siebeck, 2010), 498. Even if present tense verbs are not used, the force of these sections involves a present emphasis.

spiritual offspring within ethnic Israel" (p. 172). But Paul does not distinguish spiritual offspring within ethnic Israel in 9:7–13. The implied Ishmael (in contrast to Isaac) and then Esau (in contrast to Jacob) are outside Israel and the seed line of Israel; they are heads of non-Jewish people groups. In Psalm 83:1–6 "Ishmaelites" and "Edom" are pictured as enemies of Israel. Paul's point in 9:7–13 is that the chosen seed line of promise that will eventually bless the world runs through Isaac and Jacob, not Ishmael and Esau. National election of Israel is in view here. So even this section affirms the importance of Israel as the seed line of promise in God's electing purposes.

Second, Merkle has a quantitative or numerical understanding of *plērōma* ("full number") in both 11:12 and 11:25. This view is not impossible, but of the fifteen other references to *plērōma* in the NT, including Romans 13:10 and 15:29, there are no cases of a numerical sense of this term. A qualitative understanding in these two passages is more likely. The "fullness" of 11:12 likely refers to Israel becoming complete and everything God intends for her. The "fullness" in 11:25 probably refers to God's intended role for Gentiles as provokers of Israel's jealousy in this age. If Paul wanted to convey a full number concept here, he probably would have used *artithmos* like he did in 9:27.

Third, concerning Paul's olive tree analogy in 11:17–24, Merkle says, "[Paul's] point is that when *individual* Jews believe in Christ, they will be grafted back in" (p. 193). Supposedly, individual Jews primarily are in view. But corporate national Israel, not the remnant, makes much better sense in 11:17–24. Concerning v. 17 Paul says, "some of the branches were broken off." Later, v. 24 states, "how much more will these who are the natural branches be grafted into their own olive tree?" This speaks of a reinstatement after being cut off. Verse 23 also says, "God is able to graft them [Israel] in *again*." The "again" reveals reinstatement to something once possessed. *Only national Israel fits this picture of reinstatement after being cut off for a time.* The believing remnant of Israel is not cut off from Abrahamic covenant blessings for a while and then reinstated again at a later time.

But corporate Israel can and will be. Israel as a whole was given the Abrahamic covenant and then later cut off from its blessings because of disobedience. This situation will be reversed when the mass of Israel believes. This threefold scenario of (1) connection to Abrahamic covenant blessings, (2) removal, then (3) later reinstatement to covenant blessings was explicitly predicted for corporate Israel in Deuteronomy 30 and Leviticus 26. Also, in the olive tree analogy Paul does not speak of Israel's reinstatement to the place of blessing as happening concurrently with that of the Gentiles in the present. It comes after, which fits best with a future mass-conversion of Israel view.

Fourth, Merkle posits a terminative understanding of *achris hou* ("until") with no reversal for national Israel's unbelief in Romans 11:25 when Paul says, "a partial hardening has happened to Israel until the fullness of the Gentiles has come in." But most uses of *achris* in the NT indicate a reversal of circumstances, and the previous olive tree analogy predicts just such a reversal for Israel. Plus, the use of *achris hou* in Luke 21:24 concerning the similar "times of the Gentiles" indicates a reversal of circumstances for Jerusalem after its trampling by Gentiles ends. So usage and context heavily favor a reversal understanding of *achris hou* in 11:25, not a terminative view.

Fifth, for Merkle *kai houtōs* ("and so/thus/then") in 11:26 must be understood in a modal sense, for if a temporal sense of "then" exists, this would indicate national Israel's salvation chronologically follows the "fullness of the Gentiles" mentioned in 11:25. In my essay I note that a growing number of scholars think a temporal sense of "then" is best. This understanding is very possible. But even if the modal understanding is primary, this must include a temporal or time element in this context. Paul offered a chronology of events in the olive tree analogy (11:17–24), and then he used the chronological indicator "until" in 11:25. So the manner of Israel's salvation involves the *sequence* of corporate Israel coming to faith after the fullness of the Gentiles. A modal understanding with no temporal implications is unlikely in this context.

Sixth, Merkle believes "all Israel" in 11:26 is used in a diachronic way for the cumulative remnant of believing Jews in history. But this is a major problem. Merkle's understanding is without precedent. The vast majority of uses, if not every use, of "all Israel" in Scripture are synchronic concerning the whole of Israel at a specific point in time. A synchronic understanding of "all Israel" is likely in 11:26 and makes sense in this context. For Merkle's view to be accurate, a rare or non-existent understanding of "all Israel" must be correct in 11:26.

Seventh, Merkle believes there are two referents concerning Israel in 11:25–26, the broader nation as a whole in v. 25 and then allegedly the remnant in v. 26. But context indicates reversal for the same group—the mass of Israel. A distinction between the whole of Israel and the remnant is clear in 9:6, but this distinction is not found in 11:25–26. Appealing to 9:6 for two referents for Israel does not work since the context is different in 11:25–26, describing changing conditions for the same group.

Eighth, concerning Romans 11:26b, Paul reveals that when the "Deliverer" (Jesus) comes from Zion, "HE WILL REMOVE UNGODLINESS FROM JACOB." Context and the future tense of "will remove" point to the second coming of Jesus and the dramatic removal of ungodliness from Israel as a whole. But Merkle takes this as a reference to the first coming of Jesus and the removal of ungodliness as applying to the Jewish remnant only. But this understanding does not work for at least two reasons. First, when "Jacob" is used in the Bible beyond the individual Jacob, it refers to Israel as a whole (Num. 32:9; 1 Chron. 16:17; Ps. 14:17), not a remnant. And second, the return of the Deliver is connected with the removal of ungodliness from Israel (see Zech. 13:1–6), something that did not happen with Jesus's first coming. At that time Israel missed its time of visitation (Luke 19:41–44). The cities of Israel that rejected Jesus are headed for judgment (Matt. 11:20–24). It is difficult to see ungodliness being removed from Israel with Jesus's first coming. That awaits his second advent.

Finally, concerning 11:30–31, Merkle asserts that the threefold use of "now" emphasizes Israel's present situation not the future. Since the authenticity of the last "now" is so heavily contested,[4] it is best not to make too much of it for one's view. Yet even if the last "now" is original, in this context in which there is much emphasis on what God will do for Israel in the future, the last "now" in 11:31 is better understood in the sense of imminence. What God is doing with the Gentiles in the present means Israel is now positioned to receive God's mercy at any time. This fits with Paul's eschatology that the coming of Jesus could occur at any moment.

Objections against the Mass-Conversion View

Merkle's essay is also a polemic against the idea of a future mass-conversion of Israel. But I think his arguments here fall short.

First, he asserts that belief in a future mass-conversion of national Israel in Romans 11 is inconsistent with Paul's earlier argument concerning the remnant in chapters 9 and 10. Allegedly, if one correctly grasps Romans 9:6, one would see that Romans 11:26 cannot teach a future salvation of corporate Israel. But there is no contradiction. Romans 9:6 affirms that not all ethnic Israelites are saved. Romans 11:26, on the other hand, predicts that the mass of Israel will be saved at a coming point in time. These are not mutually exclusive ideas. It would be a contradiction only if Paul affirmed that all Israelites throughout history are saved in 11:26, which he does not. The corporate salvation of Israel view is not saying all Israelites will be saved or even that all Israelites in the future will be saved. It is just asserting that a day is coming when Israel as a whole will transition from unbelief to belief.

Also, Merkle is incorrect that the Bible does not teach a corporate salvation of Israel. In a passage where God speaks of the coming new covenant for "the house of Israel" and "the house of Judah," God says, "they [Israel] will all know Me,

---

4. See David A. Kaden, "The Methodological Dilemma of Evaluating the Variation Unit in Romans 11:31," *NovT* 53 (2011): 165–82.

from the least of them to the greatest of them" (Jer. 31:31, 34). Zechariah 12 predicts the Spirit of grace (Holy Spirit) being poured out on the inhabitants of Jerusalem, where deep-seated mourning will occur among the families of Israel (Zech. 12:10–14). Deuteronomy 30:1–10 reveals that the nation to be judged and dispersed will someday be saved and restored to the land of promise in connection with a circumcised heart (30:6). Leviticus 26:40–45, too, predicts that with national repentance Israel as a whole will be saved and participate again in the Abrahamic covenant, including the land.

Israel experienced many events as a corporate people, including the exodus, the receiving of the Mosaic covenant, the possession of the promised land, the Babylonian captivity, and the destruction of Jerusalem in A.D. 70. If all Israel can be judged and dispersed as a national entity in the past, certainly all Israel can be saved and restored as a national entity in the future. Jesus predicted both national judgment and national salvation in Matthew 23:37–39. So Merkle's approach does not account for the biblical motif of Israel's reversal from national judgment to national restoration.

Second, Merkle believes the idea of further blessings for Gentiles after national Israel's salvation is a problem. He says, "If the salvation of 'all Israel' occurs *after* the fullness of the Gentiles is saved ('has come in,' v. 25), how can there be a subsequent time of salvation for the Gentiles?" (p. 191). But Paul in 11:25 is emphasizing the place and role of Gentiles *in this age* concerning Israel, particularly Gentile blessings and provoking Israel to jealousy. When these reach completion, then national Israel will be saved, and more blessings for the world will ensue as 11:12 and 15 indicate. So the present role of Gentiles in God's purposes and future blessings for the world after the salvation of corporate Israel harmonize well.

Third, Merkle says that some who believe in a future mass salvation of Israel could be prejudiced concerning Paul's question in Romans 11:1: "Has God rejected his people?" Allegedly proponents of a mass-conversion view subconsciously might

read the question in a way that "prejudices one toward interpreting the rest of the chapter as advocating a special future for
Israel." A similar claim is made concerning 11:11, where again
some are allegedly reading a mass-conversion of Israel into the
question. But Paul's overall argument will determine what he
meant in 11:1 and 11:11. The question in 11:1 focused on the
remnant (vv. 1–6), while the question at 11:11 addressed Israel as
a whole (11:11–32). So, yes, Paul had a future mass-conversion
in mind, particularly with his question in 11:11, because the
context indicates this. Adherents of a future-mass-conversion
view are not prejudiced; they think Paul's overall argument
affirms a mass-conversion idea.

In sum, I do not think Merkle's essay presents any real
problems for the mass-conversion of Israel view that cannot be
answered sufficiently.

Conclusion

Merkle's presentation is well-written and rightly draws attention to the significance of the Jewish remnant. But I do not
think his position is accurate since it does not recognize the
significance of national Israel's coming salvation and restoration and what these will mean for the world. The twin truths
concerning both the remnant *and* the nation of Israel as a whole
function like two wings on an airplane, and both are needed
according to Paul. For the reasons stated above, I do not think
the typological non-mass-conversion view is an accurate
understanding of Romans 9–11.

RESPONSE TO MERKLE

Fred G. Zaspel
and James M. Hamilton Jr.

It is a pleasure to read behind Ben Merkle. Although we of course do not share his position on Romans 9–11, it is a plausible one, and we appreciate both his skillful defense and his focus on the leading points of exegetical concern that are determinative in the discussion. We happily acknowledge our agreement with Merkle that it is ethnic Israel that remains in view throughout the apostle's discussion in these chapters and that Israel's remnant plays an important role in it. But in our judgment Paul's discussion ultimately concerns not the remnant only but Israel as a people, and our assigned task now is to point out what we consider to be critical mistakes in his exposition. Rather than summarize what follows here in the introduction, we have subtitled the material, which begins and ends with reflections on the remnant.

Salvation for the Remnant Only?

It may be best to begin with Merkle's broad assertion: "In the OT it is clear that God never promises to save the majority of Israel, but he does promise to save a remnant" (p. 172). This is a surprising claim, for, as we have point out in our essay, the prophets plainly hold out exactly this promise in such passages as Jeremiah 24:5–7 and the new covenant prophecies of Jeremiah

31:31–37 and Ezekiel 16:60. After Isaiah was commissioned
to harden Israel (Isa. 6:9–10), through the rest of the book he
prophesies that the ears, eyes, and hearts the Lord used him to
shut will one day be opened (see Isa. 29:18; 30:21; 32:3–4; 35:5–
6; 42:7, 16, 18–20; 43:8; 44:1; 50:5). This reversal of the hardening points to more than the salvation of the remnant that was not
hardened. The OT prophets at points used terms and categories
from the old (Mosaic) covenant when they pointed forward to
the new covenant salvation. We don't have to maintain a literal
fulfillment of old covenant categories transcended by the new as
we look forward to the day when the hardening will be lifted. It
is difficult to understand expressions such as "they shall be my
people . . . they shall all know me, from the least of them to the
greatest" (Jer. 31:33–34) in any other way. The new covenant
promise very explicitly concerned more than the believing old
covenant remnant. And, in fact, the OT passages that Paul holds
in view in 11:26–27 (Isa. 27:9; 59:20–21; Jer. 31:31–34) speak
explicitly also of a time of conversion for all Israel, a turnaround
for blessing to Israel herself, corporately, following its time of
unfaithfulness. All this, as we have argued, grows out of Moses's
prophecy for Israel in Deuteronomy 32—that after her time of
judgment God will again bless his people Israel. This prophetic
expectation for Israel as a people is precisely what the apostle Paul
has in view when he claims that his hope for Israel's future is
grounded in the OT Scriptures.

The elect "remnant" within Israel does indeed play an
important role, and Merkle marshals evidence from 9:6–18
and 11:1–10 to demonstrate that Paul has this remnant in view.
We wholeheartedly agree. But Merkle wants this notion then
to control Paul's entire discussion throughout chapter 11. It is
critical to his position that we understand 11:1 and 11:11 as
asking the same question, and he demands that Paul's answer to
the first question (11:1) control his answer to the second question (11:11). But this is not at all self-evident, and the argument
loses force when we find indications in 11:11–27 that Paul's
argument develops and expands with Israel as a whole in view.

Romans 9:6 and the Rest of the Argument

In his treatment of Romans 9:6, Merkle very pointedly presents what he considers to be a problem for our position:

> This question represents a serious flaw in the future-mass-conversion view. All along Paul's main point has been that God is not, and has ever been, obligated to save every individual Israelite (Israel[1]) or even the majority of Israelites. He has promised to save only all those who receive his sovereign grace. To argue that God must save all (or the majority) of ethnic Jews at one period of time (because of his OT promises) is to claim something more than the apostle Paul argues. (p. 178)

Once again, we agree that this is all the apostle is arguing *at this point*. But we do not at all agree that the remainder of Paul's discussion must be controlled and limited by what he says here. Israel's future conversion is not "more than the apostle Paul argues" but precisely what he argues in the latter half of chapter 11. The majority of interpreters understand Paul's latter argument similarly, and in fact there are good reasons that the NIV translators render the question of 11:11 interpretively, "Did they stumble as to fall *beyond recovery*?" We can only review and highlight some of those reasons here.

- "The rest" (11:7, majority Israel) who are presently hardened seems to parallel the "they" and "their" of 11:11–12 who will be made jealous so as to be saved. That is to say, Paul's concern in 11:11–27 is to demonstrate that the "hardness" of "the rest" is not irrevocable or final.
- The "they" in v. 12 who will reach "full inclusion" are identified as majority Israel who are presently in unbelief.
- The inferential *oun* ("therefore") and the interrogative with which Paul begins each of these passages (11:1 and 11:11) seem to mark the beginning of new steps in Paul's argument, and the accompanying scriptural catenas

(11:8–10 and 11:26–27; cf. 9:25–29 and 10:18–21) seem to mark the respective conclusions.[1]

- In 11:23 Paul argues, "If they do not continue in their unbelief, [they] will be grafted in, for God has the power to graft them in *again*" (emphasis added). Merkle cautions us not to read too much into this and insists that it speaks only of what God *could* do, not what he *will* do. But one wonders, in this case, what purpose such a statement would serve? It contributes nothing to Paul's argument simply to affirm that God *could* save Israel but in fact may or may not. On the face of it the affirmation seems to look to what Paul says in 11:25–27, with the affirmation that all Israel will be saved in 11:26. Indeed, the metaphor of the natural branches being stripped away and then grafted in again seems on the face of it to describe Israel's temporary rejection and future restoration, not merely the continuous trickle of remnant salvation.

- Paul's lament and concern that give rise to this passage is that the majority of Israel has fallen into unbelief and therefore has forfeited the promised blessing. On the "remnant only" interpretation, this concern remains unanswered.

Again, it is for good reasons that the majority of interpreters have understood the questions of 11:1 and 11:11 as distinct. In v. 1 Paul asks, "Is Israel's failure *total*?"—hence the discussion of the remnant. In v. 11 he asks, "Is Israel's failure *final*?"—hence the discussion of future acceptance, fullness, re-grafting in, and deliverance.

Will the Hardening Be Lifted?

In 11:25 Paul affirms that Israel's hardening will continue only "until the fullness of the Gentiles has come in." It seems easi-

---

1. Jason C. Meyer, *The End of the Law: Mosaic Covenant in Pauline Theology*, NAC Studies in Bible and Theology 7 (Nashville: Broadman & Holman, 2009), 178n2; cf. James W. Aageson, "Scripture and Structure in the Development of the Argument in Romans 9–11," *CBQ* 48 (1986): 265–89.

est to understand this as affirming a reversal of Israel's present unbelief and rejection at the end of this age (v. 26, at the coming of Christ). Merkle argues, rather, "Paul is not suggesting a time when the hardening will be reversed but a time when the hardening will be eschatologically fulfilled." This would be an unusual understanding of "until," not only in this context, but in the NT broadly. Moo summarizes,

> The preposition ἀχρί occurs 48 times in the NT. . . . Eleven do not fall to consideration here because they involve a spatial rather than a temporal concept. Of the 37 remaining occurrences, 25 rather clearly denote a period of time that will come to an end and be followed by a change of those circumstances denoted (Luke 1:20; 4:13; Acts 1:12; 3:21; 7:18; 13:11; 20:6, 11; 22:22; 27:33; Rom. 1:13; 1 Cor. 11:26; 15:25; Gal. 3:19; 4:2; Phil. 1:6; Heb. 3:13; 6:11; Rev. 2:25, 26; 7:3; 15:8; 17:17; 20:3, 5). Significantly, 14 of these are followed by an aorist verb (as in Rom. 11:25), while only two of ten occurrences of ἀχρί where it means "right up to" use the aorist.[2]

That is, the understanding of "until" in v. 25 that is necessary to the remnant-only interpretation of this passage is unusual. As we have argued, in Romans 11 the apostle is describing a future turn-around for Israel, and the usual sense of "until" in v. 25 fits this understanding very well; indeed, it would seem to support it. The present hardness of Israel, despite the remnant (11:1–10), will finally be reversed (11:25–26). And this is in accordance with the prophetic expectation of Israel's future conversion (11:26–27; cf. Isa. 59:20–21; 27:9; Jer. 31:33–34).

The Meaning of Israel in 11:25–26

The position that Merkle supports also requires that we understand "Israel" in a different sense in vv. 25 and 26. In v. 25,

---

2. Douglas J. Moo, *The Epistle to the Romans*, NICNT (Grand Rapids: Eerdmans, 1996), 717n30.

according to Merkle, "Israel" refers to the entire Jewish nation, while in v. 26, "all Israel" refers only to the remnant. An understanding of "all Israel" as but a remnant in contrast to "Israel" as the whole nation strikes us as strained, and we think this would strike the average reader as unlikely also.

Objecting to our understanding of the meaning of Israel in 11:25 and 26, Merkle quotes Sam Storms to claim that we use Israel in two different ways: first, as "the ethnic nation as a whole during the inter-advent period," and second, as "one generation of ethnic Jews living at the time of the parousia." In response, we maintain that our interpretation is consistent with what Paul intended to communicate for two reasons. First, Paul's concern throughout Romans 11 is to contrast *ethnic* Gentiles with *ethnic* Israel. We hold that "Israel" refers to *ethnic* Israel in both 11:25 and 26. Second, on the restoration pertaining only to one generation of ethnic Israel, this would seem to be consistent with prophetic expectation. That is, Isaiah and Jeremiah, for instance, clearly expected those who suffered the destruction of Jerusalem and the exile to experience the curses of the covenant. As they prophesy about the new exodus and return from exile, the restoration pertains not to the generations that died under the curse but to the future generation that will experience the blessing. These prophecies include, however, promises of resurrection from the dead for past generations. Among the mysteries to be resolved by new covenant revelation are the questions of the relationship between the physical return to the land, the suffering of the Messiah, the inclusion of the Gentiles, the resurrection of the dead, and the return to (a new and better) Eden. In Romans 11, Paul is contributing to the new covenant revelation of the answer to these questions, explaining that the Messiah came, suffered, and was rejected by the Jews that the gospel might go to the Gentiles, but he will return to save Israel and raise the dead, and the King of glory will take his people through gates with uplifted heads, through the ancient doors, to Eden land.

The Pronouns in Romans 11:12

Merkle seeks to buttress his argument by suggesting an analogy to the way Paul distinguishes between the nation as a whole and the remnant within the nation in 9:6. The problem for this proposed analogy is that there is no indication in 11:25–26, as there is in 9:6, that Paul is using the term "Israel" in different ways. Merkle makes a similar move in his reading of the pronoun "their" in 11:12, as he claims that the first two instances of "their" in 11:12 refer to the nation as a whole, but the third instance of "their" refers only to the remnant. Consider the words of 11:12: "Now if their trespass means riches for the world, and if their failure means riches for the Gentiles, how much more will their full inclusion mean." Paul does not introduce a new subject after the second "their" to which the third "their" refers. What Merkle claims is simply not how pronouns work. Pronouns refer to an already identified noun. If an author means to distinguish between different groups, he will not designate them all with the plural pronoun "their" with no intervening nouns to which the pronouns refer. Any author wishing to distinguish between groups will refer to one, then name the other. As 11:12 and 11:25–26 stand, we need Merkle or someone who takes a view like his to tell us that Paul is using the pronouns and "Israel" to refer to different groups because Paul's own phrases make no such distinction. The authority of the asserted distinction depends on the interpreter who claims it, not on the manifest meaning of Paul's words.

Merkle's position depends on this understanding, but we think it fails to measure up to Paul's argument and language. This culminating point of the apostle's argument seems easier to understand, rather, in terms of the reversal of non-remnant Israel's unbelief and hardening that has been anticipated throughout the passage and in the prophets that Paul cites.

The First or Second Coming?

Verse 26 ("The Deliverer will come from Zion; he will banish ungodliness from Jacob") is easiest to understand in reference to the second coming of Christ. The prophecies that Paul has in view (Isa. 59:20 [cf. vv. 1–20]; Jer. 31:34 [cf. vv. 1–40]) entail Israel's eschatological hope that will finally be realized fully only when Christ returns. That this should be understood merely in reference to Christ's first coming is, in our judgment, not likely. Merkle claims that our view entails Paul referring to a heavenly Zion from which the Redeemer would come, whereas Isaiah referred to an earthly Zion. Note, however, that in Psalm 2:6 the Lord says he has installed his king "on Zion, my holy hill." In the very next psalm, David says in 3:4 that the Lord answered his prayer "from his [the Lord's] holy hill." Assuming Davidic authorship of Psalm 2 (see Acts 4:25), and following those who see the references to the Lord's holy hill in 2:6 and 3:4 as link-words joining these psalms,[3] the idea of Zion as a place not merely earthly but also heavenly was well established by Isaiah's time. Merkle further claims that the use of the term "deliverer" in Pauline texts that do not refer to the second coming indicates that here we should understand Paul to refer to the deliverance accomplished on the cross. Readers can judge for themselves whether in the context of Romans 11 Paul is discussing the cross in the past or the deliverance Christ will accomplish in the future at his return. The context in which a word like "deliverer" is used should inform our understanding of what deliverance is being referenced.

Too Much Special Pleading

As a broad summary assessment on an exegetical level, it is just these "unlikely" aspects of the remnant-only position that in our judgment leave it so difficult to accept. It is not a likely inter-pretation of the OT prophets that understands them as nowhere promising national conversion for Israel. It is not likely that Paul's affirmation that God is able to graft Israel in "again" means only that he could and not that he will. It is not likely that "until" has

---

3. See esp. Robert L. Cole, *Psalms 1–2: Gateway to the Psalter* (Sheffield: Sheffield Phoenix, 2013).

the significance Merkle gives it. It is not likely that "all Israel" indicates something less than "Israel" in the previous sentence. It is not likely that the prophecy of Israel's coming Deliverer is exhausted at Christ's first advent. And so on. In our judgment this position depends on too many improbable interpretations of critical points of Paul's discussion, and so, in the end, fails. The continued existence of the remnant among Israel is but one step to Paul's answer to the overall problem of Israel's failure. The second step is that Israel's current status will be reversed.

The Typology of Adam, Israel, Christ, and the Church

That reversal is necessary *both* for the fulfillment of God's promises *and* for a right understanding of the typological relationships between Adam, Israel, Jesus, and the church. The difficulty is that the promises are often communicated in relationship to metaphors that employ typological concepts and patterns. Here we want to address two related claims that Merkle makes. In a section titled "God Does Not Have a Special Plan for Israel That Excludes the Church" (p. 206), Merkle writes, "Some may claim that my view of typology, as it relates to Israel and Jesus, is inconsistent. That is, if Jesus fulfills all of the promises to ethnic Israel, how is it that Paul can also state that the promises to Israel are fulfilled by the Jewish remnant?" (p. 207). Earlier he writes, "If Israel is the *type*, then what is the *antitype*? *Jesus* is the antitype since he is the fulfillment of Israel" (p. 164). This kind of assertion works for some (but as will be shown below not all) aspects of the typology in the Bible.

For instance, Adam is God's son (Gen. 5:1–3; Luke 3:38), and later God identifies the nation of Israel as his son, a kind of corporate new Adam (Exod. 4:22–23). This sonship is still later granted to the king from David's line, whom God "begets" as a new Adam, the one who represents the many (2 Sam. 7:14; Ps. 2:7). When Jesus comes as the Son of God, he is the new Adam, the true Israel, the promised king from

David's line, the one who represents the many. In that sense, what Merkle says about Jesus being the antitype as the true Israel holds.

With other metaphors, however, the typological imagery is different. For example, the Sinai covenant is clearly treated as a marriage between Yahweh and Israel, the Lord referring to it in Jeremiah 31:32 with the words, "my covenant that they broke, though I was their husband." This same imagery informs Hosea 2, where the Lord says through Hosea in 2:2, "she is not my wife, and I am not her husband." Later in the chapter, the Lord asserts through Hosea, "I will betroth you to me forever. I will betroth you to me in righteousness and in justice, in steadfast love and in mercy. I will betroth you to me in faithfulness. And you shall know the LORD" (2:19–20). What is the Lord saying? In context, the assertion in 2:2 that the marriage is over means that the Sinai covenant is broken and the curses of the covenant will fall upon Israel (cf. Jer. 31:32). They will be exiled from the land. Hosea also prophesies, however, that Yahweh will save his people in the future as he saved them at the exodus from Egypt, and this is why I am referring to all this as typological. The pattern of the exodus, with the marriage covenant at Sinai, will be fulfilled at the new exodus, and that new exodus will come with a new marriage in the form of the new covenant, as Jeremiah refers to it in 31:31. With this imagery we cannot say that Jesus alone is the antitype because though he is of course the bridegroom who comes to initiate the new marriage covenant (Matt. 9:15; John 3:29), the metaphor works only if the bridegroom has a bride. Similar things can be said about the typology of the new exodus—if a *people* are not redeemed when "Christ, our Passover lamb, has been sacrificed" (1 Cor. 5:7), the correspondence to the exodus breaks down. That is to say, if Jesus is the antitype of the Passover lamb, the redeemed are the antitype of those who came out of Egypt. If Jesus is the antitype of the bridegroom in the covenant, the church is the antitype of the bride, the typological fulfillment of the nation of Israel in covenant with Yahweh at Sinai.

Further Reflections on the Remnant and Returns

What, then, of ethnic Israel? Here we can address two more of Merkle's claims. First, as noted above, Merkle asserts that the OT does not promise the future salvation of all Israel but only the remnant. Second, Merkle suggests that if only the end-time generation is saved, "It would in fact include only a small fraction of Jews, which is not as climactic as it might first appear." God did say that Israel would be left few in number (Lev. 26:22; Deut. 4:27; 28:62), but once again the nature of the promises can be brought to bear on these reflections. Adam and Eve were exiled from Eden, and the nation experienced the curses of the covenant in the form of exile from the land. The land was itself a kind of new Eden, and the prophets often spoke of return from exile as a return to Eden (e.g., Isa. 51:3; Ezek. 36:35). The book of Ezra narrates how the nation physically returned to the land, but only the coming of the Messiah opened the way to the return to Eden—the new heaven and new earth, where righteousness dwells. As we note in our essay, what Moses says in Deuteronomy 32:20–36 about making Israel jealous but not utterly wiping them out, vindicating them when their strength is gone, is exactly what Paul builds out in Romans 11.

As the prophets made the promises, it was always a future generation that would experience the fulfillments of the new exodus, new covenant, return from exile, and return to Eden. That is to say, some future generation alive once the exile was over would be the one that would be led by the new Moses, the new Joshua, the new David, the new Adam, into the new land. So the promises of ultimate restoration always pertained to the Jews who will be alive when the deliverer comes from Zion (Rom. 11:26).

As for previous generations, the prophetic word from Moses and those who followed him offered (and offers) them the opportunity to repent, believe, and hope for the resurrection from the dead (Deut. 32:39). Yes, Isaiah in particular promises salvation to the remnant, but that remnant would consist of those who survived the devastation Yahweh would visit in the curses of the covenant and the destruction of the nation.

The remnant remains; the others have perished in judgment. All living Israelites would be reckoned as remnant, and all living Israelites would be expected to be saved because, as noted above, Jeremiah said they would all know God (Jer. 31:34), and Joel said they would all prophesy (Joel 2:28–29).

What of the relationship between these promises and the Gentiles? Paul explains in Romans 11:30 that there was a time when the Gentiles were disobedient, and he appears to have in mind the time of the old covenant, when God was in covenant with Israel alone among the nations. Now, however, because of Israel's disobedience in their rejection of the gospel, the Gentiles have received mercy, but this is so that the Jews might receive mercy (11:31) once "the fullness of the Gentiles has come in" (11:25).

In the church, Jews and Gentiles are one new man in Christ (Eph. 2:15), and yet the kinds of things Paul addresses in Romans 14 (and 11:17–24!) persist. Furthermore, as Paul explains in 11:25–32, under the old covenant God showed mercy to Israel, but he hardened them (Isa. 6:9–13; cf. Deut. 29:4, 18–20) and brought an end to that covenant. That hardening continued through the ministry of Jesus (Isa. 6:9–12 is quoted in all four Gospels—Matt. 13:14–15; Mark 4:12; Luke 8:10; John 12:39–40) and remained on Israel through Paul's time (Acts 28:26–27). Apparently because some Jews did believe in Jesus, Paul refers to this hardening as partial in Romans 11:25, but the hardening that resulted in exile remains on Israel. Once God has lavished all the mercy he has planned for the Gentiles, he will turn and again show mercy to Israel (11:25–27, 31). Moses's response to this plan in Deuteronomy 29:29 is not unlike Paul's in Romans 11:33–36: the secret things belong to the Lord our God; what is revealed is given to us that we might obey, and God's wisdom is unsearchable and inscrutable. He owes no one. All is from, through, and to him. To him be glory forever. Amen.

CONCLUSION

Jared Compton

Before concluding with a synthesis of our authors' agreements and disagreements, let me first take a step back and say something once again about what this book is trying to do.

1. Framing Our Authors' Arguments

The idea for this book grew out of a seminar on biblical theology I led a few years back at Detroit Baptist Theological Seminary. In the seminar I had students read Peter Gentry and Stephen Wellum's book *Kingdom through Covenant*,[1] which argues for a fresh way of putting the Bible together (*progressive covenantalism*) and, especially, of understanding the relationship between Israel and the church. One of the ways we tried to evaluate their thesis was by putting it into conversation with a handful of relevant NT texts since the book deals primarily with the OT.[2] One of these NT texts was Romans 9–11. It was during our discussion of this text that I was reminded about just how central Romans 9–11 is for putting the Bible together.

---

1. Peter J. Gentry and Stephen J. Wellum, *Kingdom through Covenant: A Biblical-Theological Understanding of the Covenants* (Wheaton, IL: Crossway, 2012).

2. This isn't a slight against Gentry and Wellum's book, which is nearly 800 pages and, as well, admittedly provisional (see, e.g., Wellum's note about his theological syntheses on p. 716). For a fuller extension of their thesis into the NT, see Stephen J. Wellum and Brent Parker, eds., *Progressive Covenantalism: Charting a Course between Dispensational and Covenant Theologies* (Nashville: Broadman & Holman, 2016).

Paul in this text *explicitly* reflects on the relationship between Israel and the church to show how what God is presently doing in salvation history fits with what he promised. In other words, Paul is doing in Romans 9–11 the same sort of thing Gentry and Wellum are doing in their book—showing how the Bible fits together. He's doing *biblical theology*.[3]

The exercise of putting Gentry and Wellum's thesis in conversation with Paul got me thinking about how helpful it would be to have biblical theologians from various perspectives do the same thing. What would happen if each looked afresh at what Paul says in Romans 9–11 and then reflected on what Paul's argument implies about biblical theology? A "views" book seemed the best format since these, at their very best, prevent authors from talking past one another. And having these authors focus specifically on Romans 9–11 instead of, for example, Israel's place in the Bible's storyline would give each author's essay a helpful constraining focus. Moreover, I had just read Russell Moore's book on the kingdom,[4] which talks about the narrowing chasm between the old, entrenched biblical-theologies within evangelicalism and about the growing consensus that is emerging. And, I admit, I hoped that a book like this—with this format and focus—would further that consensus, even if marginally.

With Andy Naselli's help, we carved out the "views" we wanted to see represented and contacted our prospective authors. We intended to have someone argue that Paul anticipates in Romans 9–11 the salvation and the restoration of Israel—the *nation* of Israel, which, we thought, would lead to the conclusion that Israel's role in biblical theology is *non-typological*.[5] Israel, in other words, was not a type because Israel, rather than the church or Jesus, is still the referent of OT promises predicting Israel's salvation and restoration (i.e., restoration

---

3. For a definition of this discipline, take a look at Andy's introduction, p. 15n7.
4. Russell D. Moore, *The Kingdom of Christ: The New Evangelical Perspective* (Wheaton, IL: Crossway, 2004).
5. For a definition of typology, see Andy's introduction, p. 15n8.

to a specific place and role). We thought we would need a traditional dispensationalist for this view.

We also intended to have someone who would argue that when Paul talks about the salvation of Israel in Romans 9–11, he is talking about the salvation of the *new* Israel, the church, composed of Jews and Gentiles, which occurs not at Jesus's return but throughout the present era. This sort of conclusion would imply that Paul views Israel's role *typologically*, since the church—or perhaps Jesus and by extension the church—is the true referent of OT predictions about Israel. For this one, we anticipated needing an amillennialist or a traditional proponent of covenant theology.

Finally, we also intended to have someone do what middle views in three-views books invariably do—carve out a *via media* between the polarities created by the first and third views. Here we wanted someone to argue that while Paul anticipates the salvation of Israel—understood to refer to ethnically Jewish people—he does not anticipate the restoration of the nation. On this reading, therefore, Paul would view Israel's role in biblical theology—at least certain promises about Israel's restoration—typologically, but Paul would also view Israel—for reasons we were eager to discover—as maintaining something of a "special status." Here we thought someone representing Gentry and Wellum's progressive covenantalism would work well. After all, George Ladd was not available.

As astute readers will quickly recognize, the views represented in our book do not precisely line up with this planned taxonomy. Michael Vlach is perhaps the closest. Fred Zaspel and Jim Hamilton do carve out a middle way, though it is not precisely the middle way of *Kingdom through Covenant*.[6] And

---

6. Zaspel and Hamilton, e.g., argue that Romans 9–11 suggests that Jews in the church are referents of OT promises that Gentiles in the church are not (i.e., corporate salvation). This implies a less typological understanding of Israel than is found in progressive covenantalism. Cf., e.g., Brent Parker, who asks, "How Jewish Christians can be recipients of OT . . . promises apart from Gentile Christians . . . is confounded by the fact that *all* believers have their identity in Christ . . . and *all* the promises and the inheritance are theirs through him"

Ben Merkle blew up our taxonomy, with his dual insistence that Israel is a type of Christ (and the church) *and* that Romans 9–11 anticipates the salvation of a lot of ethnic Jews, referring to these Jews with the term *Israel*. Merkle's view, however, ended up giving us the best elements of the view we had originally intended as the "third view" without, in our opinion, that view's implausibilies, specifically, that Paul uses "Israel" in Romans 9–11 to refer to Jews *and* Gentiles. Merkle, in other words, still argues against a future mass-conversion of Israel, while at the same time for the persistent salvation of a remnant of *Jewish* people throughout the present era.

I say all this simply to remind our readers about what this book is trying to do and to explain why we have gone about it the way we have. This book explores the way one apostle puts his Bible together. And it does this by putting authors with different biblical theologies in conversation with this apostle *and* each other. Our aim all along has been clarity and consensus. We wanted to gain clarity about the precise nature of our authors' disagreements about Romans 9–11 and about what these disagreements imply for their differing biblical theologies. We also hoped that some new consensus might emerge through the exercise. I think we have achieved the clarity we

---

("The Israel-Christ-Church Relationship," in *Progressive Covenantalism: Charting a Course between Dispensational and Covenant Theologies*, ed. Stephen J. Wellum and Brent Parker [Nashville: Broadman & Holman, 2016], 63–64). I have edited Parker's claim (removing "nationalistic" and "in a future millennial age"), but, nevertheless, preserved his point and, in doing so, have highlighted the difference in approaches. For another difference, this one perhaps less significant, compare Zaspel and Hamilton's claim that Paul's "olive tree" (Rom. 11:17–24) refers, at least at this point in salvation history, to the church ("Response to Vlach," p. 82) and, e.g., Richard Lucas's, who suggests it is "Israel itself"—the "spiritual Israel within Israel" ("The Dispensational Appeal to Romans 11 and the Nature of Israel's Future Salvation," in *Progressive Covenantalism: Charting a Course between Dispensational and Covenant Theologies*, ed. Stephen J. Wellum and Brent Parker [Nashville: Broadman & Holman, 2016], 253, citing Doug Moo, "Paul's Universalizing Hermeneutic in Romans," *The Southern Baptist Journal of Theology* 11, no. 3 [2007]: 77). Interestingly, Merkle's view of typology, which he suggests "differ[s] at points" from Zaspel and Hamilton's ("Response to Zaspel and Hamilton," p. 151n1), may actually be slightly closer to progressive covenantalism's (see Merkle, "Essay," e.g., p. 163).

were aiming for, but I am not as confident we achieved any new consensus. The success of that aim will have to rest on our authors and, specifically, on how persuasive our readers find their individual essays.

2. Synthesizing Our Authors' Arguments

This synthesis highlights how our authors agree and (especially) disagree. And it pays special attention to the arguments underlying the disagreements. Here and there, moreover, I raise issues and questions deserving further thought, drawing upon the response essays.[7] We begin with what our authors say about Paul's argument in Romans 9–11 and then turn to what each suggests this implies about how Paul does biblical theology.

2.1. What Paul Says about Israel in Romans 9–11

2.1.1. Agreement

Each of our authors agrees that when Paul talks about Israel in Romans 9–11, he is talking about Jews not Gentiles, nor even Jews *and* Gentiles.[8] That is not to say, of course, that our authors think Paul *always* uses Israel this way. Merkle, for example, thinks Paul uses "Israel of God" in Galatians 6:16 to refer to Jews and Gentiles.[9] The point is simply that none of this book's authors thinks that is what is happening in Romans 9–11. Moreover, each agrees that when Paul talks about Israel's salvation (e.g., 11:26), he is referring to Jews believing in Jesus. Added to this, each agrees that the basis for Paul's claim is the OT, specifically promises God made to Israel in the OT.

---

7. I will draw upon the response essays especially when they raise new questions or give additional evidence beyond that found elsewhere in the book (i.e., in the responding author[s]'s original essay).
8. See, e.g., Vlach, "Essay," pp. 26, 55, 68; Zaspel and Hamilton, "Essay," p. 121; Merkle, "Essay," pp. 167 and 196.
9. Merkle, "Essay," p. 167n16. Cf., however, Vlach's opposite conclusion, "Essay," p. 31n15, along with Zaspel and Hamilton's discussion, "Response to Vlach," p. 78n1.

Granted, none points to exactly the same OT texts.[10] Nevertheless, each agrees that Paul's argument for God's faithfulness in Romans 9–11 *hinges* on Israel remaining the referent of certain OT promises.

It is at this point, however, that we begin to see our authors part ways, both in their understanding of the nature of those OT promises and in their understanding of Paul's argument.

2.1.2. *Disagreement about the Nature of Old Testament Promises*
Merkle argues that the OT does not promise anything beyond God's continued preservation of a remnant within Israel. Merkle does insist, however, that this remnant, while contrasted with the whole nation, will not be small. He makes this claim by appealing to Isaiah 11:11–12, 16, Isaiah 37:31–32, and Micah 2:12, 4:7.[11]

In contrast, Vlach and Zaspel and Hamilton argue that the OT promises that God will save all of Israel—viewed corporately—and not simply a remnant *within* Israel. For proof, they point to many of the same texts, including Deuteronomy 30:1–10, Isaiah 27:9, Isaiah 59:20–21, and Jeremiah 31:31–34. It is interesting at this point to note that Zaspel and Hamilton also point to the texts Merkle cites above, not to prove that the remnant will be a certain size (large) but, rather, to prove that the remnant anticipates God will save Israel *as a whole*.[12] In other words, both see the same texts anticipating a sizeable number of Jewish believers. Merkle sees a large number of Jews *constituting* the remnant; Zaspel and Hamilton see a group *in addition to* the remnant.[13] Whether there is an actual numerical difference between the two conclusions is an open question.

2.1.3. *Disagreement about the Nature of Paul's Argument*
Our authors' disagreements over Paul's argument center almost entirely on Romans 11:11–31, specifically whether Paul's argu-

---

10. See below for some of the specific texts each appeals to.
11. Merkle, "Essay", p. 204n120.
12. Zaspel and Hamilton, "Essay," p. 125.
13. Zaspel and Hamilton, "Essay," p. 175.

ment advances beyond the claim that God's faithfulness to his word is proven by his preservation of a Jewish remnant (cf. Rom. 9:1–11:10). Merkle insists it does not; Vlach and Zaspel and Hamilton insist it does.

Merkle: *Paul argues for the salvation of a remnant.* Merkle's claims about Romans 11:11–31 turn on how he understands Paul's argument in Romans 9:6. If, as he puts it, "11:26 is the key verse" for our book's debate, then "9:6 is the key to correctly understanding 11:26."[14] In 9:6 Paul argues that God never promised to save Israel in its entirety; therefore, were Paul to turn around in 11:11–31 and affirm God had promised to save Israel in its entirety, Paul would flatly contradict himself.[15]

Beyond this, Merkle makes the following arguments to support his reading that Israel's salvation in Romans 9–11 refers to God's continual preservation of a remnant *within* Israel and not to the future salvation of Israel in its entirety.

(1) *Romans 11.* Paul focuses on what is happening to Israel now, which pushes against the future-mass-conversion view. Paul speaks of his own salvation (11:1), the present remnant (11:5), his present ministry to Israel (11:13–14), and Israel's present experience of mercy (11:30–31).[16]

(2) *Romans 11:1, 11.* The question in Romans 11:11 recapitulates the question in 11:1. In both cases, Paul's answer is essentially the same—namely, "There is still a remnant of believing Jews, and there will always be such until Christ returns."[17]

---

14. Merkle, "Essay," pp. 169 and 175 (respectively).
15. "If Paul's point is that God is not, and has ever been, obligated to save every individual Israelite (or even the majority of Israelites), but only those he elects according to sovereign grace, how is it consistent to also maintain that God will (indeed must) also save all (or the majority) of ethnic Jews in the future" (Merkle, "Response to Zaspel and Hamilton," p. 153).
16. Merkle, "Essay," pp. 181.
17. Merkle, "Essay," p. 180, incl. 180n42.

(3) *Romans 11:12, 15*. Both verses refer to the full salvation of the remnant ("fullness" and "acceptance"), not to Israel in its entirety. Plus, since "fullness" in 11:25 refers to the salvation of "the full number of elect Gentiles throughout history," as most admit, why could it not connote the same thing about Israel in v. 12?[18]

Zaspel and Hamilton raise an interesting point, however, when they complain that Merkle's reading requires that the third reference to Israel in Romans 11:12 has a different referent (i.e., the remnant [Israel²]) than the previous two (i.e., Israel corporately [Israel¹]) and that it does this without any textual warrant. Merkle's reading: "Now if their [Israel¹] trespass means riches for the world, and if their [Israel¹] failure means riches for the Gentiles, how much more will their [Israel²] full inclusion mean."[19] Zaspel and Hamilton insist that this "simply is not how pronouns work." Rather, "if an author means to distinguish between different groups, he will not designate them all with the plural pronoun 'their' with no intervening nouns to which the pronouns refer."[20]

(4) *Romans 11:23–24*. The "re-grafting" of Israel—"the natural branches"—into its own tree describes the present and continuing salvation of the Jewish remnant.[21]

(5) *Romans 11:25–26a*. Paul refers to Israel's partial—not temporary—hardening, which terminates, but is not reversed, when the fullness of the Gentiles comes in. And it is in this manner—by the remnant's salvation throughout this new era prompted by Gentile salvation—that God will save all the elect within Israel. Paul, moreover, refers to this whole process—this "strange interdependence of the salvation of Israel and that of the gentiles"—as

---

18.   Merkle, "Essay," p. 190.
19.   Merkle, "Essay," p. 189.
20.   Zaspel and Hamilton, "Response to Merkle," p. 229.
21.   Merkle, "Essay," p. 192.

a "mystery."[22] Moreover, "Israel" changes referents from v. 25 to v. 26 (from unbelieving to believing Israel) in the same way that "Israel" changes referents in 9:6 (from all Israel to the elect within Israel).[23] Zaspel and Hamilton respond to this last assertion, insisting that while Paul indicates this change of referents in 9:6, he does not do the same thing here.[24]

(6) *Romans 11:26b–27.* When Paul cites Isaiah, he refers to Jesus's first advent, not his second, and therefore connects Israel's salvation in 11:26 with the present and not with the future.[25]

Vlach and Zaspel and Hamilton: *Paul argues for the salvation of all Israel.* Vlach, as well as Zaspel and Hamilton, insist that Paul's argument in Romans 11:11–31 advances beyond the discussion of the remnant's salvation in Romans 9:1–11:10. They argue that in these verses Paul describes the future salvation of all Israel. Their reading rests on the following lines of evidence.[26]

(1) *Romans 9–11.* The issue in Romans 9–11 is why only a remnant has believed, but Israel, as a whole, has not. Therefore, "merely to affirm the salvation of the remnant would leave" this larger problem "unanswered."[27]

(2) *Romans 11:1, 11.* These verses ask slightly different questions. Verse 1 asks whether Israel's present rejection is total, and

---

22. Merkle, "Essay," p. 194, citing Herman Ridderbos, *Paul: An Outline of His Theology*, trans. John R. De Witt (Grand Rapids: Eerdmans, 1975), 359–60; see also Merkle, "Essay," pp. 184–189.

23. Merkle, "Essay," pp. 194–197. Here we should probably add Merkle's remark that if 11:25–26 implies a sequence of events, beginning with Gentile salvation and concluding with Jewish salvation, then this suggests a time when Israel can be saved but Gentiles cannot be (Merkle, "Essay," p. 187).

24. Zaspel and Hamilton, "Response to Merkle," p. 227.

25. Merkle, "Essay," pp. 197–199.

26. Here I simply combine the evidence from Vlach's and Zaspel and Hamilton's essays, since each argues for this same point. The notes show the provenance of each claim, including those places where the essays overlap.

27. Zaspel and Hamilton, "Essay," p. 124; see also their "Response to Merkle," p. 225.

v. 11 asks whether it is temporary.[28] Moreover, there are literary clues that suggest v. 11 advances, rather than recapitulates,
the line of reasoning begun in v. 1. Paul begins v. 11 with *oun*,
which in at least two other places in Romans 9–11 signals the
beginning of a new section (9:30; 11:1). Added to this, Paul
concludes sections of his argument in at least two other places
in Romans 9–11 by citing the OT (9:25–29; 10:18–21). This
may suggest, therefore, that he intends to do the same with the
OT citations in 11:8–10 and 11:26b–27.[29]

(3) *Romans 11:12, 15.* "Fullness" and "acceptance" (along with
the "all" in v. 26) refer to the salvation of Jews who are not part
of the remnant, not simply to the expansion of the remnant.
This distinction between the remnant and the rest ("their" in
vv. 12 and 15) is signaled earlier in the "rest" (v. 7) who are
hardened (cf. "transgression" and "rejection" in vv. 12 and 15)
over against the remnant of "the present time" who are not (v.
5).[30] Thus, vv. 12 and 15 suggest that God will reverse present
circumstances: a time will come when the "rest" will believe,
and therefore "*all* Israel will be saved."

(4) *Romans 11:16.* The holiness of "the whole batch" and
"branches" implies and anticipates the salvation of Israel corporately, especially if, as Vlach argues, the "firstfruits" (of dough)
refers to the remnant.[31]

(5) *Romans 11:17–24.* Those branches that are "broken off" and
"re-grafted" refer not to the salvation of the remnant but to the

---

28. Zaspel and Hamilton, "Essay," p. 108.
29. Zaspel and Hamilton, "Essay," p. 109; see also their "Response to Merkle," p. 226.
30. Zaspel and Hamilton, "Essay," pp. 124; see also their "Response to Merkle," p. 225; Vlach, "Essay," pp. 40–43. (I confess that I am not sure I am able to completely distinguish between Zaspel and Hamilton's third and fifth arguments on pp. 124–126.)
31. Vlach, "Essay," p. 44; Zaspel and Hamilton, "Essay," p. 113, who say the "firstfruits" is the patriarchs.

salvation of that part of Israel that has presently been hardened (cf. v. 7) in contrast to the remnant.[32]

(6) *Romans 11:25–26a*. "Mystery" refers to the manner of Israel's salvation: Gentiles and remnant now, Israel as a whole later.[33] "Israel" in both verses has the same referent—corporate Israel.[34] "Until" implies Israel's present hardening will be undone—reversed—in the future.[35] *Houtōs* is modal ("in this way"), but it implies a temporal sequence since the "way" it describes involves Israel's future salvation *following* Israel's present hardening (and Gentile salvation).[36]

(7) *Romans 11:26b–27*. When Paul cites Isaiah, he refers to Jesus's return, which connects Israel's salvation in v. 26a with a still-future event.[37] Isaiah's reference to Jesus's "turn[ing] godlessness away from Jacob," moreover, refers to the actual (and immediate) application of Jesus's death and not simply to its accomplishment (or provision) and progressively realized application.[38] And Isaiah's reference to "Jacob" refers to Israel corporately since this is its common referent in the Psalms and Prophets. Jacob, in fact, is sometimes *contrasted* with the remnant.[39]

(8) *Romans 11:28*. The "enemies" who are also "loved" refer to that part of Israel that is presently hardened but will one day be saved.[40]

---

32. Vlach, "Essay," pp. 47–47; Zaspel and Hamilton, "Essay," p. 128; see also their "Response to Merkle," p. 226.
33. Zaspel and Hamilton, "Essay," p. 126.
34. Zaspel and Hamilton, "Essay," pp. 126–127; Vlach, "Response to Merkle," p. 220.
35. Vlach, "Essay," pp. 49–53; Zaspel and Hamilton, "Essay, pp. 119–121.
36. Vlach, "Essay," pp. 52–54.
37. Zaspel and Hamilton, "Essay, pp. 120–121; cf. also Vlach, "Essay," pp. 55–57.
38. Vlach, "Response to Merkle," p. 219, who sees something similar to what Isaiah describes in Zechariah 13:1–6.
39. Zaspel and Hamilton, "Essay," p. 128.
40. Zaspel and Hamilton, "Essay," p. 129; Vlach, "Essay," pp. 59–60.

(9) *Romans 11:30–31*. These verses refer to a historical process, moving from Israel's present disobedience to its future reception of mercy.[41]

Vlach: *Paul also argues for the restoration of all Israel.* Vlach goes a step further than Zaspel and Hamilton, arguing that both the OT and Romans 9–11 anticipate Israel's salvation *and restoration*. By "restoration" Vlach principally means the restoration of Israel's "vocational role to [bless] the nations."[42] Vlach's argument rests on the following evidence.

(1) *Old Testament*. The same OT texts that anticipate Israel's salvation also anticipate Israel's restoration (see Deut. 30:1–10; Lev. 26:40–45; Isa. 2:2–4; et al.).[43]

(2) *Romans 9:4–5*. The OT "covenants" and "promises" that Paul says continue to belong to Israel include, among other things, Israel's vocational role to the nations and Israel's land.[44]

(3) *Romans 11:12, 15*. "Fullness" refers not simply to Israel's salvation but to Israel's experience of "everything God intended Israel to be" (qualitative not quantitative, with special reference to Israel's vocational role),[45] something evidenced by the beneficial effect of Israel's fullness on the world ("much greater riches," v. 12; "life from the dead," v. 15).[46] The same definition applies to Gentile fullness in 11:25.

Merkle raises a problem with how Vlach defines "fullness" in v. 25 and, therefore, by implication in v. 12. What does it

---

41. Cf. Zaspel and Hamilton, "Essay," p. 129, who do not comment on the second *nun* in v. 31, with Vlach, who notes that if original the second *nun* refers to Israel's "imminent" reception of mercy ("Essay," pp. 61–62; see also his "Response to Merkle," p. 219).
42. Vlach, "Essay," p. 29; see also pp. 61 and 68–70.
43. Vlach, "Essay," p. 29.
44. Vlach, "Essay," pp. 28–29.
45. Vlach, "Essay," p. 69.
46. Vlach, "Essay," p. 69.

mean, he wonders, to talk about "fullness" in this qualitative sense "coming in" (v. 25)?[47]

(4) *Romans 11:26b–27.* Paul cites OT texts that in context refer not simply to Israel's salvation but also to Israel's restoration.[48] And if Paul anticipates the straightforward fulfillment of the one, why not the other?[49]

(5) *Romans 11:29.* The "gifts" and "call" that are "irrevocable" refer, respectively, to Israel's promises and covenants in 9:4–5 and to Israel's vocational role to the nations.[50]

2.2. What Paul's Argument Implies about Israel's Role in Biblical Theology

So what does all this imply for Israel's role in biblical theology? None of our authors concludes that Israel is a type, at least in the same way that the Levitical priesthood is a type. Paul's argument, with its insistence on the necessary salvation of Jews in fulfillment of OT promises, simply will not allow for this. Two of our essays, however, do insist that Israel is a kind of type, though in a sense that allows for both typological fulfillment (i.e., in Jesus or the church) and more straightforward fulfillment (i.e., by Israel itself).[51]

2.2.1. Vlach: Israel Is Not a Type

Vlach does not think Israel should be called a type of the church since, according to his understanding of typology, this would suggest the church has taken Israel's place.[52] Vlach acknowl-

---

47. Merkle, "Response to Vlach," pp. 91–92.
48. Vlach, "Essay," p. 68.
49. Vlach, "Essay," p. 70.
50. Vlach, "Essay," p. 69–69.
51. NB: Vlach admits that there are "typological connections . . . between national Israel and Jesus" while still calling his approach "non-typological" ("Response to Merkle," p. 212).
52. Vlach, "Essay," pp. 22–23; see also pp. 63 and 71. And see Vlach's citation of Karlberg: "If one grants that national Israel in OT revelation was truly a

edges that there are "correspondences" between Israel and the
church, but he insists these do not imply that the church has
superseded Israel.[53] Vlach considers the present remnant—
"believing Israelites"—as part of the church and as part of Israel.[54] Upon Jesus's return, Vlach argues, Israel as a nation will
be saved and incorporated into the people of God *alongside* not
within the church.[55] Also, as we have already noted above, Vlach
argues that once Israel is saved, the nation will be restored to its
role as a "vehicle for universal blessings."[56]

Vlach also concludes that Jesus is the "true" or "ultimate"
Israelite, but Jesus's status does not make Israel "irrelevant."[57]
By this he means that Jesus represents Israel; he does not replace
Israel. Jesus represents Israel by taking on the guilt incurred by
Israel's failure in order to save and restore Israel "to be every-
thing God intended" the nation to be.[58] Jesus is the means
of securing promises made to Israel, while Israel remains the
referent of those promises.[59]

One question I have about Vlach's view is why Israel's
future inclusion into the people of God must be alongside and
not within the church, especially considering the status of the
presently existing Jewish remnant within the church (i.e., part
of Israel *and* part of the church). It seems to me to be a short step
from recognizing the existence of natural and wild branches
within the church—of *Israelites* within the church—to the exis-

---

type of the eternal kingdom of Christ, then it seems that, according to the canons
of Biblical typology, national Israel can no longer retain any independent status
whatever" (Mark W. Karlberg, "The Significance of Israel in Biblical Typology,"
JETS 31, [1988]: 259, cited in Vlach, "Essay," p. 22n2). Vlach indicates in
another place, however, that not all types work this way. He says, "*In some cases,*
once the NT antitype or reality arrives, the OT type fades away in significance"
("Response to Zaspel and Hamilton," p. 145, emphasis added).

53. Vlach, "Essay," pp. 68–68.
54. Vlach, "Essay," p. 71: "Believing Israelites are still identified with Israel (11:1–
    6) as they participate in Jesus's church."
55. Cf. Vlach, "Essay," p. 70.
56. Vlach, "Essay," p. 68.
57. Vlach, "Essay," pp. 23, 64, 67
58. Vlach, "Response to Merkle," p. 212; Vlach, "Essay," p. 68.
59. Cf. Vlach, "Response to Merkle," pp. 212–213.

tence of natural and wild *nations* within the church—of restored *Israel* within the church, not least considering John's description of nations in the new creation (Rev. 21:24, 26; 22:2).[60]

2.2.2. Merkle: Israel Is a Type

At the other end of the spectrum is Merkle. Merkle insists that Israel is a type of Jesus. As he puts it, "Jesus is the 'true Israel' because he fulfills (typologically) all that the nation of Israel was to accomplish *as well as all that they hoped for and anticipated.*"[61] And again, "all [the promises to Israel] are fulfilled in Jesus the Messiah, the perfect Israelite."[62] In light of this, Merkle notes that the church "is not the replacement of Israel."[63] Rather, the church has "access" to Israel's promises "only because of [its] union with Christ."[64] Or as he puts it elsewhere, "God *incorporates* the church into his people through [the church's] union with Christ."[65]

---

60. Along this same line, it seems to me that the Jewish remnant's role, along with the church's generally, of being "God's instrument for worldwide gospel proclamation" (Vlach, "Essay," p. 70) is not all that far from Israel's role, as Vlach conceives of it, once restored—that is, of being an "instrument for worldwide blessings" (ibid., p. 64). Could this further blur the distinction Vlach makes between Israel now (in the church) and Israel later (alongside the church)? I also wonder why Israel's role couldn't be typological (i.e., fulfilled by Jesus; cf. Isa. 49:6; see Vlach, "Essay," pp. 67–69), even while Israel's salvation is not. Perhaps Romans 11:12 and 15 do not refer so much to what *Israel* does for the world but to what Jesus does for the world *when* he fully saves Israel.

61. Merkle, "Essay," p. 164, emphasis added.

62. Merkle, "Essay," p. 167. See also, "Christ was the promised Messiah and . . . he fulfills what God promised in the Old Testament to ethnic Israel" (p. 200); "If we interpret the many OT restoration prophecies regarding the nation of Israel literalistically, then such prophecies do not find their fulfillment in God's greatest work" (i.e., Christ; p. 202); "'All the promises of God find their Yes in him' (2 Cor. 1:20). Jesus fulfills OT prophecy by embodying and completing the expectations of the nation of Israel" (p. 203); "In one sense, then, God gave the new covenant to the house of Israel and the house of Judah because Christ fulfilled it" (p. 203; the "other sense" may refer, e.g., to Merkle's earlier insistence that Christ "is the one who secures the new covenant benefits for his people," p. 167); and, finally, "Christ, the perfect representative Israelite, fulfills what God originally prophesied to a single nation" (p. 203).

63. Merkle, "Essay," p. 165.

64. Merkle, "Essay," p. 203.

65. Merkle, "Essay," pp. 205–205, emphasis original.

Merkle says all this while at the same time arguing, as we have seen, that God still *must* save ethnic Jews if he is to be faithful to his OT promises. In other words, Merkle argues that *Jews*—the *type*—remain the referent to at least some OT promises.[66] Thus, after noting Paul's citation of Isaiah 10:22–23 in Romans 9:27–28, Merkle writes, "In the Old Testament it is clear that God never promises to save the majority of Israel, but he does promise to save a remnant."[67] Merkle, in other words, suggests that Jews—beyond Jesus—are the intended referent of Isaiah's promise and that God's faithfulness in Romans 9–11 is proved by his faithfulness to this very promise. As he puts it, "If God made promises to the people of Israel but did not deliver on those promises, what kind of assurance do believers have regarding his promises to them?"[68]

One wonders if Merkle can indeed affirm both. Can he affirm that Jesus fulfills all that Israel "hoped for and anticipated" *and* that the remnant fulfills at least some of what Israel hoped for? Merkle acknowledges the tension: "Jesus is the fulfillment of certain OT promises to Israel, *and* Israel has a unique place in salvation history."[69] Perhaps we might have expected the second half of that sentence simply to say, "*and* Israel is the fulfillment of certain OT promises," not least considering Merkle's earlier comments about what God's faithfulness required (i.e., to preserve Jews *beyond* Jesus).

It is at this point that I think Zaspel and Hamilton's response to Merkle could be especially helpful. They draw attention to the fact that Israel can be in different kinds of typological relationships with Jesus. They give, on the one

---

66. Merkle, "Essay," p. 204n120.
67. Merkle, "Essay," p. 172. See also later, "God never promised to save every ethnic Jew but only an elect remnant" (p. 177) and "God's promises attain fulfillment not in the nation as such (that is, all of ethnic Israel) but rather in the remnant according to the election of grace" (p. 177, citing Charles Horne, "The Meaning of the Phrase 'And Thus All Israel Will Be Saved' [Romans 11:26]," *JETS* 21 [1978]: 333).
68. Merkle, "Essay," p. 170.
69. Merkle, "Essay," p. 207, emphasis original.

hand, the example of Jesus fulfilling the typological trajectory of "the son of God," which Adam, Israel, and David partici-pate in. "In [this] sense," they conclude, "what [Merkle] says about Jesus being the antitype as the true Israel holds."[70] On the other hand, they give the example of the typology of the marriage between YHWH and Israel, where Jesus is not the antitype of Israel; rather, he is the antitypical bride-groom, which suggests there is still room for (i.e., Jesus has not replaced) the bride.[71] This suggests, perhaps, a more plau-sible way for Merkle to affirm an Israel–Jesus typology and still preserve his exegesis of Romans 9–11. That is, Jesus is the antitype of Israel, at least in the ways that Zaspel and Hamil-ton (and, indeed, Vlach) affirm, without his being the referent to the OT promises of Israel's future salvation.

2.2.3. Zaspel and Hamilton: Israel Is and Is Not a Type

In the middle of the spectrum are Zaspel and Hamilton. So we are not surprised they argue that Israel is *and* is not a type of the church. Paul, they say, "understands Israel and the church as related typologically . . . and he *also* argues for Israel's yet-future blessing on OT grounds."[72] After all, "typological fulfill-ments"—in this case Israel and the church—"do not imply that the implications of the promises God has made . . . have been exhausted."[73] This, they argue, allows them to take on board all the connections the NT makes between Israel and the church,[74] while still recognizing the place Paul gives Israel in his argu-ment in Romans 9–11.

---

70. Zaspel and Hamilton, "Response to Merkle," p. 232.
71. In Zaspel and Hamilton's response, the bride is the church; so Israel is still, in some sense, replaced. But this need not dull the more general point that Jesus sustains different kinds of typological relationships with Israel. Thus, it is possible to imagine Jesus as the antitype of Israel *and* Israel as the continuing referent to some OT promises—which is to say, it is possible to imagine Paul's argument in Romans 9–11.
72. Zaspel and Hamilton, "Essay," p. 135, emphasis original.
73. Zaspel and Hamilton, "Essay," p. 135.
74. See, e.g., Zaspel and Hamilton, "Response to Vlach," pp. 77–78.

Zaspel and Hamilton insist, however, that while God's promises about Israel's salvation remain to be fulfilled non-typologically, his promises about Israel's restoration, principally to the land, do not. Here their argument is that Canaan, like Eden, was a "beachhead" from which God's image-bearers were to extend God's life-giving rule.[75] Israel, however, like Adam, failed in its role. And now the world awaits not the reclamation and then extension of Canaan by Israel but simply Jesus's return, which will itself fill the world with the glory God intended from the very beginning.[76] Whether this automatically rules out his doing it "from Zion" and, therefore, through Israel, as Vlach insists, is perhaps an open question.

Vlach in a couple of places complains that Zaspel and Hamilton's view of typology is overly "complicated."[77] And at least at one point, I would have to agree. They seem to suggest that the OT promises regarding Gentile salvation are fulfilled *both* straightforwardly and typologically in Romans 9–11.

1. Straightforwardly: Both Moses (Deut. 32:21) and Isaiah (65:1–2) anticipated that God would "show his favor to the Gentile nations."[78]
2. Typologically: "Gentiles . . . inherit Israel's promises . . . [which] typologically fulfill[s] the Old Testament's patterns and promises."[79]

I bring up the point not to disagree with Zaspel and Hamilton but to confess that I am not sure how both can be true, which is to say, I too wonder if their view of typology is not more complicated than necessary. Slightly beyond this, it is not clear

---

75. Zaspel and Hamilton, "Essay," p. 138.
76. Zaspel and Hamilton, "Essay," p. 138.
77. Vlach, "Response to Zaspel and Hamilton," pp. 141 and 149.
78. Zaspel and Hamilton, "Essay," p. 107. See also their discussion of Hosea 1:10 and 2:23 in Romans 9:24–25 (pp. 103–106), including the echo they discern of Genesis 17 and 22. "Gentile inclusion in the people of God is not a new concept to Paul. It is a hope rooted in the patriarchal promise itself" (p. 104).
79. Zaspel and Hamilton, "Essay," p. 134.

to me how they determine what is typological (e.g., Israel's restoration) and what is not (e.g., Israel's salvation) and, for that matter, what is *both* (e.g., Gentile salvation).[80] Something similar could be said about Vlach's and Merkle's typologies as well.

3. Conclusion

These one or two pushbacks notwithstanding, Andy and I are very grateful for the amount of clarity our authors have brought to Paul's argument in Romans 9–11, to its implications for biblical theology, and to the nature of their lingering differences with one another. So much of this owes to the patient way each has listened to Paul and to one another. We would be remiss not to commend this virtue to our readers, who, we trust, will continue this conversation where our book leaves off. It is imperative that we sympathetically listen to and understand our theological "opponents" *before* disagreeing with them. This is one practical way Christians put into practice Jesus's admonition to "love your neighbor as yourself" (Rom. 13:9). In fact, perhaps the best thing readers could do to cultivate this virtue would be to turn back to the essay they disagreed with the most . . . and read it *again*!

---

80. See Vlach's similar query, "Response to Zaspel and Hamilton," pp. 145–147.

SCRIPTURE INDEX

NAME AND SUBJECT INDEX

FOUR
VIEWS
ON THE
WARNING
PASSAGES
IN HEBREWS

HERBERT W. BATEMAN IV
GENERAL EDITOR

GARETH L. COCKERILL • BUIST M. FANNING
RANDALL C. GLEASON • GRANT R. OSBORNE
CONCLUSION BY
GEORGE H. GUTHRIE